101 976 349 3

D1382103

Sheffield Hallam University
Learning and Information Services
Withdrawn From Stock

General Editors: Professor Ian Brownlie CBE, QC, FBA
Former Chichele Professor of Public International Law in the
University of Oxford and Member of the International Law Commission, and
Professor Vaughan Lowe, *Chichele Professor of Public International Law in*
the University of Oxford and Fellow of All Souls College, Oxford

INTERNATIONAL JUSTICE AND THE INTERNATIONAL CRIMINAL COURT

ONE WE

OXFORD MONOGRAPHS IN
INTERNATIONAL LAW

The aim of this series is to publish important and original pieces
of research on all aspects of international law. Topics that are
given particular prominence are those which, while of interest
to the academic lawyer, also have important bearing on issues
which touch upon the actual conduct of international relations.
None the less, the series is wide in scope and includes
monographs on the history and philosophical foundations of
international law.

RECENT TITLES IN THE SERIES

Just War or Just Peace?
Humanitarian Intervention and International Law
Simon Chesterman

State Responsibility for Transboundary Air
Pollution in International Law
Phoebe Okowa

The Responsibility of States for International Crimes
Nina H. B. Jørgensen

The Law of International Watercourses: Non-navigational Uses
Stephen C. McCaffrey

Human Rights in International Criminal Proceedings
Salvatore Zappalà

FORTHCOMING TITLE:

Universal Jurisdiction: International and
Municipal Legal Perspectives
Luc Reydams

INTERNATIONAL JUSTICE AND THE INTERNATIONAL CRIMINAL COURT: BETWEEN SOVEREIGNTY AND THE RULE OF LAW

BRUCE BROOMHALL

OXFORD

UNIVERSITY PRESS

*This book has been printed digitally and produced in a standard specification
in order to ensure its continuing availability*

OXFORD
UNIVERSITY PRESS

Great Clarendon Street, Oxford OX2 6DP

Oxford University Press is a department of the University of Oxford.
It furthers the University's objective of excellence in research, scholarship,
and education by publishing worldwide in

Oxford New York

Auckland Cape Town Dar es Salaam Hong Kong Karachi
Kuala Lumpur Madrid Melbourne Mexico City Nairobi
New Delhi Shanghai Taipei Toronto
With offices in
Argentina Austria Brazil Chile Czech Republic France Greece
Guatemala Hungary Italy Japan South Korea Poland Portugal
Singapore Switzerland Thailand Turkey Ukraine Vietnam

Oxford is a registered trade mark of Oxford University Press
in the UK and in certain other countries

Published in the United States
by Oxford University Press Inc., New York

© B. Broomhall 2003

The moral rights of the author have been asserted

Database right Oxford University Press (maker)

Reprinted 2009

All rights reserved. No part of this publication may be reproduced,
stored in a retrieval system, or transmitted, in any form or by any means,
without the prior permission in writing of Oxford University Press,
or as expressly permitted by law, or under terms agreed with the appropriate
reprographics rights organization. Enquiries concerning reproduction
outside the scope of the above should be sent to the Rights Department,
Oxford University Press, at the address above

You must not circulate this book in any other binding or cover
And you must impose this same condition on any acquirer

ISBN 978-0-19-927424-6

SHEFFIELD HALLAM UNIVERSITY
WL
345,01
BR
COLLEGIATE LEARNING CENTRE

General Editors' Preface

Globalization and the decline of State sovereignty are prominent among the clichés of the age. The rise of 'international criminal law' and in particular of international criminal tribunals is often said to reflect these phenomena. The extent to which this represents the reality of international criminal law is a question of importance, both for the future of attempts to promote the broad aims of international justice, and more generally for the understanding of the bases upon which international law rests. Dr Broomhall's study subjects these developments to a critical analysis, and offers a balanced and informed assessment of their true significance. His sharply focused study of one particular aspect of globalization is a valuable contribution to the contemporary debate.

IB
AVL

Preface

As this work was being finalized, press releases from governments, non-governmental organizations and the United Nations celebrated the entry into force of the Rome Statute of the International Criminal Court, even as the newspapers and broadcast news were filled with reports of escalating violence in Israel and the Occupied Territories and of a potential shift of military action towards Iraq in the next phase of the American-led 'war on terrorism'. In an important—if often oblique—sense, the work that follows is about the stark divide between the former celebrations and the latter crises.

This work takes the developing field of international criminal law as a prism through which to view a basic tension at work in the world today: that between the sovereignty of States—and especially of very powerful ones—and the pursuit of collective goods like peace, justice, and human rights. With some adjustments, the international regulation of climate change, of peace and security, of HIV/AIDs, or of weapons of mass destruction (to name but a few) might equally have made the point. Nonetheless, this work looks at specific aspects of the emerging system of international justice, and in particular of the International Criminal Court, to underscore the point that the pursuit of global responses to common problems has not prevented States from fundamentally shaping these responses in ways that serve their own interests, notwithstanding claims of 'globalization', the 'decline of sovereignty', and the ascendancy of 'international civil society'. The events of September 11, 2001 and their aftermath have only made us more aware of the fragility of efforts to establish collective, multilateral regimes for contemporary international crises.

An underlying assumption of this author is that the machinery of international justice that is presently putting down roots and articulating its institutions and principles in the international system is ultimately viable; international justice *could* work. There will be those who say it should not work (as among conservative circles in the United States and elsewhere) and there will be some who say it cannot work, urging that we turn our attention instead to truth commissions or processes of democratization or something else. There will be many who say that international justice could, should, and will work, but who will offer no or unrealistic solutions for, and little or no acknowledgement of, the enormous difficulties facing the project. International justice can work; but to work in a legitimate and a politically, legally, and financially viable way requires that problems be honestly appraised and the first steps taken towards defining solutions. At this early stage, with the Rome Statute having just entered into force, this work aims to provide a modest step towards such an approach.

This book arose from a Ph.D. thesis produced at the School of Law of King's College London and, like any thesis, it owes its positive qualities to many people (its negative ones being solely my own). I owe warm thanks to my supervisor, Professor Rein Müllerson, for his unfailing support and rich juridical imagination. My work in the human rights community has also enriched my thinking, and for that I owe deep thanks to the Lawyers' Committee for Human Rights and its Executive Director, Michael Posner. For their many years of love and support, I dedicate this work to my parents, Sylvia and Norman.

Table of Contents

Introduction

Since the early 1990s, international criminal law has undergone a pace of development unknown since the days of the Nuremberg Tribunal. Norms have been refined and expanded, institutions established, and seminal judgments handed down both nationally and internationally. Above all, these developments crystallized in the July 1998 adoption of the *Rome Statute of the International Criminal Court* (the 'Rome Statute' or 'the Statute')[1] which entered into force with unforeseen rapidity on 1 July 2002.

The movement to establish a permanent international criminal court ('ICC'), revived after almost half a century's dormancy, has enjoyed broad and enthusiastic support from governments and non-governmental organizations ('NGOs') alike. This is a surprising turnaround for an institution that during the Cold War tended to be derided as Utopian, when it was mentioned at all. Great hopes have now been vested in the Court. United Nations Secretary-General Kofi Annan called the ICC 'a gift of hope for future generations'[2] and (with many others) lauded it as a means to promote the rule of law, to render accountable the perpetrators of the worst atrocities, and to deter future abuses. If fulfilled in the Court's actual practice, such achievements would make its establishment a major turning point in the development of the post-War international legal order.[3] Rather than turning a blind eye to egregious acts of governments against the population of their own or other countries, the international system of the twenty-first century will, we are led to hope, respond effectively to redress and even to prevent the heinous acts which so plagued the twentieth.

Are these hopes justified? How likely is the promise attributed to the ICC to be fulfilled? Accountability for abuse of power, the prevention of atrocities, and reparation for victims are to be wished and striven for, without doubt.

---

[1] 17 July 1998, U.N. Doc. A/Conf.183/9, as corrected by the procès-verbaux of 10 November 1998 and 12 July 1999; reprinted in M. Cherif Bassiouni, *The Statute of the International Criminal Court: A documentary history* (Ardsley, NY: Transnational, 1998) 39. For a survey of efforts to establish an international criminal court up to and through the Rome Diplomatic Conference, see M. Cherif Bassiouni, 'Historical Survey: 1919–1998' in ibid. 1; for the negotiating dynamics of the Conference, see Philippe Kirsch and John T. Holmes, 'The Rome Conference on an International Criminal Court: The negotiating process' (1999) 93 A.J.I.L. 2; a detailed examination of the negotiation of various parts of the Statute is found in Roy S. Lee, ed., *The International Criminal Court: Issues, negotiations, results* (The Hague: Kluwer, 1999); an article by article explication of the Statute is found in Otto Triffterer, ed., *The Rome Statute of the International Criminal Court: Observers' notes, article by article* (Baden-Baden: Nomos, 1999).

[2] 'Secretary General says establishment of International Criminal Court is major step in march towards universal human rights, rule of law', U.N. Press Release L/2890 (20 July 1998), at 4.

[3] Lamberto Dini ('. . . it will mark not only a political but a moral stride forward by international society'), ibid. at 5, and M. Cherif Bassiouni, 'Preface' in Triffterer (1999), n. 1 above, at xix ('. . . the United Nations' most significant accomplishment since its establishment in 1945').

Nonetheless, oversimplifications will not achieve these aims. This study hopes to go beyond the seemingly straightforward statements proffered in support of the ICC and of international justice generally: statements which conceal a host of assumptions about international law, the international system, and inter-State relations which are anything but simple and indisputable. To accept such assumptions without reflection in fact hampers our ability to foresee accurately the problems and promise of the emerging system of international justice and, more importantly, to find the means of making the system work more effectively. One might be excused for believing that the need for a just and effective means of enforcing the legal norms within ICC jurisdiction, for want of which millions have died in the past half-century, demands a clear-eyed assessment of the international system and its dynamics. To strive, if imperfectly, towards such an assessment can only facilitate the discernment of the regime best able, given the present system and its present constraints, of halting and redressing the abuses that have so far regularly—even systematically—taken place. Ultimately, the task is therefore to ask, if the system has not so far been able or willing to enforce international criminal law with regularity, on what terms will it be willing and able to do so in the foreseeable future, and does the system coalescing around the ICC fulfil those terms? Such questions can only be approached through a careful understanding of both the emerging machinery of international criminal law and the international system in which it is embedded.

It is a central theme of this work that between international criminal law and the international system as it presently exists there is a relationship of tension, of conflicting demands, sometimes of contradiction. Between the sovereignty-limiting rationale of the Nuremberg legacy and the sovereignty-based control over enforcement that continues to characterize the present, essentially Westphalian, system there lies a gulf that is yet to be spanned, even in the wake of the Rome Statute's entry into force. The regular enforcement of criminal law has always required coercion, and the authority to deploy coercive power internationally remains firmly in the hands of States—States that make their decisions on the basis of national interest calculations bearing no necessary relationship to the needs of international justice. It may be that the tension between regular enforcement and the discretion of sovereign States will lessen over time as the end of the Cold War, the establishment of the ICC, and the process of globalization bring about changes in the international environment of legitimation in which States operate. Enforcement decisions take place in an increasingly 'legalized' context in which pressure to vindicate the rule of law is sometimes great. Nonetheless, the fundamental conditions of the modified Westphalian system of the post-War era show little sign of radical change, and extra-legal (economic, strategic, and political) factors related to national interest continue to inform crucial decisions. Important changes have been wrought and great progress toward accountability made, but an institutionalized rule of law, in the robust sense, remains fundamentally at odds with the world system as it now exists. Taken to its logical extreme, routine enforcement of international criminal law would call for a qualitatively different approach to the deployment of coercive power, that is, to the management of international peace and security; but such deployment remains a pre-eminently 'politicized' area of international law. Given that a fundamental change in the system is unlikely (and indeed looks less and less likely in the context of the counter-terrorism drive which has followed the events of 11 September 2001) the best remaining hope for the entrenchment of international criminal law as a regular feature of the international system is the development of a deeply rooted culture of accountability that leads to a convergence of perceived interests and of behaviour on the part of the States responsible for enforcing this law. The ICC and related developments may in fact contribute to the emergence of such a culture, although the present signals are not uniformly positive.

This study consists of this Introduction and three further parts. In Part I, the Nuremberg legacy is set apart from other areas of law that are sometimes included under the rubric of 'international criminal law'. The unique character of this legacy appears in setting the 'core crimes' of international criminal law apart from the primarily domestic law that has developed to deal with the burgeoning phenomenon of transnational crime ('inter-State criminal law'), as well as from the international instruments that call on States to prohibit conduct domestically ('suppression conventions') and the norms that apply to States rather than to individuals (so-called 'international crimes of State'). The distinguishing features deriving from Nuremberg lie in the engagement of individual responsibility directly under international law, and in the subsidiary doctrines that make the effective imposition of that responsibility possible. The latter doctrines include the absence of the defences of prior legality and of superior orders, as well as loss of immunity for acts committed in the course of official functions. Having described the unique cluster of doctrines that make up 'international criminal law' in this narrow sense, Part I goes on to examine how the principles of clarity and non-retroactivity have been brought to bear upon international criminal law, in particular in the negotiation of the Rome Statute of the ICC. It then treats the rationale that legitimates the intrusion of international criminal law into the otherwise sacrosanct domain of sovereignty. This rationale rests on two basic principles underlying the core of international criminal law: 'international peace and security' and 'the collective conscience of humankind'. While of uncertain scope, these principles can be characterized as a condition of membership in the international community and as justifying an infringement of sovereignty to that extent.

With the scope of international criminal law so defined, Part I concludes by raising questions that the enforcement of this law provokes. By calling

for the regular enforcement of international criminal law, is the accountability literature calling for the international recognition of 'the rule of
law'?[4] If so, the proposition need not be controversial so far as the formal
aspects of this doctrine (clarity, non-retroactivity, impartial and non-
discriminatory application of the law, etc.), originally developed with a view
to municipal law, are concerned. Yet calls for the 'rule of law' with respect
to international criminal law often carry with them an express or implied
endorsement of a reduction in sovereignty and an increased willingness to
use force in support of this law. As such, this trend in opinion comes into
conflict with basic characteristics of the post-War modified 'Westphalian'
system. The latter system establishes a divide between the increasing legal
regulation of areas once considered purely sovereign or internal, and the
abiding role of the independent discretion of States acceding to, interpreting,
and applying international law in practice. State discretion is not unfettered,
free of all constraints, but it is a discretion in which law is but one constraint, and in which diplomatic, economic, strategic, and other 'political'
factors also have an integral role.

Part II examines, in six chapters, how this tension between the normative
curb on sovereignty represented by the doctrines of international criminal
law and the factual role of State discretion in the processes of international
law has played out, and is likely to play out, in the development of select
areas essential to the promotion of international justice. Chapter IV finds in
the basic features of the Rome Statute a balance between the needs of a
credible system of justice and the desire to induce wide State support for the
ICC, with the result that real strengths in the definitions, general principles,
and some of the mechanisms of the Rome Statute are tempered by the fact
that the ultimate effectiveness of the Court remains in the hands of States,
individually and collectively. In Chapter V the 'complementarity' mechanism of the Rome Statute, whereby States (and particularly those where the
crime took place, or those of which the nationals stand accused) are given
priority in proceeding against international crimes, is shown to be one of the
real potential strengths of the ICC regime, although issues such as the
role of prosecution in relation to peace and reconciliation remain, along
with the related question of amnesties that it raises. Should the territorial or
national State fail to act, Chapter VI argues that the Rome Statute provides
at least an indirect rationale for the use of universal jurisdiction by other
States, although serious questions arise in attempting to apply this

---

[4] For example, Diane Orentlicher, 'Settling Accounts: The duty to prosecute human rights
violations of a prior regime' (1991) 100 Yale L.J. 2537; M. Cherif Bassiouni, 'Searching for Peace
and Achieving Justice: The need for accountability' and Madeline H. Morris, 'International
Guidelines Against Impunity: Facilitating accountability' in M. Cherif Bassiouni and Madeline
Morris, eds., *Accountability for International Crime and Serious Violations of Fundamental
Human Rights* (1996) 59 Law & Contemp. Probs. 9 and 29 respectively.

doctrine in practice. In Chapter VII a potential block to national proceedings is examined, as the developing law of immunities reveals something of a conflict between the needs of justice and the functioning of inter-State relations, with the result that one of the central tenets of the 'accountability' school (that immunities are unavailable with respect to international crimes) must now at least in part be brought into question. Should national proceedings for any reason be blocked, the ICC will become the main forum for ensuring accountability, and Chapter VIII shows how the Rome Statute mechanisms for State (and Security Council) cooperation, essential to the functioning of the ICC, leave the likelihood of effective enforcement open to question. More than this, the ultimate success of the Court will, it seems, depend on the willingness of the Security Council to support the enforcement of ICC decisions. Yet Chapter IX shows that the United States has to date made strenuous efforts against a Court that could have even an extremely narrow jurisdiction over its own nationals, seriously reducing the prospects for Security Council backing.

The concluding part of this study, Part III, offers a discussion of whether the changes that have taken place or are underway in the international system are likely to lead to increased regularity in future enforcement practice. It is sometimes asserted that the end of the Cold War, globalization, or the alleged decline of sovereignty could lead towards an international society significantly more committed to strong and regular compliance with international law. Yet while the end of the Cold War did broaden the possibilities for Security Council action, and accelerated the development of international criminal law, it did not fundamentally alter the role of State decision-making in the key decisions underlying the enforcement of international criminal law and of international peace and security. As to the decline of sovereignty and globalization, which have given rise to extensive debates, it can be asserted that the institution of sovereignty, at least in areas relevant to international criminal law, is in no danger either of being replaced or of its importance being radically diminished in the foreseeable future. Indeed, the relatively secondary role of the United Nations in the U.S.-led response to the events of 11 September 2001 makes it clear that the development of robust multilateral institutions in the area of peace and security is less likely than ever. Recent developments thus do not provide evidence of the formal changes to the international legal order that would be required in order to establish the preconditions for regular, impartial enforcement. Nonetheless, the growth of international civil society and an intensified interdependency between States has (especially in light of the end of the Cold War) created a new 'legitimation environment' in which States are under increased pressure to justify their decisions and account for their conduct towards their own citizens. The international rule of law is therefore related to the concept of legitimacy and it is possible that, although deep changes to the international system are unlikely, developments in the decision-making environment in which States operate may considerably heighten future support for enforcement. It is in this context that the impact of the ICC and international criminal law are most likely to be felt.

Part I

International Criminal Law

I

Scope

'International criminal law' in the broadest sense cannot be considered a unified or coherent body of law. While one area of this law has, over the last decade of the twentieth century, enjoyed increasing cohesion and developed with unprecedented rapidity through the establishment of the tribunals for the Former Yugoslavia and Rwanda and through the process of establishing an International Criminal Court, overall developments have often had an *ad hoc*, fragmentary character. The different areas of this law, as most broadly conceived, and the distinct dynamics of those areas reflect the divergent, and sometimes conflicting, nature both of international law and of the global system from which it emerges. Around a core of agreed customary or treaty norms lies a wide penumbra of what is either disputed custom, 'soft law', mere proposal, or treaties binding on some but not on all (or substantially all) members of the international community.

Schematically speaking, the phrase 'international criminal law' encompasses increasingly narrow concentric rings of doctrine. Outermost is the whole area of comparative transnational or inter-State criminal law, that is, of national laws that deal with the international or cross-border aspects of substantive and procedural criminal law. Next is the area of the 'suppression conventions', whereby international treaties define offences (such as drug trafficking or hijacking) and set out procedures (including the characteristic obligation to extradite or prosecute) that States agree to follow in taking action through their national systems. In this case, individual responsibility arises only under national law, while a State's failure to act (whether by passing laws or by commencing proceedings under those laws) gives rise to its own international responsibility in accordance with the ordinary principles of international law. A related but *sui generis* phenomenon is that of proposed 'international crimes of State', which would apply criminal responsibility not to individuals but to the abstract collective entity of the State. Finally, at the core of international criminal law are the doctrines by which international law imposes criminal responsibility directly upon individuals, regardless of the national law.[1]

Unless otherwise indicated, this work uses the term 'international criminal law' in the latter, narrow sense, focusing on the 'core crimes' derived from the

---

[1] See generally D.H. Derby, 'A Framework for International Criminal Law' in M. Cherif Bassiouni, ed., *International Criminal Law* (3 vols.) (Dobbs Ferry, NY: Transnational, 1986) (vol. I) 33; also M. Cherif Bassiouni, 'The Sources and Content of International Criminal Law: A theoretical framework', in M. Cherif Bassiouni, ed., *International Criminal Law* (2d ed., 3 vols.) (Ardsley, NY: Transnational Publishers, 1999) ['Bassiouni (1999b)'] (vol. I) 3.

legacy of Nuremberg (crimes against peace, war crimes, crimes against humanity, and genocide). With the 'core crimes', unlike most of the other crimes that might legitimately fall within a broader conception of international criminal law, individual responsibility arises directly under international law, with no need (as a matter of international law) to have domestic legislation in place. As a result, individuals accused of these few, most serious crimes are subject to prosecution either by a successor regime in his or her own State, by foreign authorities acting on the basis of universal jurisdiction, or by an international (including a Security Council) tribunal, regardless of whether national law prohibited (or indeed permitted or required) the conduct at the time and place of its commission. The justification for this departure from the requirement of domestic legality—of prohibition at national law as a precondition to imposing criminal responsibility upon individuals—lies in the assumption that these crimes undermine the international community's interest in peace and security and, by their exceptional gravity, 'shock the conscience of humanity'. It is through this link to deep principles of the international order that these crimes are often considered to be violations of *jus cogens* norms giving rise to obligations *erga omnes*. The underlying premise, of course, is that criminal prohibition acts as a general deterrence, thus promoting stability and basic norms of conduct, especially by governments. While, as a practical matter, one might challenge aspects of these basic assumptions, the contemporary resurgence of international criminal law, culminating in the establishment of the International Criminal Court, ensures a distinct doctrinal place for the core crimes.

By outlining the limits of three potential definitions of 'international criminal law' (inter-State criminal law, suppression conventions, and 'international crimes of State') the discussion below highlights the special character of the fourth (the core 'Nuremberg' doctrines). At the same time, the link between the 'core crimes' and the fundamental interests of international order (in particular, that of international peace and security) can be seen as one source of the very problems that have beset efforts to put this area of law into practice (see pp. 44–51 below).

1. INTER-STATE OR TRANSNATIONAL CRIMINAL LAW

The broadest definition of international criminal law would catch within the phrase all national law relating to crimes with transboundary elements and to inter-State legal cooperation in criminal matters. In recent decades, rapidly developing transportation and communication technology have enormously enhanced the ability of crime (and especially organized crime) to traverse borders and of suspects to evade authorities. National legislatures, courts, and enforcement authorities have responded with new doctrines of law and innovative enforcement strategies while a multi-layered international machinery for coordinating policy development and enforcement has developed, producing international agreements, and international friction, in a number of areas.[2] Where international agreements have arisen, they focus on procedural and jurisdictional questions to allow national authorities to respond more effectively to conduct that remains criminal only under domestic law. Particularly noteworthy, in this regard, are the treaty-making efforts of the Council of Europe, which has undertaken more concrete work to promote mutual assistance than any other intergovernmental organization,[3] as well as the proliferation of instruments in response to the needs of U.S. law enforcement agencies.[4]

As with private international law, there are as many potential ways to regulate this area as there are States to regulate it.[5] In the words of Doudou Thiam:

There has developed within internal law a discipline which is wrongly called, in French at least, 'international penal law['], but which is in fact an internal discipline, its subject matter being the internal laws which delimitate [*sic*] the jurisdiction of foreign courts and the authority of judgements outside the territory of the State in which they are rendered. The fact that, because of the need for co-operation in this field, countries

---

[2] For a sampling of discussions from Europe and the United States, see Roman Boed, 'United States Legislative Approach to Extraterritorial Jurisdiction in Connection with Terrorism', and Bert Swart, 'The European Union and the Schengen Agreement', both in Bassiouni (1999b) (vol. II) 145 and 177. In 1990, the United Nations produced a model instrument: *Model Treaty on Mutual Assistance in Criminal Matters*, 14 December 1990, Annex to G.A. Res. 45/117, U.N. Doc. A/45/49, G.A.O.R., 45th Sess., Supp. No. 49A, at 215; see Herman F. Woltring, 'The United Nations', in Bassiouni (1999b), n. 1 above, (vol. II) 795.

[3] Ekkehart Müller-Rappard, 'Inter-State Cooperation in Penal Matters within the Council of Europe Framework' (surveying twenty treaties and many resolutions and recommendations over forty years) and Peter Wilkitzki, 'Council of Europe' (reviewing the Council's efforts towards integrated codification of mutual legal assistance), both in Bassiouni (1999b) n. 1 above, vol. II 331, 755; M. Cherif Bassiouni and Ekkehart Müller-Rappard, eds., *European Inter-State Cooperation in Criminal Matters: The Council of Europe's legal instruments* (Dordrecht: Martinus Nijhoff, 1993).

[4] Alan Ellis, Robert L. Pisani, and David S. Gualtieri, 'The United States Treaties on Mutual Assistance in Criminal Matters', in Bassiouni (1999b), n. 1 above, (vol. II) 403.

[5] On the distinction between private and public international law, see Sir Robert Jennings and Sir Arthur Watts, eds., *Oppenheim's International Law* (9th ed.) (London: Longman, 1994) at 5–7: 'Whereas [public international law] governs the relations of states and other subjects of international law among themselves, [private international law] consists of the rules developed by states as part of their domestic law to resolve the problems which, in cases between private persons which involve a foreign element, arise over whether the court has jurisdiction and over the choice of the applicable law: in other terms, public international law arises from the juxtaposition of states, private international law from the juxtaposition of legal systems' (at 6–7). As North and Fawcett remark, '[t]here is, at any rate in theory, one common system of public international law . . . but . . . there are as many systems of private international law as there are systems of municipal law': P.M. North and J.J. Fawcett, *Cheshire and North's Private International Law*, (12th ed.) (London: Butterworths, 1992) at 12–13. Of course, the words 'between private persons' in the passage from Jennings and Watts makes clear that the analogy to criminal law is inexact.

decided to make the principle of territoriality of penal law less rigid may have been misleading, and this discipline was styled 'international penal law'. But the crimes to which the discipline relates are, as a rule, crimes under internal law, the courts competent to try them are national courts, and they may become international crimes only by virtue of conventions or of the circumstances in which they are committed. In this respect, they are different from crimes that are international by their very nature, which fall directly under international law irrespective of the will of States.[6]

As Derby remarks, '[w]ell might one puzzle about the genesis of "international law irrespective of the will of States" . . .';[7] the basic thrust of the passage is nonetheless accurate. 'Comparative transnational' or 'interjurisdictional' criminal law would best describe this important sphere of contemporary legal inquiry.

2. SUPPRESSION CONVENTIONS

International obligations pursuant to what are sometimes called 'suppression conventions' often impel governments to pass national laws bearing on crimes with transboundary implications.[8] Such conventions impose on States Parties the obligation to prohibit certain conduct.[9] The conduct, such as terrorist-related activities or drug trafficking, invariably has an international component or global impact that attracts State interest in the first place.[10] These treaties typically include provisions requiring parties to exercise jurisdiction over a specified crime or crimes and to provide cooperation to other States Parties.[11]

A distinguishing feature of many of these treaties, or at least of modern ones, is their recognition of what is often described (inaccurately) as 'universal jurisdiction', which permits, or more often obliges, States Parties either to prosecute individuals suspected of the relevant crime or to extradite them to States Parties willing to do so, regardless of their nationality or of where the

---

[6] *First Report on the Draft Code of Offences Against the Peace and Security of Mankind*, U.N. Doc. A/CN.4/364 (29 April 1983) at 9, cited in Derby, n. 1 above, at 57 n. 108.

[7] Ibid.

[8] See for example national legislation implementing the obligations under the *Convention for the Suppression of Unlawful Acts Against the Safety of Civil Aviation*, 23 September 1971, 974 U.N.T.S. 177 ['1971 Montreal Convention']: see *Criminal Code*, R.S. 1985, c.C–46, ss.7(1) and 7(2) (Canada); 18 U.S.C. s. 32 (United States).

[9] 1971 Montreal Convention, Art. 1 (definition of offences), Art. 3 ('Each contracting State undertakes to make the offences mentioned in Article 1 punishable by severe penalties').

[10] 1971 Montreal Convention, Preamble, para. 1 ('unlawful acts against the safety of civil aviation . . . undermine the confidence of the peoples of the world in the safety of civil aviation'), Art. 4 (establishing various international jurisdictional requirements, e.g. that the place of take-off or landing is situated outside the territory of the State of registration of the aircraft).

[11] 1971 Montreal Convention, Art. 5 (duty to establish jurisdiction under national law), Art. 6 (duty to arrest), Art. 7 (duty to submit case to competent authorities for prosecution if the individual is not extradited), Art. 8 (extradition), Art. 11 (mutual assistance).

crime took place (see pp. 105–27 below).[12] The jurisdiction created by the duty *aut dedere aut judicare* ('either to extradite or to prosecute') embedded in these conventions is not truly 'universal' but is in fact jurisdiction between the parties (*inter partes*); non-States Parties are not obliged to act unless so required under customary law or another applicable treaty. At the same time, it appears that the 'extradite or prosecute' requirement arising under suppression conventions could result in the arrest and extradition or arrest and trial of individuals accused of a relevant crime, provided they are within the jurisdiction of the arresting State, and regardless of whether they themselves are citizens of a State Party.[13]

The obligations under these conventions, for example to take measures to suppress certain conduct, arise at international law while the enforcement of prohibitions against individuals takes place only through national judicial systems. Failure to enact the requisite domestic laws could therefore either constitute or lead to a breach of a State's obligations and give rise to its international responsibility. Yet it does not follow that any *international* responsibility attaches to the individual engaging in the conduct aimed at by the instrument. Suppression conventions by themselves impose no duties and no responsibility directly on the individual; only a State exercising jurisdiction under national legal systems prohibiting the conduct (and not, for example, an international tribunal in the absence of such laws) could normally prosecute her or him.

The phrase 'international criminal law' sometimes encompasses suppression conventions.[14] This broader conception is not unjustifiable, given the internationally important subject matter of these conventions, although the discussions do not always adequately distinguish the levels at which individual responsibility arises. Yet because there is no direct link between international law and individual responsibility in this area, the present study touches on suppression conventions only where they affect the operation of the 'core crimes' of international criminal law, which do entail such a link.

---

[12] The emergence of this innovation in the modern treaties, beginning with the 1949 Geneva Conventions, is carefully traced by Roger S. Clark, 'Countering Transnational and International Crime: Defining the agenda', in Peter J. Cullen and William C. Gilmore, eds., *Crime Sans Frontiers: International and European legal approaches* (Hume Papers on Public Policy, vol. 6, nos. 1 & 2) (Edinburgh: Edinburgh University Press, 1998) 20 at 25–8; and idem, 'The Development of International Criminal Law', paper presented at the conference 'Just Peace? Peace making and peace building in the new millennium', Massey University, Auckland, New Zealand, 24–8 April 2000 (unpublished).

[13] For a review of US legislative and judicial practice in cases of international drug trafficking and terrorism, see the discussion in Michael P. Scharf, 'The ICC's Jurisdiction over the Nationals of Non-Party States: A critique of the U.S. position' in Madeline Morris, ed., *The United States and the International Criminal Court* (2000) 63 Law & Contemporary Problems 67.

[14] See 'Introduction' in M. Cherif Bassiouni, *International Criminal Law Conventions and their Penal Provisions* (Irvington-on-Hudson, NY: Transnational, 1997) 14; and Bassiouni (1999b), n. 1 above.

The dividing line between the responsibility of individuals imposed by international law and the responsibility of States to prohibit conduct under national law is, however, not always easy to draw, with the result that suppression conventions inevitably bear upon discussions of the 'core crimes'. Treaties requiring States Parties to exercise 'universal jurisdiction' over certain acts may support the emergence of international custom imposing individual responsibility for the same acts, as the 1949 Geneva Conventions did in part.[15] This movement from responsibility imposed by conventional obligation under national law to responsibility directly under international law is discussed further below (at pp. 25–6 and pp. 34–9). Multilateral conventions may also articulate a duty for States Parties to exercise jurisdiction over acts already giving rise to individual responsibility under customary law, as did the 1984 Convention Against Torture.[16] Suppression conventions thus clarify the national legal consequences that should flow from international crimes, and also define crimes for purposes of national prohibition in a way that might over time give rise to individual responsibility directly under international law.

3. 'INTERNATIONAL CRIMES OF STATE'

Another use of the phrase 'international criminal law'—not adopted here—would encompass the responsibility of States, characterized as *criminal* responsibility, arising from certain exceptionally serious violations of international law. This approach arose in the course of the work of the International Law Commission ('ILC') on the subject of State responsibility for breaches of international obligations. First appearing in 1976, the category of 'international crimes of State'[17] was set out in the Draft Articles on State Responsibility provisionally adopted at first reading by the ILC in 1996.[18] Article 19 of that draft bears the title 'International crimes and international delicts' and declares that: '2. An internationally wrongful act which results from the breach by a State of an international obligation so essential for the protection of fundamental interests of the international community that its breach is recognized as a crime by that community as a whole constitutes an international crime.'

---

[15] See Theodor Meron, 'Geneva Conventions as Customary Law', in Theodor Meron, *War Crimes Law Comes of Age: Essays* (Oxford: Clarendon, 1998) ['1998b'] 154.

[16] See Chapter VI below at n. 21 and related text.

[17] *Report of the International Law Commission on the Work of its Twenty-Eighth Session, 3 May–23 July 1976*, U.N. Doc. A/31/10, G.A.O.R., 31st Sess., Supp. No. 10 (1976) 175 ['1976 ILC Report'].

[18] *Draft Articles on State Responsibility*, in the *Report of the International Law Commission on the Work of its Forty-Eighth Session, 6 May–26 July 1996*, U.N. Doc. A/51/10, G.A.O.R. 51st Sess., Supp. No. 10 (1996) ['1996 ILC Report'] at 125.

Sub-article (3) provides a non-exclusive list of areas of law giving rise to such 'essential obligations', and included, among others, the prohibitions of aggression, slavery, genocide, apartheid, and massive pollution to the natural environment.

From its first appearance, this proposed category of international responsibility was highly contentious.[19] In particular, critics debated the status of the category (whether it exists or is emerging, and within what scope, or whether it is antithetical to the international system as now constituted), its desirability, as well as the normative and institutional elaboration to which it should be subject.

These debates finally led the ILC, first, to suspend consideration of Article 19, owing to a lack of consensus on its inclusion, to return to it at a later date,[20] and then, in adopting on second reading its renamed Draft Articles on Responsibility of States for Internationally Wrongful Acts, to drop all references to 'crimes'. Instead, the Commission chose to refer to 'serious breaches of obligations under peremptory norms of general international law' and to provide that such breaches 'can attract additional consequences, not only for the responsible State but for all other States' and that 'all States are entitled to invoke responsibility for breaches of obligations to the international community as a whole'.[21] States have a duty to cooperate by lawful means to bring an end to, and have a duty not to recognize as lawful a situation created by, a serious breach of a peremptory norm (Article 41); with regard to obligations 'owed to the international community as a whole', the Draft Articles allow any State to seek cessation of the offending conduct, guarantees of non-repetition, as well as performance of the obligation of reparation on

---

[19] See in particular the consideration of Art. 19 in the 1976 ILC Report, n. 17 above, 226–92, as well as the *Report of the International Law Commission on the Work of its Fiftieth Session, 20 April–12 June 1998, 27 July–14 August 1998*, U.N. Doc. A/53/10, G.A.O.R., 53d Sess., Supp. No. 10 (1998) 118–47 ['1998 ILC Report']; and Joseph H.H. Weiler, Antonio Cassese, and Marina Spinedi, eds., *International Crimes of State: A critical analysis of the ILC's Draft Article 19 on State Responsibility* (Berlin: Walter de Gruyter, 1989). Further, see the Symposium on State Responsibility, and in particular: Georges Abi-Saab, 'The Uses of Article 19'; Giorgio Gaja, 'Should All References to International Crimes Disappear from the ILC Draft Articles on State Responsibility?'; Alain Pellet, 'Can a State Commit a Crime? Definitely, yes!', in (1999) 10 E.J.I.L. 339, 365, 425. See also Derek William Bowett, 'Crimes of State and the 1996 Report of the International Law Commission on State Responsibility' (1998) 9 E.J.I.L. 163 at 164, 167; Ian Brownlie, *System of the Law of Nations: State responsibility, Part I* (Oxford: Clarendon, 1983) at 32–3; N. Jørgensen, *The Responsibility of States for International Crimes* (Oxford: Oxford U.P., 2000); Robert Rosenstock, 'An International Criminal Responsibility of States?' in *International Law on the Eve of the Twenty-First Century: Views from the International Law Commission* (New York: United Nations, 1997) 265; and C. Tomuschat, 'International Crimes by States: An endangered species?', in K. Wellens, ed., *International Law: Theory and practice: Essays in honour of Eric Suy* (The Hague, Nijhoff, 1998).
[20] 1998 ILC Report, at 147.
[21] *Report of the International Law Commission on the Work of its Fifty-Third Session, 23 April–1 June, 2 July–10 August 2001*, U.N. Doc. A/56/10, G.A.O.R., 56th Sess., Supp. No. 10 (2001) ['2001 ILC Report'] at 282.

behalf of those entitled (Article 48). The Draft containing these provisions was forwarded to the General Assembly, which took note of the Draft Articles 'without prejudice to their future adoption or other appropriate action'.[22] While the latter language fell short of the ILC's request that the Assembly 'consider, at a later stage, . . . the possibility of convening an international conference of plenipotentiaries . . . with a view to adopting a convention on the topic', it is not impossible that further action will be taken on the Draft Articles in future.[23] Thus, while it appears unlikely, the notion of 'international crimes of State' may yet resurface.

There is good reason to set 'international crimes of State' to one side when considering 'international criminal law' either narrowly or broadly. It is true that, if international law came to recognize such crimes, there would be some reason to treat them under the broad rubric of 'international criminal law', as the same subject matter and overlapping norms would often be involved. Crimes of State would nevertheless define a unique sub-field of their own, applying to legal rather than natural persons, and ultimately forming a part of the international law of State responsibility rather than that of individual criminal responsibility. It is unlikely that crimes of State will enjoy such recognition in the foreseeable future, owing to the deeply rooted difficulties to which 'international crimes of State' will surely give rise if they become the subject of concerted State negotiations. Three such difficulties may be touched upon here.

First, not all the acts that would give rise to this criminal responsibility can be said to be stipulated under international law with the uniform clarity needed to satisfy the principle of *nullum crimen sine lege*, and thus to win the support of States.[24] It would be no easy task, for example, to arrive at a list of those obligations, related to self-determination or to the protection of the natural environment, the violation of which a substantial majority of States could agree should give rise to their criminal responsibility. The threshold for agreement would certainly be very high, and negotiations arduous.[25]

Secondly, there is no institution with jurisdiction to try and convict States accused of such crimes. The main possibilities discussed by the ILC include the International Court of Justice, the Security Council, an Arbitration

---

[22] G.A. Res. 56/83, U.N. Doc. A/RES/56/83 (12 December 2001), para. 3.

[23] 2001 ILC Report, at page 42, paras. 72–3.

[24] Bowett (1998), n. 19 above, at 164, 167; for the State interest in seeing the requirements of the *nullum crimen* principle satisfied in the context of crimes included within the jurisdiction of the International Criminal Court, see pp. 30–4 below.

[25] The 2001 ILC Report speaks of the prohibitions related to aggression, slavery and the slave trade, genocide, racial discrimination and Apartheid, torture, basic rules of international humanitarian law applicable in armed conflict, and the obligation to respect the right of self-determination, as giving rise to peremptory norms: at 283–4, paras. 4–5. Definitions with respect to some crimes could be borrowed from various sources (for the ICC PrepCom's work on the crime of aggression, see Chapter II below at n. 85 and related text). This does not resolve the problem with respect to all possible 'crimes', however.

Tribunal (perhaps preceded by the finding of a Conciliation Commission) and individual States (as an initial step). Arbitration was the most favoured option, but none is without serious problems.[26] Conferring jurisdiction on either of the first two presents issues regarding the scope of the mandate set out in their constituent instruments. Apart from this, it would be very difficult politically to give adjudicative responsibility to the Security Council for the same reasons that its role was contentious during the drafting of the ICC Statute (see pp. 70–6 below). As discussed below (pp. 52–62) with regard to the potential for embedding the rule of law in the international system, the legitimacy of the system *as a legal one* encourages that criminalization be followed by enforcement that is both reasonably consistent and seen to be so. It is doubtful that judicial powers put directly in the hands of the Security Council could ever satisfy this standard, however far current practice mimics this.[27] Whatever process was decided upon, the legitimacy of the enterprise would require (a) that measures be reasonably effective, (b) that the power of States to take countermeasures be subject to constraints aimed at preventing further significant disruption to international relations, and (c) that the coordinating potential of the Security Council (in the absence of any alternative) be given primacy, while (d) the rights of individual States to respond to violations of their fundamental rights (for example, by exercising their right to self-defence) not be impaired. Importantly, (e) the system as a whole would have to be seen to function at an acceptable level of fairness to sustain the support of States. Creating a mechanism or set of mechanisms to satisfy all of these demands in the current state of international law and international relations would be a delicate and challenging task. One might be forgiven for believing that the international system is not ready for such developments at present.

Thirdly, identifying the appropriate consequences of such acts has been contentious, to the extent that there has been 'no development of penal consequences for States' with respect to breaches of peremptory norms, not even to the extent of providing for punitive damages.[28] Even if the aim of creating a category of 'international crimes of State' was to 'visit a crime with the same consequences as an ordinary delict, but to add further "punitive"

---

[26] See Bowett, n. 19 above, at 168–71.

[27] Bowett, n. 19 above, at 166, argues in reply to the view that the Council's capacity to deal with international crimes was demonstrated by the measures it imposed in response to Iraq's invasion of Kuwait, that this was not dealt with as a crime *per se*, but as a breach of international peace and security. To have dealt with the situation as criminal in a directly judicial manner would have exceeded the Council's powers, in his view. He also points out, at 170, that the Council has not always been impartial in exercising its powers. One can see that the same measures might have been applied had Iraq's acts been treated as crimes, but due process considerations would then have played a greater role.

[28] 2001 ILC Report, at 279, para. 5; also Jennings and Watts (1994), n. 5 above, at 533, para. 157; Brownlie (1983), n. 19 above, at 32–3; Ian Brownlie, *International Law and the Use of Force by States* (Oxford: Clarendon, 1963) 150–66, esp. 152–4; 1998 ILC Report, at 141.

consequences',[29] the question of ensuring the adequacy and justness of such consequences remains. The 1996 ILC draft was willing to contemplate a right on the part of an injured State to seek restitution even if it were 'out of all proportion to the benefit the injured State would gain from obtaining restitution in kind rather than compensation', or if it were to 'seriously jeopardize the political independence or economic stability' of the offending State; similarly, the injured State would have been entitled to satisfaction even were its demands to impair the dignity of the State in question.[30] While some within the Commission may have been ready to contemplate restoration 'however painful or burdensome' to the State in question,[31] such a stance, even were it ethically justified, would risk disregarding the overriding need to see that the system of State responsibility promotes, rather than undermines, international peace and security. The same is true of the humanitarian concern arising from the attempt to define effective responses to egregious violations of international law while avoiding the imposition of collective punishments on the subject population of the State in question.[32] Needs such as these require more nuanced measures and a more circumspect consideration of elusive factors, such as dignity and stability, than the rush to 'criminalization' always allows.

As the ILC's development of clear rules for ordinary forms of State responsibility has been arduous and slow, it is hard to believe that governments, gathered together in greater numbers and often with less expertise than in the ILC, could easily reach agreement on even weightier forms of State responsibility. Such considerations may have led the Commission, in its second reading (2001) Draft Articles, to seek instead greater clarity on the distinct consequences flowing from serious breaches of peremptory norms and of obligations owed to the international community as a whole. This approach, without setting up a new category of 'crimes', is likely to take on momentum as a result of the evolution of international criminal law, which will focus international attention on many of the same norms.

---

[29] Bowett n. 19 above, at 171. Whether the consequences suggested by the ILC are properly labelled 'punitive' is open to question. Theodor Meron, in 'Is International Law Moving Towards Criminalization?' (1998) 9 E.J.I.L. 18 ('1998a') at 21, states that 'international crimes [of State] do not necessarily have penal consequences. Rather, these articles address certain obligations for all states and reinforce the principle that an injured state's entitlement to restitution or satisfaction is not subject to certain restrictions stated in the articles.' Professor Abi-Saab adds, importantly, that the concept is intended also 'to emphasize that such violations cannot be reduced to a mere bilateral relation between the victim and the perpetrator . . .': George Abi-Saab, 'The Concept of "International Crimes" and its Place in Contemporary International Law', in Weiler *et al.* (1989), n. 19 above, 141 at 146. Rosenstock, n. 19 above, at 280, points out that this is true of any *erga omnes* violation, and that the concept of 'crimes of State' is not needed to make the point.

[30] 1996 ILC Report, at 142–3, Art. 52, Art. 43(c) and (d), and Art. 45(3).

[31] 1996 ILC Report, at 168.

[32] 1998 ILC Report, at 141, para. 315.

There is good reason to support the emergence of effective legal means of redressing and preventing the most disruptive violations of international law, even if the term 'crimes' is ill suited to describe acts of States and misleading with respect to the process that should address these acts. Clear consequences in the area of fundamental norms, applied with enhanced consistency, and reinforced by the international law of individual responsibility, would be a significant mark of the maturity, strength, and legitimacy of the international legal apparatus as a whole. Even with such formal elaboration, however, regular and impartial enforcement cannot be expected to be imminent. The norms included under the ILC formulation of 'international crimes of State' include those that have hitherto been least subject to legal and most to political (if any) regulation (such as aggression). Moreover, the closer international regulation of political and diplomatic power implicit in attempting to adopt such rules would require a fundamental shift in priorities on the part of a number of influential States. Even were the rule of law to evolve piecemeal internationally, 'international crimes of State' are not likely to be at the front line.

4. THE NUREMBERG PRINCIPLES

The Nuremberg Principles comprise a cluster of principles that has defined the core of international criminal law from the time of the International Military Tribunal to the Rome Statute.[33] These Principles mark out a doctrinal field establishing what was, at the end of the Second World War, a new relationship between the individual, the State, and the international community based on an awareness that national interdependence and industrialized warfare created new exigencies and demanded new and stronger safeguards for the stability of international life. In this, the Principles joined the UN Charter as part of the revolution in public consciousness that followed the return to peace following the War.

Several features of 'international criminal law', understood as a coherent body of doctrine surrounding the 'core crimes', stand out. First, the responsibility of the individual (for crimes against humanity, genocide, war crimes,

---

[33] *Charter of the International Military Tribunal, Annex to the Agreement for the Prosecution and Punishment of Major War Criminals of the European Axis*, London (8 August 1945), 82 U.N.T.S. 279, reprinted in (1945) 39 A.J.I.L. (Supp.) 257 and in M. Cherif Bassiouni, *Crimes Against Humanity under International Law* (Dordrecht: Martinus Nijhoff, 1992), at 579 ['Nuremberg Charter/Tribunal']; for formulation and consideration of the Nuremberg Principles by the International Law Commission and the General Assembly respectively, see Part II Introduction, n. 4 and related text below; see also Judgment, *Trial of the Major War Criminals before the International Military Tribunal, Nuremberg, 14 November 1945–1 October 1946* (Nuremberg: I.M.T., 1947) (vol. 1) 171, reprinted in (1947) 41 A.J.I.L. 172.

and crimes against peace)[34] arises immediately under international law. Secondly, criminal responsibility attaches regardless of the official position of the individual. Thirdly, responsibility reaches the individual regardless of whether national law is silent, condones, or actually requires the behaviour in question (through superior orders or otherwise). Fourthly, this form of criminal responsibility gives rise to the potential for enforcement through international (including Security Council) tribunals as well as through national courts exercising universal jurisdiction. Finally, and of key importance, there are close historical, practical, and doctrinal links between the core prohibitions of this law and the foundations of the post-War international order.

International law does not apply solely to States, although this was the position of leading theorists for much of its history.[35] Yet States remain the subjects *par excellence* of international law, having a fuller range of rights and obligations than any other entity recognized as having (limited) international legal personality. Such other entities do exist and include, to a greater or lesser extent, intergovernmental organizations, 'peoples', and individuals.[36] It is the application to individuals that is of concern here. While public international law has been known to confer rights upon individuals from time to time, and does so increasingly in the context of human rights protection, it is in the case of international criminal prohibition that this law strikes most forcefully what was traditionally the strictly national sphere of the individual: 'Although international law generally establishes rights and duties between and among states, international criminal law imposes obligations on individuals, making them liable to criminal punishment'.[37]

In the famous, if not gender-neutral, words of the judgment of the International Military Tribunal which sat at Nuremberg to apply international and not German law to the defendants before it: 'Crimes against international law are committed by men, not by abstract entities, and only by punishing individuals who commit such crimes can the provisions of international law be enforced'.[38]

---

[34] Nuremberg Charter, Art. 6(a), (b) and (c) respectively. 'Crimes against peace' are now more commonly referred to as 'the crime of aggression'. Genocide, an offshoot of crimes against humanity, was given definitive recognition apart from crimes against humanity by the 1948 Genocide Convention (see Part II Introduction, n. 6 and related text below).

[35] Jennings and Watts (1994), n. 5 above, at 16ff. It was 'well established' in the eighteenth century that individuals could be punished for certain breaches of the law of nations, but support for this approach declined in the positivist consensus of the nineteenth century, which restricted both the sources and the binding effects of international law to States, until the human rights and humanitarian developments which followed World War II lent it new vigour: Diane Orentlicher, 'Settling Accounts: The duty to prosecute human rights violations of a prior regime' (1991) 100 Yale L.J. 2553.

[36] Jennings and Watts (1994), n. 5 above, at 16ff. and 85, n. 29.

[37] Orentlicher (1991), n. 35 above, at 2552 (footnotes omitted).

[38] Judgment, n. 33 above, at 223.

At Nuremberg, the justification for so invading the normally circumscribed sphere of the individual depended greatly on the status of the individuals involved (i.e. as officials) and on the link between the core crimes and fundamental interests of the international community (see pp. 44–51 below).

As accused persons will most often be real or *de facto* State agents rather than private individuals, the suspension of sovereign immunity is essential to the effective enforcement of international criminal, and hence to any movement towards the rule of law in this sphere. Individual responsibility for the commission of these acts in the performance or purported performance of official functions was central to the conceptual innovation represented by Nuremberg. The abuse of power inherent in these acts aggravated their heinous character while the deployment in their commission of the resources available to the State made possible a threat to international peace. The Nuremberg Charter 'pierces the veil' of State sovereignty, making officials directly responsible *as individuals* under international law for the acts they carry out in the name of the State. The aim was, of course, to control State conduct by controlling the conduct of the officials behind the State, thus indirectly promoting international peace.

Under the Nuremberg doctrines, the status of an accused as a Head of State or otherwise is immaterial. The doctrines of 'act of State' and of immunity were effectively dismissed, while command responsibility and the absence of any defence of superior orders or of prior legality was confirmed. Thus, at least in principle, the individual was exposed to investigation and prosecution by successor regimes, by foreign authorities using universal jurisdiction, or by international tribunals (whether treaty-based, such as the Nuremberg Tribunal or the ICC, or based on resolutions of the Security Council), regardless of the condition of national law at the time and place of the alleged crime. Individual responsibility could not be left to national law precisely because it would not be enforced by the totalitarian regimes at which aim was taken. Nor could responsibility under international law be made effective unless immunities were unavailable and unless national law provided no excuse, whether by making the acts in question legal (prior legality) or by binding an individual with orders to commit the acts (superior orders). It must be added, however, that the law of immunity has not and is not likely to reflect this doctrinally coherent view for some time (see pp. 128–50 below).

The *jus cogens* roots frequently asserted for the core of international criminal law testify to the link between this law and the foundations of the post-War international order.[39] Such an assertion is tantamount to grounding this law in the constitutional order of the international community, at the foundations of which lie the fundamental interests in international peace and

---

[39] See, e.g. M. Cherif Bassiouni, 'International Crimes: *Jus cogens* and *obligatio erga omnes*' in Bassiouni and Morris eds., *Accountability for International Crime and Serious Violations of Fundamental Human Rights* (1996) 59 Law and Contemp. Probs. 63.

security and 'the collective conscience of humanity'. Like much that stems from the Nuremberg Principles, these roots, while coherent at the level of principle, do not correspond to any straightforward subsequent development of the law (see pp. 41–3 below). Also, the underlying rationales of this law have diversified, with the result that while the perpetration of relevant crimes by the State, pursuant to policy, in the context of an armed conflict, remains important, no one of these factors is now indispensable to the character of a core crime under international law, as they were at the time of Nuremberg (see pp. 44–51 below).

Without each of the above factors forming a coherent doctrinal whole, the core of international criminal law would not have had the elements necessary at the level of principle to fulfil its proclaimed purposes of deterrence and punishment. The link between the Nuremberg Principles' affirmation of the international responsibility of individuals and basic rationales of international order justifies the distinction between the 'core crimes' and other crimes within 'international criminal law' (as broadly conceived), and is essential in assessing how core crimes might best be enforced, given the involvement of highly political as well as legal issues in the consideration of these crimes (see pp. 41–3 below). In criticizing a study that treated 'international crimes' (widely defined) in an undifferentiated manner,[40] Derby was right to state that:

[g]iving the same consequences and label to such disparate forms of conduct not only fails to correspond to past and existing practice but also fails to reflect a clear and acceptable policy basis. It . . . seems to establish that straightforward principles operating on the international plane and seeking to provide a single definition for 'international crimes' may have limited utility.[41]

Rather than adopt a definition of international criminal law that offers no differentiation but between procedure and substance,[42] or one that offers a great

---

[40] M.C. Bassiouni, *International Criminal Law: A Draft international criminal code* (Alphen aan den Rijn, The Netherlands: Sijthoff & Noordhoff, 1980).

[41] Derby, n. 1 above, at 45.

[42] G.O.W. Mueller and D.J. Besharov, 'Evolution and Enforcement of International Criminal Law', in Bassiouni (1986), n. 1 above, (vol. 1) 59 at 61, state:

. . . I.C.L. seems to consist of (1) adjective criminal law (accommodation norms) [i.e. matters of mutual assistance, extradition, conflict of laws, etc., referred to at pp. 10–12 above as 'comparative transnational or interjurisdictional law'] and (2) substantive criminal law (deviant conduct regulation which sovereigns have ceded to higher authority or general international supervision) [including Nuremberg law, piracy, the range of treaty-based offenses, and even human rights standards involving international scrutiny into criminal justice areas].

That this distinction lacks sufficient subtlety, or even a clear distinction, is apparent. G. Schwarzenberger, in 'The Problem of an International Criminal Law' (1950) 3 Current Leg. Probs. 262 set out six possible meanings of the phrase 'international criminal law'. Derby, n. 1 above, at 34, complained that ICL as a discipline had yet to decide which of these meanings was 'appropriate'.

deal of differentiation but ultimately fails to justify its approach,[43] the present work takes the view that by distinguishing from the entire pool of 'international crimes' those 'core crimes' having the strongest 'peace and security' element or the strongest link to 'the collective conscience of humanity', one can understand better both why these prohibitions have not been—and how they might be—better enforced.

5. NOTE: PIRACY AND SLAVERY

Piracy and slavery have both been identified as crimes under customary international law, and indeed as *jus cogens* crimes. Piracy on the high seas, the oldest recognized crime under international law, has had that status since at least the seventeenth century, and was most recently codified in the 1982 Convention on the Law of the Sea, which defines the crime and commits all States Parties to its repression, permitting universal jurisdiction to be exercised over the offenders.[44] Slavery, slave-trading, and slavery-related practices, while initially prohibited on the basis, essentially, of territorial and

[43] Even as accomplished a thinker as Bassiouni has declared that 'there are no common or specific doctrinal foundations that constitute the legal basis for including a given act in the category of international crimes', making the broad assertion that: '. . . an empirical or experiential observation supports the conclusion that an international crime is any conduct which is designated as a crime in a multilateral convention with a significant number of state parties to it, provided the instrument contains one of the ten penal characteristics described below'.

The 'ten characteristics' include criminalization of the conduct, duty or right to prosecute, establishment of criminal jurisdictional basis, and so forth. Bassiouni would, in this study, require that 'international crimes' have nothing more in common than that they possess at least one (but share perhaps none) of these characteristics: M. Cherif Bassiouni, 'Characteristics of International Criminal Law Conventions', in Bassiouni (1986) n. 1 above, (vol. I) at 2–3. Bassiouni believes that all of his ten characteristics should ideally be present in every ICL convention, and remarks (at 4) that 'those crimes containing a significant ideological or political component have the least number of the ten penal characteristics, while those that are devoid of it have the largest number (compare aggression with drugs . . .)'. Annex 2 to the same essay (at 11–13) provides a table in which aggression is listed as involving a direct threat, while other crimes (including war crimes, crimes against humanity, and racial discrimination or *Apartheid*) involve a threat to world peace and security. He does not take the next step and conclude that the threat to peace and security empirically does or normatively should lead to a difference in approach, however. This reflects a shortcoming in applying a pure criminal justice model to matters involving international peace and security. The same approach is carried forward to Bassiouni (1999b), n. 1 above, which asserts the need to differentiate between and to establish a hierarchy among international crimes, and which then provides five different lists with a total of 26 different criteria for so doing. None of these give adequate weight to the peace and security interest or to the related international/national distinction in locating the source of individual responsibility (at 95–100). Such an agglomerative approach results in an unhelpfully undifferentiated pool of 'international crimes'.

[44] Chapter VI, n. 6 see more generally Bassiouni, n. 1 above, at 83; Clark, 'Countering Transnational and International Crime: Defining the agenda', n. 12 above, at 25–7; Jennings and Watts (1994), n. 5 above, at 746–55; Jacob W.F. Sundberg, 'Piracy', in Bassiouni (1999b) n. 1 above, (vol. I) 803; and Kenneth C. Randall, 'Universal Jurisdiction under International Law' (1988) 66 Tex. L. Rev. 785, at 791–8.

national jurisdiction under international instruments dating back to the early nineteenth century, has been prohibited by twentieth century law as well.[45] By comparison to the times in which these prohibitions arose, both of these crimes have been radically curtailed, although neither has been eliminated. Trade liberalization and other factors have given rise to a marked increase in piracy in recent years, particularly in the South China Seas.[46] Similarly, slavery itself and a range of slavery-like practices (such as debt bondage and trafficking in persons) continue to occur around the world.[47]

Despite ongoing incidents of each crime, they are not treated as part of the 'core crimes' for purposes of this work, simply because these crimes are, on their own, less a focus of international concern than they were in times past, with the result that the contemporary discussion on accountability has largely neglected these crimes (with the exception of the inclusion of enslavement and sexual slavery within the Rome Statute definition of crimes against humanity).[48]

[45] M. Cherif Bassiouni, 'Enslavement' in Bassiouni (1999b), n. 1 above, 663; Clark, n. 12 above; Jennings and Watts (1994), n. 5 above, at 979; relevant provisions of the applicable conventions are reproduced in Bassiouni (1997) n. 14 above, at 637–733. Jennings and Watts (1994) at 981–2, acknowledge the customary law status of the prohibition of slavery, but express doubt as to whether slavery, and particularly 'slavery-like practices' have *jus cogens* status; Sunga affirms such status for slave-trading and slavery, based in part on the ICJ's classification of the prohibition of slavery as an obligation *erga omnes* (see Chapter II, n. 117 below): Lyal S. Sunga, *Individual Responsibility in International Law for Serious Violations of Human Rights* (Dordrecht: Martinus Nijhoff, 1992), at 92. See also Randall (1988), at 798–800.

[46] International Maritime Organization, 'IMO acts to combat piracy' (Press Release, February 1998); also Keith Harper, 'Violence threatens booming world sea trade' *The Guardian* (18 September 1999).

[47] See e.g. *Report of the Working Group on Contemporary Forms of Slavery on its Twenty-Sixth Session,* U.N. Doc. E/CN.4/Sub.2/2001/30 (16 July 2001); and 'Despite abolition efforts, slavery persists, says Secretary-General, calling for united action to outlaw all forms', U.N. Press Release SG/SM/7649 OBV/188 (1 December 2000).

[48] Rome Statute Art. 7(1)(c) and (g); the crime of enslavement as a crime against humanity was the object of trial and conviction by the International Criminal Tribunal for the Former Yugoslavia in the *Foca* case: *Prosecutor* v. *Dragoljub Kunarac et al.,* Judgment, ICTY Case No. IT–96–23-T & IT–96–23/1-T (22 February 2001), in particular paras. 515–43.

II

From National to International Responsibility

Once it is acknowledged that there is a core of international criminal law that imposes responsibility upon individuals directly under international law, the question arises how individuals become responsible under international and not merely under national law. In other words, how do crimes rise to the level of being core crimes, particularly from being crimes under suppression conventions?

That a crime be of concern to the international community is, of course, a prerequisite to its being subject to international regulation at all. Normally, some cross-boundary element in the crime itself (or occurrence outside the jurisdiction of any State, as with piracy on the high seas) or the prevalence of cross-boundary factors in the occurrence of the crime (as with international drug trafficking and terrorism) is what engenders the concern. Such international concern underlies both cooperation regimes, including suppression conventions, and core crimes. To distinguish a core crime, attracting responsibility without the intermediation of national law (pp. 19–23 above), something more is required. That a State is responsible under international law for failing to suppress torture or drug trafficking clearly does not by itself decide whether individuals are or are not also internationally responsible.

Any suppression convention prohibition could in principle give rise over time to direct individual responsibility under international law. States would be reluctant to recognize new developments in international responsibility as legitimate, however, unless the effect of the conduct in question on fundamental interests of the international community was so great and so immediate as to warrant it. This was the case following the Second World War, when prior legal developments, the official position of the accused, the monumental disruption of international peace, and the enormity of the acts charged all converged to justify what amounted to a quantum leap in the progressive development of the law.

While the type of leap represented by Nuremberg is not impossible in the present day, it is more likely that gradual efforts towards codification through multilateral negotiations, in particular through amendment of the Rome Statute of the ICC, will characterize the expansion of international criminal law in future. This is not least because of expectations that will have been established by the decision, taken early in the course of ICC negotiations, to include express definitions of crimes within the Rome Statute. Before examining again the question of how prohibitions rise to join the 'core' of crimes under international law (at pp. 34–9 below) the principle of legality (or *nullum crimen sine lege*) and its role in promoting the codification of international criminal law is reviewed.

1. CLARITY AND PROSPECTIVITY

(a) The Principle nullum crimen sine lege in international law

Clarity and non-retroactivity are key components of the principle of legality, *nullum crimen sine lege* ('no crime without law'), a basic maxim of any criminal justice system claiming to be guided by the rule of law.[1] It is now codified in Article 22 of the Rome Statute.

The principle of legality promotes a legal system's legitimacy by limiting the interventions of its criminal process to those clearly prescribed in advance by law. It assumes a rational, autonomous legal subject and a known or knowable law. It posits that the deterrent potential of the law, its power to influence the decision-making of individuals in a socially constructive way, arises from its rational and knowable character. Where legal subjects make choices relying on the apparent sense of the law, and nonetheless find themselves tried and convicted, the law has effectively been applied *ex post facto* to them, and the administration of justice is accordingly brought into disrepute.[2] A system supporting retroactive application and vagueness in definition lends increasing discretion to the judiciary and (in national systems) to the police. In its extreme form, neglect of this principle coincides with an abandonment of the rule of law and is a characteristic of unfettered authoritarianism.[3]

The principle plays a 'constitutional' role in maintaining the separation of powers as well. As a principle of legislation, *nullum crimen sine lege* constrains law-makers to set out their intentions clearly and in advance of the conduct over which they wish the courts to exercise jurisdiction.[4] It thereby seeks to protect the subjects of the law from indeterminate executive interference. As a principle of interpretation, *nullum crimen* aims to limit the power of the (unelected) judiciary to extend the interference with liberty beyond that which a reasonable individual could infer from the words of the relevant prohibition. Just as subjects are presumed capable of knowing and have a duty to

---

[1] See Chapter 3, nn. 1–3, below.

[2] See the discussion in Andrew Ashworth, *Principles of Criminal Law* (Oxford: Clarendon, 1991) at 59–62, and in John Calvin Jeffries, 'Legality, Vagueness and the Construction of Penal Statutes' (1985) 71 Virg. L. Rev. 189, at 205–10.

[3] See Bassiouni *Crimes Against Humanity under International Law* (Dordrecht: Martinus Nijhoff, 1992) at 98–9, for a description of retroactive and open-ended laws under National Socialism, and ibid. at 91–5 for the roots of the principle of legality in the struggles of the Enlightenment to limit the abuses of absolute monarchs.

[4] This constraint is constitutionally enforced in some jurisdictions, such as Canada, where judges are empowered to strike down legislation for vagueness and retroactivity: Peter W. Hogg, *Constitutional Law of Canada* (3d ed.) (Scarborough, Ont.: Carswell, 1992) 1045–6.

obey the law, so too is the law-maker responsible for making the law clear and ascertainable, while the judiciary is obliged in principle to refrain from penalizing conduct not intended by the legislator to be criminal.[5]

As is the case with criminal law doctrine generally, the principle of legality and its corollaries originated in municipal law. Its lineage can be traced to Roman law, although in its modern manifestation it is a product of the Enlightenment. Its entrenchment as a cornerstone of national law took place over the course of the late eighteenth and in the nineteenth centuries.[6] By the start of the First World War, it was recognized in the legal systems of all developed countries and their dependent territories, although not always in the same way. In particular, there was a major difference between common law jurisdictions—in particular the United Kingdom—and Continental (Romano-Germanic) systems. For the former, the rule against retroactivity was a presumption that could be refuted by clear statutory wording. In the latter, the principle was more firmly adhered to. In the former, crimes could be developed by analogy as part of the gradual development of the law, while in the latter, such development was strictly limited to minor infractions. Its Constitution made the United States an exception among the common law systems, since retroactivity was constitutionally prohibited.[7]

The movement from being a principle primarily of national law to being one clearly and firmly entrenched in international law was a product of the Second World War and its aftermath. Between the wars, some jurisdictions retreated from the principle as totalitarian governments sought to extend the powers of a politicized judiciary by recognizing broad powers to criminalize by analogy. Such efforts led, at the end of the Second World War, to the recognition of the principle of legality in the judgment of the Nuremberg Tribunal, in the Universal Declaration of Human Rights ('UDHR'), and later in the International Covenant of Civil and Political Rights ('ICCPR').[8]

---

[5] See Ashworth (1991), n. 2 above, at 61 and Edward M. Wise, 'General Rules of Criminal Law', in M. Cherif Bassiouni, ed., *The International Criminal Court: Observations and issues before the 1997–98 Preparatory Committee; and administrative and financial implications,* (1997) 13 Nouvelles Études Pénales 267, at 272. The line between the 'legislative' and the 'judicial' is a matter of judgement and is never fixed however: Jeffries (1985), n. 2 above, at 189 and 202–5.

[6] 'Although there may have been ancient antecedents, the categorical insistence on advance legislative crime definition is clearly a modern phenomenon. In fact, the legality ideal is an explicit and self-conscious rejection of the historic methodology of the common law': Jeffries (1985), n. 2 above, at 190.

[7] See generally Bassiouni (1992), n. 3 above, at 87–146.

[8] Ibid. at 91–146, and esp. 141–4. *Universal Declaration of Human Rights,* G.A. Res. 217A (III) (10 December 1948), U.N. Doc. A/810 at 71; *International Covenant of Civil and Political Rights,* 16 December 1966, 999 U.N.T.S. 171, both reprinted in Brownlie, ed., *Basic Documents in International Law* (4th ed.) (Oxford: Clarendon, 1995) 255, 276.

Article 15(1) of the ICCPR recognizes *nullum crimen* in its usual form as protecting against retroactivity, and echoes Article 11(2) of the UDHR.[9] Article 15(2) emphasizes that absence of criminal prohibition under national law is no bar to prosecution for conduct criminal under international law at the time of its commission.[10] That the state of national law is not determinative for purposes of international criminality is a necessary corollary of the prohibition of any defense of prior legality in the Nuremberg Charter. The latter 'defense', and the objection that national law did not prohibit the international crime at the time it was committed, may sometimes be raised on the basis of *nullum crimen*, but only by misunderstanding the principle's proper scope.[11] The international criminal law pertaining to the 'core crimes' recognized from the Charter and Judgment of the Nuremberg Tribunal to the Rome Statute of the International Criminal Court is based on the assumption of individual responsibility directly under international law. As such, the international principle of *nullum crimen*,[12] at least with respect to these crimes, does not require prohibition by national law. To allow otherwise would be to allow individual States to legislate their agents out of their international responsibility.[13]

(b)   The Draft Code of Crimes Against the Peace and Security of Mankind

The first effort to establish a definitive codification of international criminal law was the work of the International Law Commission on a Draft Code of Crimes Against the Peace and Security of Mankind.

The Draft Code shares common origins with the Nuremberg Principles and the International Criminal Court. The General Assembly first asked the ILC to prepare a draft Code in the same resolution that asked it to formulate the principles of international law recognized in the Nuremberg Charter and

---

[9] The first sentence of Art.15(1) reads: 'No one shall be held guilty of any criminal offence on account of any act or omission which did not constitute a criminal offence, *under national or international law*, at the time when it was committed (emphasis added)'. But for using the word 'penal' instead of 'criminal', Art. 11(2) of the UDHR is the same.

[10] Art. 15(2) reads: 'Nothing in this Article shall prejudice the trial and punishment of any person for any act or omission which, at the time it was committed, was criminal according to the general principles of law recognized by the community of nations'.

[11] See Otto Triffterer, 'Efforts to Recognize and Codify International Crimes (General Report, Part I)', in *Les Crimes Internationaux et le Droit Pénal Interne: Actes du Colloque Préparatoire tenu à Hammamet, Tunisie, 6–8 Juin 1987* (1989) 60 Revue Internationale de Droit Penal 31, at 60 for statements exhibiting the belief that national prohibition is required even with respect to 'core' international crimes in order for *nullum crimen* to be satisfied.

[12] On the application of the international principle of *nullum crimen* to any 'treaty crimes' incorporated into the Rome Statute in future, see the discussion of Art. 22 at pp. 34–9 below.

[13] It has also been argued that international law allows criminalization of individual conduct by analogy in broader circumstances than does national law: Bassiouni (1992), n. 3 above, at 112. This may affect the application of *nullum crimen* as a principle of international law outside the scope of the Rome Statute.

Judgment.[14] After submitting its formulation of the Nuremberg Principles to the General Assembly in 1950,[15] the Commission adopted draft Codes in 1951 and 1954.[16] Despite this early progress, the draft Code fell victim to Cold War paralysis in the same way as did the establishment of a permanent ICC.[17] It was not until 1981 that the ILC, at the General Assembly's request,[18] resumed the project, intensifying its work to adopt provisionally at first reading a draft Code in 1991 and to adopt at second reading a further and substantially modified draft in 1996. While the 1991 draft contained twelve categories of crimes, the 1996 draft contained only five (aggression, genocide, crimes against humanity, crimes against United Nations and associated personnel, and war crimes). The Commission reduced the scope of the Draft Code 'in response to the interest of adoption of the Code and of obtaining support by Governments'.[19] The Commission recommended that the General Assembly decide whether the Code be adopted as an international convention, be incorporated into the Statute of an international criminal court, or be adopted as a declaration of the General Assembly.[20] Understandably, the General Assembly has not proceeded with the Code. Once the decision was made to make the Rome Statute of the International Criminal Court a *de facto* criminal code by including exhaustive definitions of crimes, defenses, and general principles of criminal law, the impetus to bring the Draft Code to fruition could only diminish (see below).[21] The provision in the Rome Statute of a clause allowing inclusion of further crimes at a later date (Article 121(5)) increased the potential of the Statute to deplete the Draft Code of any

[14] GA Res. 177(II) (21 November 1947), U.N. Doc. A/519 (1948), G.A.O.R., 2nd Sess., at 11. The Code was originally titled a code of *offences*; the change from 'offences' to 'crimes' was made by GA Res. 42/151 (7 December 1987), U.N. Doc. A/42/49 (1988), G.A.O.R. 42nd Sess., Supp. No. 49, at 292.

[15] See Part II Introduction, n. 4, below.

[16] *Report of the International Law Commission covering the Work of its Sixth Session, 3 June–28 July 1954*, U.N. Doc. A/2693, G.A.O.R., 9th Sess., Supp. No. 9 (1954) 9.

[17] The General Assembly asked the Commission to put off work on the draft Code and on the ICC until a Special Committee established to address the definition of aggression had submitted its report: GA Res. 897 (IX) (4 December 1954) (Draft Code) and GA Res. 898 (IX) (14 December 1954) (ICC), both in U.N. Doc. A/2890, G.A.O.R., 9th Sess., Supp. No. 21 (1954), at 50. A definition of aggression based on the Special Committee's recommendations not adopted until 1974: GA Res. 3314 (XXIX) (14 December 1974), U.N. Doc. A/9631 (1974), G.A.O.R. 29th Sess., Supp. No. 31, Vol. I, at 142.

[18] GA Res. 36/106 (10 December 1981), U.N. Doc. 36/51 (1982), G.A.O.R., 36th Sess., Supp. No. 51, at 239.

[19] 1996 ILC Report.

[20] Ibid. at 13–14.

[21] The ILC's adoption in 1996 of a new version of the Draft Code of Crimes against the Peace and Security of Mankind made the question of the relationship between the ICC and the Draft Code more pressing. Rayfuse, after noting that the General Assembly put off consideration of the Draft Code until after 1998, concluded that following establishment of the ICC 'the Code will have no relevance in the international arena': Rosemary Rayfuse, 'The Draft Code of Crimes against the Peace and Security of Mankind: Eating disorders at the International Law Commission' (1997) 8 Crim. L. Forum 43, at 83, 85.

independent *raison d'être*. As a result, one can conclude that the half-century effort to adopt a Draft Code has now been superseded by the negotiation of the Rome Statute for the ICC.

(c) Nullum crimen *in the negotiation of the Rome Statute*

As a principle of legislation, *nullum crimen* was brought to bear on the processes leading to the adoption of the Rome Statute. Offering a means both of limiting exposure to the obligations imposed by the Statute and of fostering codification and development of the law, the principle encouraged clearer stipulation of procedural detail, exhaustive definitions of crimes, movement of general principles from the proposed Rules to the Statute, and much else.[22] This function of the principle was merely a continuation of its role in driving efforts to codify international criminal law, primarily through the work of the International Law Commission, from 1946 onwards.[23] It similarly reflected a desire to forestall any repetition of the criticisms aimed at the Nuremberg Tribunal, which had already been taken into account in the establishment of the ICTY and ICTR.[24]

The 1994 Draft Statute of the International Law Commission[25] applied the *nullum crimen* principle so as to reflect that Draft's proposed jurisdictional distinction between crimes under general international law (which applied directly to individuals) and treaty crimes (which normally applied only through national law). With respect to the former, Article 39(a) provided that an accused would not be held guilty of genocide, aggression, serious violations of the laws and customs applicable in armed conflict, or crimes against

---

[22] That *nullum crimen* requires the definition of general principles in addition to those of crimes is not undisputed. Wise concedes that it may not, but arrives at the same effect by speaking of more general 'requirements of precision and certainty expected in criminal proceedings': Wise, n. 2 above, at 271. Criminal prohibitions under international law have often been declared sufficiently precise and their incorporation by mere reference into national law satisfactory for purposes of the *nullum crimen* principle: see Jordan J. Paust, '*Nullum crimen* and related claims', in Bassiouni (1997), n. 5 above, 275, esp. at 275–6 and 282–8. Art. 22(3) makes clear that the *nullum crimen* principle within the Statute is not intended to affect the characterization of conduct as criminal under international law outside of the Statute.

[23] 1996 ILC Report, n. 19 above, paras. 30–46, at 9–13. For the ILC process to 1996 in this context, see pp. 28–9, and Wise, n. 5 above. For views from a wide range of countries on codification efforts as they stood at the time, see generally Triffterer (1989), n. 11 above.

[24] See Morris and Scharf *The International Criminal Tribunal for Rwanda* (2 vols.) (Irvington-on-Hudson, NY: Transnational, 1998) at 39–42 and esp. 124–32, demonstrating that the ICTY Statute, being based on acknowledged customary law, satisfied the *nullum crimen* principle at the time of its establishment, and that the ICTR Statute, although initially less certain, soon did no more than reflect such custom.

[25] International Law Commission, Draft Statute for an International Criminal Court ['ILC Draft Statute'], in *Report of the International Law Commission on its Forty-Sixth Session*, U.N. G.A.O.R., 49th Sess., Supp. No. 10, U.N. Doc. A/49/10 (1994) 43 ['1994 ILC Report'], at 112; reprinted in Bassiouni, ed., *The Statute of the ICC: A documentary history* (Ardsley, NY: Transnational, 1998) 657, at 667 (omitting the ILC's commentary to the Draft Statute).

humanity unless the act or omission in question constituted a crime under international law at the time it occurred. It therefore did no more than apply the prohibition against retrospective application of the criminal law. Provided the conduct was criminal under international law at the time of occurrence, the ICC would be able to exercise jurisdiction, even where national courts, because of a failure to incorporate the relevant prohibitions into national law[26] or because of national laws contrary to them, could not.

As a constraint on law-making, the principle of legality was relied upon by those seeking to have the crimes within the jurisdiction of the Court defined expressly in the Statute, rather than leaving the Court to interpret general international law. The rationale was that general international law might not set out the elements of the offences with sufficient precision, particularly where the crime in question was not defined by a general treaty (as with aggression).[27] The result was a move towards the vision, finally affirmed in the Rome Statute, of a Court whose subject-matter jurisdiction is exhaustively defined in its constitutive instrument. Motivated in part by legitimate uncertainty as to customary international law's definitions of the offences in question, the move also resulted from the awareness of governments that they were designing an institution that could possibly bring indictments against even their highest-ranking officials. This awareness put a premium on the clear delimitation of Court jurisdiction.

Responding to such pressures, the ILC replaced its earlier proposal to define the Court's jurisdiction by reference to 'crimes under general international law'[28] with a list specifying four such crimes (as well as treaty crimes).[29] Despite acceding to Sixth Committee criticisms on this point, the ILC maintained that the Statute should be 'primarily an adjectival and procedural instrument. It is not its function to define new crimes. Nor is it the function of the Statute authoritatively to codify crimes under general international law'.[30] Thus, the Court would determine the exact contents of the

---

[26] Commentary to Art. 39, ILC Draft, paras. 2 & 4, n. 25 above at 113–14.

[27] That international law does meet *nullum crimen* standards has frequently been asserted, and incorporation by reference of definitions under international law (as proposed in the ILC Draft) has been allowed under both national and international law: see Paust, n. 22 above, at 275–6 and 282–8.

[28] For the previous Draft to emerge from the ILC, see 'Report of the Working Group on the Draft Statute for an International Criminal Court', Annex to *Report of the International Law Commission on the Work of its Forty-Fifth Session*, U.N. Doc. A/48/10, 48 G.A.O.R. Supp. No. 10 (1993).

[29] 1994 ILC Report, para. 60 at 36 and Commentary to ILC Draft, paras. 5–6 at 66–7 and para. 1 at 71, n. 25 above.

[30] The ILC continued: 'With respect to certain of these crimes, this is the purpose of the Draft Code of Crimes against the Peace and Security of Mankind, although the Draft Code is not intended to deal with all crimes under general international law': Commentary to Art. 20, ILC Draft, para. 4, n. 25 above at 71–2.

listed prohibitions by resort to the relevant sources of international law. While the ILC was willing to contemplate a gradual, judicially led process to determine the scope and content of much of the ICC's legal substance and procedure, the subsequent process saw the adoption of a more cautious approach, in which express and near-exhaustive definitions of crimes, of defenses, and of most principles of criminal law were included in the Statute itself. The ILC approach aimed to keep the task of establishing the ICC from becoming bogged down in the elaboration of a *de facto* criminal code, thus taking advantage of the delinking of the ICC from the Draft Code of Crimes Against the Peace and Security of Mankind, with which it had been paired off and on since 1948.[31] The ILC may have been concerned in part that too firm a link between the Draft Code and the ICC might prove fatal to the negotiation of the latter.

Concerns about the ILC approach were raised in the 1995 Ad Hoc Committee, where the view was expressed that the principle of legality required the definition and not merely the enumeration of crimes, and indeed that it required definitions of general principles, defenses, and the applicable procedural and evidentiary law as well.[32] At the 1996 Preparatory Committee, there was widespread agreement that 'the crimes within the jurisdiction of the Court should be defined with the clarity, precision and specificity required for criminal law in accordance with the principle of legality (*nullum crimen sine lege*)' and that the fundamental principles of criminal law and the 'general and most important rules of procedure and evidence' should be clearly set out in the Statute for the same reason.[33] Only by knowing the scope of the crimes and defenses, and the basic principles involved, could States gauge the extent to which their leaders and agents would be vulnerable to international prosecution.[34]

The 1996 Preparatory Committee text contained three proposals. The first changed little of the content of the ILC Draft,[35] but introduced the precursor to the present Article 22(3) and a stipulation that the more lenient law would

[31] G.A. Res. 260B (III), U.N. Doc. A/810, at 177 (1948); see Part II Introduction, n. 8 below and pp. 28–30 above.

[32] *Report of the Ad Hoc Committee on the Establishment of an International Criminal Court*, U.N. G.A.O.R., 50th Sess., Supp. No. 22, U.N. Doc. A/50/22 (1995), paras. 52 & 57 at 10 & 12; reprinted in Bassiouni (1998), n. 25 above, 667 at 677 and 678.

[33] *Report of the Preparatory Committee on the Establishment of an International Criminal Court*, U.N. G.A.O.R., 51st Sess., Supp. No. 22, U.N. Doc. A/51/22 (1996) (2 vols.) paras. 52, 180, and 185 at 16, 41, and 42 (vol. I), reprinted in Bassiouni (1998), n. 25 above, 363 at 383–4 and 408–9. For contemporary commentary, see Wise, n. 5 above. The extent to which the principle of *nullum crimen* requires such a codification of the general part is not free from uncertainty.

[34] As remarked above (pp. 29–30) it may well be that the decision to make the ICC Statute a *de facto* criminal code reduced the impetus to complete and adopt the Draft Code.

[35] 'Article A' of Part 3*bis* of the 1996 Preparatory Committee Report was compiled by an informal group and did not represent a text agreed by delegates: ibid., vol. 2 at 79; Bassiouni (1998), n. 25 above, at 500.

apply in case of an amendment between the commission of the offence and final judgment. It also introduced the requirement that any commission of a 'core' crime occur after the entry into force of the Statute. The second and third proposals also contained this latter requirement.[36] The second proposal contained a further prohibition on the use of analogy in construing punishable conduct or imposing sanctions.

With the moving of the provisions on jurisdiction *ratione temporis* into a separate provision, the February 1997 Preparatory Committee text reflected a modified version of the first 1996 proposal, with a two-pronged paragraph on non-retroactivity of core crimes and treaty crimes, a bracketed paragraph prohibiting analogy, and a precursor to paragraph 22(3).[37] This version, the basis for the present Article 22, appeared without significant changes in the text prepared at the inter-sessional Zutphen meeting in January 1998.[38] The same wording appeared with insubstantial changes in the final Preparatory Committee Draft that was placed before the Diplomatic Conference.[39]

At the Diplomatic Conference, the basic structure devised for Article 22 by the Preparatory Committee underwent little change. The suggested text of Per Saland, Chair of the Working Group on General Principles of Criminal Law,[40] added to the prohibition on analogy in the second paragraph the requirement of strict construction and disallowed the proscription of conduct not clearly prohibited by the Statute.[41] A note pointed out that the principle of legality would apply equally to all crimes within the jurisdiction of the Court, including crimes against the integrity of justice.[42] The Working Group Report which followed[43] incorporated the strict construction requirement and, with the changes made by the Drafting Committee subsequently,[44]

---

[36] The third proposal was the precursor of current Art. 11 (Jurisdiction *ratione temporis*).

[37] *Decisions taken by the Preparatory Committee at its Session held from 11 to 21 February 1997*, U.N. Doc. A/AC.249/1997/L.5 (1997), Art. A (*Nullum crimen*) and Art. A*bis* (Jurisdiction *ratione temporis*, as it was to become known); Bassiouni (1998), n. 25 above, 343 at 355. Article A*bis* included the proposal to apply the more lenient version in the event of amendment.

[38] *Report of the Inter-Sessional Meeting from 19 to 30 January 1998 in Zutphen, the Netherlands*, U.N. Doc. A/AC.249/1998/L.13 (1998) Art. 15[A] at 51; reprinted in Bassiouni (1998), n. 25 above, 143 at 173.

[39] Draft Statute for the International Criminal Court, Part 1 of the Addendum to the *Report of the Preparatory Committee on the Establishment of an International Criminal Court*, U.N. Doc. A/Conf.183/2/Add.1 (1998) ['PrepCom Draft Statute'], Art. 21 at 57; reprinted in Bassiouni (1998), n. 25 above, 119 at 140.

[40] *Chairman's suggestions for Arts. 21, 26 and 28*, U.N. Doc. A/Conf. 183/C.1/WG.GP/L.1 (15 June 1998).

[41] This stipulation was dropped, presumably for superfluity, from subsequent versions.

[42] Art. 22 in its final form applies to 'crimes' within ICC jurisdiction and not to 'offences against the administration of justice' (lying under oath etc.) under Art. 70. It is likely that the Court will apply *nullum crimen* as a principle of general international law to the Art. 70 offences through Art. 21 (applicable law).

[43] *Report of the Working Group on General Principles of Criminal Law*, U.N. Doc. A/Conf.183/C.1/WGGP/L.4 (18 June 1998) Art. 21 at 2.

[44] *Draft Report of the Drafting Committee to the Committee of the Whole*, U.N. Doc. A/Conf.183/C.1/L.65/Rev.1 (14 July 1998) Art. 21 at 1.

resulted in the wording of the Bureau's Draft Statute[45] and finally of the adopted text. The Working Group, Drafting Committee, and Bureau versions reflected the growing sense that treaty crimes would not be included in the initial Statute, and so omitted provision for them.

(d) Article 22 of the Rome Statute, and the 'treaty crime'/'core crime' distinction

As finally adopted, Article 22 sets out the core prohibition on retroactive application of the criminal law, as well as two major corollaries of this prohibition, namely the rule of strict construction (including here the forbidding of extensions by analogy of the definitions of crimes) and the requirement that ambiguities be construed in favour of the suspect or accused. It reads:

Article 22
Nullum crimen sine lege
1. A person shall not be criminally responsible under this Statute unless the conduct in question constitutes, at the time it takes place, a crime within the jurisdiction of the Court.
2. The definition of a crime shall be strictly construed and shall not be extended by analogy. In case of ambiguity, the definition shall be interpreted in favour of the person being investigated, prosecuted or convicted.
3. This article shall not affect the characterization of any conduct as criminal under international law independently of this Statute.

'Without law' in the phrase 'no crime without law' does not of course mean that *any* law whatsoever will suffice. It requires a law reasonably ascertainable in advance: hence the corollaries to the principle expressly listed in Article 22. The rule of strict construction, which is not free from uncertainty and has been irregularly applied in common law jurisdictions,[46] aims to ensure that criminal prohibitions are read to the advantage of the person being investigated or prosecuted, in accordance only with their clear meaning and with residual ambiguities resolved in favour of the defence. The prohibition on extending the definitions of crimes by analogy similarly ensures that individuals will only be convicted with respect to conduct making out the offence in question, not conduct making out something similar or analogous to that offence. Each of these corollaries is based on notions of fair warning to the subjects of potential criminal sanction and on an awareness of the inequality

---

[45] *Draft Statute for the International Criminal Court*, U.N. Doc. A/Conf.183/C.1/L.76/Add.3 (16 July 1998) at 1 ['Bureau text'].

[46] The rule is said to be applied to strengthen decisions reached on other grounds: Jeffries (1985), n. 2 above, at 198–200. Jeffries adds (at 219): 'The rule [of strict construction] is still invoked, but so variously and unpredictably, and it is so often conflated with inconsistencies, that it is hard to discern widespread adherence to any general policy of statutory construction'. See also Ashworth (1991), n. 2 above, at 67–71.

of power between the individual and (under municipal law) the State. Each has the 'constitutional' rationale of ensuring that the judiciary interprets and applies, but does not make law.[47]

As embodied within Article 22, *nullum crimen* will act as a principle both of legislation and of interpretation. Legislatively, the Article will remind States Parties of the need for care in drafting amendments or additions to the crimes within the jurisdiction of the Court, as the Court will have only such scope of jurisdiction as the reasonably ascertainable and non-retroactive meaning of the words defining it. In this connection, it is interesting to note that the Court is not given the power to strike down crimes or otherwise refrain from giving effect to laws of indeterminate scope. There is no 'void for vagueness' doctrine in the law of the ICC. This is not because the safeguards of Article 22 are comprehensive: a strictly construed, non-retroactive law may still be vague. The absence of any remedy for vagueness is presumably the result of both the general trend towards limiting rather than expanding the power of the judges *vis-à-vis* States Parties, and the feeling that States Parties as legislators could be trusted to delineate clearly the crimes that might ultimately be charged against their own agents.[48] The latter feeling is given weight by the exhaustive attention paid to definitions during negotiations: a product, in large measure, of *nullum crimen* arguments.

As already stated, the *nullum crimen* principle provides certainty to both individuals and States. Individuals face the possibility of prosecution only with respect to the crimes that States Parties have clearly and exhaustively provided for in the Statute. For their part, States Parties are under an obligation to cooperate with the Court and to surrender jurisdiction to it in accordance with the complementarity provisions only in clearly delineated statutory circumstances. This is not because the provisions relating to the obligation to cooperate (for example) are subject to the rule of strict construction, but because such provisions will only come into play when crimes within the jurisdiction of the Court, which are so subject, are being addressed. It was largely because of this ability to clarify and to limit the obligations of States, and because of the likelihood that many defendants will be State agents, that the principle of legality was incorporated into the Statute as explicitly as it was.

As a result of its codification, one must now carefully distinguish the principle of *nullum crimen sine lege* as it exists under general international law from its manifestation in Article 22 of the Statute. As to the former, it will remain the case that individual responsibility arises directly under international law as it did before the entry into force of the Statute, and that the

---

[47] Ashworth (1991), n. 2 above, at 68–70.

[48] That a judicial ability to find vagueness or indeterminacy carries with it substantial power derives partly from the fact that 'indeterminacy' is itself an indeterminate concept: Jeffries (1985), n. 2 above, at 196.

principle of legality, as an principle of international law apart from Article 22, is satisfied with respect to such crimes as they exist outside the Statute. The international principle is broader in some respects than that inscribed in Article 22. One commentator asserts that it encompasses a broader allowance for prohibitions by analogy than do most domestic systems and is, in general, less rigid than its Article 22 manifestation.[49] The international principle is adapted to the much less systematic arena of general international law.[50] One result is that, anticipating indirect (national) rather than direct (international) enforcement, the principle as it exists at international law relies on supplementation by national law, and consequently does not require exhaustive *international* provision of applicable principles of procedure and evidence. In the case of the statute of an international court or tribunal, the principle may call for just such express provision.[51]

Should the Statute be amended at some future date to incorporate crimes set out in international treaties (such as drug trafficking or terrorist acts), *nullum crimen* as a principle of general international law may be interpreted so as to lead to the imposition of special requirements with respect to such crimes. Such requirements may then lead to the amendment of Article 22.

The ILC Draft adapted *nullum crimen* to the particular needs of treaty crimes in its Article 39(b). This provided that no accused would be held guilty of one of these crimes unless the treaty in question was 'applicable' to his or her conduct at the time of the relevant act or omission. Thus, a specification of applicability was added to the prohibition on retrospectivity that Article 39(b) shared with Article 39(a). The ILC understood that for the *nullum crimen* principle to be satisfied in the case of treaty crimes, the conduct in question would not only have to come within the words of the treaty's prohibition, but the treaty itself would have to apply to the conduct of the accused through the relevant State(s) being party to the instrument and, crucially, through the prohibition having been made a part of the law of the relevant State Party.[52]

---

[49] 'International criminal law as it is now . . . requires the existence of a legal prohibition arising under conventional or customary international law, which is deemed to have primacy over national law, and which defines a certain conduct as criminal, punishable or prosecutable, or violative of international law. This minimum standard of legality permits the resort to the rule *ejusdem generis* [permitting analogy] with respect to analogous conduct, and also permits the application of penalties by analogy . . .': Bassiouni (1992), n. 3 above, at 112.

[50] ' . . . the "principles of legality" in international criminal law . . . are necessarily *sui generis* because they must balance between the preservation of justice and fairness for the accused and the preservation of world order, taking into account the nature of international law, the absence of international legislative policies and standards, the *ad hoc* processes of technical drafting and the basic assumption that international criminal law norms will be embodied into the national criminal law of the various states': ibid. at 112. Outside the ICC regime, the condition described cannot be expected to change quickly or radically.

[51] M. Cherif Bassiouni and Peter Manikas, *The Law of the International Criminal Tribunal for the Former Yugoslavia* (Irvington-On-Hudson, NY: Transnational, 1996), at 269–70 (with reference to the ICTY).

[52] See the commentary to Art. 39(b), ILC Draft, n. 25 above, paras. 3–4 at 113–14.

This acknowledges that not all treaties calling for the prohibition of certain conduct also entail the internationally enforceable criminal responsibility of individuals, absent some form of incorporation of the international agreement into national law.[53] Agreements to prohibit conduct are relatively common between States, with the parties agreeing to penalize certain behaviour in their national legal systems and otherwise to cooperate in its suppression (see pp. 12–14 above). Such 'suppression conventions' create law of a different sort from prohibitions entailing individual responsibility directly under international law. With respect to treaty crimes, the ILC Draft intended in essence to provide international enforcement for national prohibitions. Under this vision, States would agree to the ICC as a supplementary enforcement mechanism, with no intention of creating international responsibility as such. Where the latter exists—for example, in the case of the 'core crimes' or 'international crimes *sensu stricto*' which originated in the Nuremberg Charter[54]—there is no need for the prohibition to be made applicable to the accused under national law. But such a requirement does exist for many conventions including, to name but one, the 1988 Vienna Convention on Narcotic Drugs.[55]

Thus conduct falling within a treaty prohibition may not entail individual criminal responsibility if the prohibition did not apply *as law* to the accused. The Court would have to decide in a given case whether the treaty in question was applicable to the individual. There is no single means by which international agreements come so to apply. Ratification and the passage of implementing legislation carrying the prohibition into national law is one, but not the only, method. A State might not be party to a treaty or, being party, might not have made it part of domestic law.[56] It may be applicable to an accused on more than one basis of jurisdiction (national, territorial, etc.) and the Court would have to examine each case individually to construe the intention

---

[53] While international criminal law, in a broad sense, is in large measure derived from conventions, the majority of these 'do not meet the test of legality under contemporary standards of western European legal systems' owing, *inter alia*, to the fact that it was foreseen that the prohibitions called for would be promulgated into national law in accordance with the principles of legality applicable under that law: Bassiouni (1992), n. 3 above, at 111.

[54] The distinction between 'international crimes *sensu stricto*' entailing individual responsibility directly under international law (essentially the 'core' or 'Nuremberg' crimes) and 'international crimes *sensu largo*' not doing so (crimes under 'suppression conventions') was generally accepted at the meetings of the Association Internationale de Droit Pénal reported in Triffterer (1989), n. 11 above, at 40, 42, 52–3, and 69–70.

[55] 1994 ILC Report, n. 25 above, para. 8 at 68. The ILC gives the opinion that cases where a treaty definition of a crime is insufficient to make the treaty applicable to individuals, thereby giving rise only to State responsibility, are 'likely to be rare, and may be hypothetical . . .': ibid. para. 4 at 113–14. This appears to be overstated: see n. 53 above. The ILC acknowledged that it proposed to include in its Draft Statute '. . .treaties which explicitly envisage that the crimes to which the treaty refers are none the less crimes under national law': n. 25 above, para. 3 at 104.

[56] Ibid., para. 3 at 113.

of the drafters. A relevant question is whether the parties to the treaty, in concluding it, intended that the prohibition in question apply directly to individuals, or whether it was intended only to entail State responsibility (i.e. for any failure to prohibit the conduct under national law).[57]

Article 22 is better suited in its present form to crimes under international law in the strict sense, that is, to the 'core crimes' now listed in Article 5 of the Statute. In the event that treaty crimes are incorporated into the Statute, Article 22 will have to be amended accordingly to give expression to the requirement that the treaty be 'applicable' to the conduct of the accused as the ILC, the Preparatory Committee, and the Diplomatic Conference all foresaw. Article 21 (applicable law) may also have to be amended to provide an expanded role to national law where treaty crimes are concerned.

To do otherwise—to amend the Rome Statute, to include e.g. terrorism or drug trafficking, without modifying the terms on which the Court holds an individual criminally responsible—would be to assume that the treaty crime had risen to the level at which responsibility is imposed directly upon individuals as a result of customary international law. A treaty prohibition may become so applicable to the individual through the action of custom or through the application of 'general principles of law'; nonetheless, it should not be assumed lightly. Rather, the determination as to which of the many norms of international law, proscribing conduct of one sort or another, have joined the 'core crimes' would ideally be guided by a test distinguishing when those prohibitions impose international responsibility directly on the individual, and when they rely upon enactment through national law. In this vein, Meron writes:

whether international law creates individual criminal responsibility depends on such considerations as whether the prohibitory norm in question, which may be conventional or customary, is directed to individuals, whether the prohibition is unequivocal in character, the gravity of the act, and the interests of the international community. Those factors are all relevant for determining the criminality of various acts.[58]

This assessment relies, of course, on judgements as to 'gravity' and 'interests', which are inherently subjective.[59] Nonetheless, this type of normative, multi-issue assessment might prove more useful than striving for quasi-algebraic exactness in isolating the factors involved.[60] Among 'the interests of the inter-

---

[57] n. 25 above, para. 3 at 113.

[58] Theodor Meron 'Is International Law Moving Towards Criminalization?' (1998) 9 E.J.I.L. 18 ['1998a'] at 24.

[59] Meron, ibid., in effect acknowledges this by stating that although there is 'a move in the direction of criminalization', 'the legal criteria for judging criminality in this area are still far from clear, as shown by the lack of clarity as to whether violations of environmental treaties, the use of land mines, or the use of blinding laser weapons, for example, involve individual criminal responsibility.' He does not attempt to clarify these criteria.

[60] This is the central difficulty with the Bassiouni list (see Chapter I, n. 43 above) which provides no means of distinguishing prohibitions containing one or more of the relevant elements from each other.

national community' to which Meron refers, it is argued below that 'shocking the conscience of humankind', disrupting 'international peace and security', and, related to these, 'State action or policy' are key factors upon which international criminalization rests. Such factors, however, can never be exhaustively defined and can, at best, provide only very tentative benchmarks by which to assess developments, as their deployment by the international community is subject to a range of circumstantial political and other forces. Because the judgement of States, individually and collectively, is subject to diverse extra-legal influences, the process of international criminalization will always be less orderly than its conceptual formulation. It is ultimately States that determine what constitutes an international crime, just as they are the ultimate arbiter of what comprises a 'threat to international peace and security', and what 'shocks the conscience of humanity'. This potential circularity finds its limit in the pressure of legitimation applied between States and applied to States 'from below' by civil society.

(e) Is 'terrorism' a crime under international law?

'Terrorism' is not treated in the present work as a 'core crime' under international law for the simple reason that this author does not believe that it currently gives rise to individual responsibility directly under international law. States proposed to include 'terrorism' within the Rome Statute, and a definition was discussed in the process leading to adoption of the Statute.[61] The only result was the commitment made, in the Final Act of the Diplomatic Conference, to re-consider the definition and inclusion of this crime, along with that of drug trafficking, at the first Rome Statute Review Conference.[62]

Rather than being a crime under international law, 'terrorism' is best viewed, at least at the present stage of development of international law, as a catch-all category for a number of crimes under suppression conventions. These crimes (hostage taking, aircraft sabotage, etc.) are punishable,

---

[61] See the above discussion, pp. 30–9. An optional definition of 'crimes of terrorism' was included in the final Draft Statute produced by the Preparatory Committee: PrepCom Draft Statute, Art. 5, at 33; reprinted in Bassiouni (1998), n. 25 above, at 129. At the Rome Diplomatic Conference, a definition of 'act of terrorism', to be included within the definition of crimes against humanity, was submitted, then later modified: *Proposal Submitted by Algeria, India, Sri Lanka and Turkey*, U.N. Doc. A/CONF.183/C.1/L.27 (29 June 1998); *Proposal Submitted by India, Sri Lanka and Turkey*, U.N. Doc. A/CONF.183/C.1/L.27/Rev. 1 (6 July 1998). As it became apparent that the proposal did not have the needed support, a 'place-holder' provision was proposed that would require the Preparatory Commission to elaborate definitions of these crimes: *Proposal Submitted by Barbados, Dominica, India, Jamaica, Sri Lanka, Trinidad and Tobago and Turkey*, U.N. Doc. A/CONF.183/C.1/L.71 (14 July 1998).

[62] *Final Act of the United Nations Diplomatic Conference of Plenipotentiaries on the Establishment of an International Criminal Court*, U.N. Doc. A/Conf.183/10 (17 July 1998) [Final Act], Resolution E.

according to the applicable treaties, only under national law.[63] While the international response to the destruction of the World Trade Center and related attacks within the United States on 11 September 2001 has made 'terrorism' the object of unprecedented world wide attention and condemnation, attempts to define a distinct crime with this name have been no more successful after 11 September than they were before.[64] Recent international instruments,[65] as well as domestic laws passed since 11 September, indicate that a comprehensive definition of 'terrorism' may yet emerge, albeit with a breadth of definition and a focus on the purported intent of perpetrators that raise real concerns about the definition's potential use against legitimate dissidents; it remains to be shown that the term can be applied impartially.[66] For the present, it appears adequate that genocide, war crimes, and crimes against humanity define most of the acts that a definition of 'terrorism' might encompass.[67] The only acts not covered by these crimes are those not committed in armed conflict, as part of a widespread or systematic attack on a civlian population, or with intent to destroy an identifiable group. Given the narrowness of the remaining 'gap' (if such it is) the drive to define a crime of terrorism is better viewed as politically rather than legally driven.

---

[63] For example, *Convention for the Suppression of Unlawful Seizure of Aircraft*, 16 December 1970, 860 U.N.T.S. 105 [1970 Hague Convention]; 1971 Montreal Convention, 23 September 1971, 974 U.N.T.S. 177; *International Convention Against the Taking of Hostages*, 17 December 1979, Annex to GA Res. 34/146, U.N. Doc. A/34/46, G.A.O.R., 34th Sess., Supp. No. 46 at 245, 18 I.L.M. 1456 [1979 Hostages Convention]; *European Convention on the Suppression of Terrorism*, 27 January 1977, 1137 U.N.T.S. 93, 90 E.T.S. 3 [European Convention]; *International Convention for the Suppression of Terrorist Bombings*, adopted by G.A. Res. 52/164 (15 December 1997) [Terrorist Bombing Convention]. For detail on the status of these instruments, see *Measures to Eliminate International Terrorism: Report of the Secretary-General*, U.N. Doc. A/56/160 (3 July 2001).

[64] The General Assembly's Sixth (Legal) Committee has come very close to adopting a final draft 'comprehensive' convention against terrorism, only to have its efforts founder on differences concerning the crimes of 'national liberation movements' and State authorities: *Report of the Working Group on Measures to Eliminate International Terrorism*, U.N. Doc. A/C.6/56/L.9 (29 October 2001), paras. 11–14 and Annex 1. For efforts to define this crime in the context of the United Nations Sub-Commission on the Promotion and Protection of Human Rights, see *Terrorism and Human Rights: Progress report prepared by Ms Kalliopi K. Koufa, Special Rapporteur*, U.N. Doc. E/CN.4/Sub.2/2001/31 (27 June 2001), paras. 24–81.

[65] See *International Convention for the Suppression of the Financing of Terrorism*, adopted by G.A. Res. 54/109 (9 December 1999), Art. 2(1).

[66] For a short discussion of some of the problems, see Michael Kinsley, 'Defining Terrorism: It's essential. It's also impossible' *Washington Post* (5 October 2001) p. A37.

[67] See Interights, 'Responding to September 11: The framework of international law' (October 2001), Part IV; available on-line at http://www.interights.org/about/Sept 11 Parts I-IV.htm#PART IV (site last accessed on 21 July 2002).

2. *JUS COGENS*, SOVEREIGNTY AND THE INTERNATIONAL INTERESTS UNDERLYING INTERNATIONAL CRIMINAL LAW

(a) Jus cogens *and sovereignty*

The core crimes of international criminal law are often cited as part of *jus cogens*, or peremptory norms of international law.[68] The sources, nature, and implications of the concepts of *jus cogens* and obligations *erga omnes* have been much debated.[69] As will be pointed out in relation to universal jurisdiction, the consequences sometimes ascribed to the *jus cogens* character of international crimes does not necessarily correspond to the reality of State behaviour in the contemporary international system.[70] Nonetheless, the

---

[68] The authoritative formulation of the concept of *jus cogens* is in the *Vienna Convention on the Law of Treaties*, 23 May 1969, 1155 U.N.T.S. 331, Art. 53:

Treaties conflicting with a peremptory norm of general international law (jus cogens)
A treaty is void if, at the time of its conclusion, it conflicts with a peremptory norm of general international law. For the purposes of the present Convention, a peremptory norm of general international law is a norm accepted and recognized by the international community of States as a whole as a norm from which no derogation is permitted and which can be modified only by a subsequent norm of general international law having the same character.

See also *Application of the Convention on the Prevention and Punishment of the Crime of Genocide (Bosnia and Herzegovina* v. *Yugoslavia (Serbia and Montenegro)), Further requests for the indication of provisional measures, Order of 13 September 1993*, (1993) I.C.J. Rep. 325, at 440 (in the separate Opinion of Judge *ad hoc* Lauterpacht, that 'the prohibition of genocide has long been regarded as one of the few undoubted examples of *jus cogens*'); Bassiouni, *Crimes Against Humanity in International Criminal Law* (2d ed.) (The Hague: Kluwer, 1999) ['1999a'] at 210–17 (crimes against humanity); Dinstein, *War, Aggression, and Self-Defence* (Cambridge: Grotius, 1988) at 98–103 (*jus cogens* nature of prohibition of inter-State use of force underlying the crime of aggression).

[69] Obligations *erga omnes* are 'the obligations of a State towards the international community as a whole', which '[i]n view of the importance of the rights involved, all States can be held to have a legal interest' in protecting; as opposed to those obligations owing to a particular State or group of States: *The Barcelona Traction, Light and Power Company, Limited (Belgium* v. *Spain) (Second phase) Judgment (5 February 1970)*, (1970) I.C.J. Rep. 4, at 32. The Court, ibid. at 32, goes on: 'Such obligations derive, for example, in contemporary international law, from the outlawing of acts of aggression, and of genocide, as also from the principles and rules concerning the basic rights of the human person, including protection from slavery and racial discrimination.' Bassiouni (1999a), n. 68 above, at 211, considers *jus cogens* norms and obligations *erga omnes* to be 'two sides of the same coin', the first indicating a norm's place within the hierarchy of international law and the second characterizing the results that flow from this. See also Ian Brownlie, *Principles of Public International Law*, (5th ed.) (Oxford: Clarendon, 1998) at 514–17; Sunga *Individual Responsibility in International Law for Serious Violations of Human Rights* (Dordrecht: Martinus Nijhoff, 1992) at 129–132 (that all crimes under international law entail violations of obligations *erga omnes*, but that not all violations of obligations *erga omnes* comprise crimes under international law); Rein Müllerson, *Ordering Anarchy: International law and international society* (The Hague: Martinus Nijhoff, 2000) at 155–9; and Giorgio Gaya, 'Obligations *Erga Omnes*, International Crimes and *Jus Cogens*: A tentative analysis of three related concepts' in Weiler *et al.*, *International Crimes of State: A critical analysis of the ILC's Draft Article 19 on State Responsibility* (New York: Walter de Gruyter, 1989) 151.

[70] See Chapter VI, nn. 26–8 and and related text below.

concept of *jus cogens* may be helpful as showing a coherent view, at least at the doctrinal level, of the legal stature and consequences of these crimes.

The characterization of the core crimes of international criminal law as *jus cogens* has been conceived as an indication of how these crimes inhabit the 'constitutional' level of the international system, or of an emerging international system. Thomas Franck has articulated the idea of fundamental rules such as those underlying international criminal law as forming conditions on membership in the international community that, contrary to the ordinary practice of international law, are not themselves subject to the specific consent of States, except in the very act of accepting membership in the community itself. According to Franck, such 'associative' norms are part of an 'ultimate canon', acting as preconditions to the very recognition of sovereignty that constitutes a given State as a participant in the international community.[71]

The consistency of this idea with what was done at Nuremberg should be noted. At and parallel to Nuremberg, it was the interest of the Allies in preserving peace and security—an interest seen with unparalleled clarity after the catastrophic destruction of the War—that justified overriding previously sacrosanct doctrines of immunity and sovereignty. This broadening of international criminal law represented a movement within international law parallel to that which gave birth to the modern system of human rights protection, and which arose out of the same historical circumstances. The importance of Nuremberg therefore extends beyond the confines of international criminal law to underpin the relationship between sovereignty and the international system in the post-War era:

> The principles of Nuremberg were not only the victory of justice over the intolerable fiction of the unassailable state, as well as an affirmation of the supremacy of a higher positive law; they were also the base upon which a positive international law of human rights could be built, namely, the identification of duties for those sharing in the exercise of power to respect, at least to a minimal extent, the dignity of those subject to that power.[72]

The imposition of individual responsibility would, it was hoped, provide a moral vindication and a practical support for the maintenance of international order. By marking the point at which sovereignty gives way to the

---

[71] Thomas M. Franck, *Fairness in the International Legal and Institutional System* (The Hague: Academy for International Law, 1993) at 57–61: Franck borrows the term 'associative' obligations from Dworkin: Ronald Dworkin, *Law's Empire* (Cambridge, MA: Belknap Press, 1986) at 195–216. On entering the international system, successor States also inherit rights and obligations vested by customary law in their predecessor States: Sir Robert Jennings and Sir Arthur Watts, eds., *Oppenheim's International Law* (9th ed.) (London: Longman, 1996) at 214.

[72] Nigel S. Rodley, 'Impunity and Human Rights' in Christopher C. Joyner, ed., *Reining in Impunity for International Crimes and Serious Violations of Fundamental Human Rights: Proceedings of the Siracusa Conference, 17–21 September 1998* (1998) 14 Nouvelles Études Pénales 71 at 73–4.

prerogatives of the international community, international criminal law's affirmation of the underlying interests of that community confirmed respect for these interests as a minimum condition of membership in international society.[73]

The idea that sovereignty does not arise in a vacuum, but is constituted by the recognition of the international community, which makes its recognition conditional on certain standards, has become increasingly accepted in the fields of international law and international relations.[74] Such limits are held always to have been imposed by the community on the recognition of its members, but to be subject to development over time. From this perspective, crimes under international law can be understood as a formal limit to a State's legitimate exercise of its sovereignty, and so in principle justify a range of international responses (subject to the rest of international law, including that relating to the use of force).

The 'international order' rationale and the functional limit to sovereignty which that arguably represents are admittedly clear and coherent at the level of principle, and not necessarily contrary to the nature of sovereignty as it has been articulated in modern theory. In practice, however, their realization has always been subject to uncertainty and resistance. The formal rationale of order is in basic tension with the actual functioning of the international system, where sovereignty and autonomy in decision-making are highly prized by States. Enforcement power in international criminal law remains in State hands and subject to extra-legal calculations, creating a deep divide between the formal rationale of international criminal law and its effective realization. This tension has characterized the development of international criminal law from its origins to the present day (see pp. 63–6 above/below) and there is no reason to expect that it will not continue to characterize it after the entry into force of the Rome Statute (see pp. 151–62 above/below).

---

[73] Here it should be noted that both obligations *erga omnes* and *jus cogens* norms rely upon the concept of 'the international community as a whole', the first being obligations owed to that community and the second being norms authorized by that community: Sunga (1992), n. 69 above at 131–2.

[74] J. Samuel Barkin, 'The Evolution of the Constitution of Sovereignty and the Emergence of Human Rights Norms' (1998) 27 Millenium 229, at 232; David Beetham, *The Legitimation of Power* (London: Macmillan, 1991), at 122; Abram Chayes and Antonia H. Chayes, *The New Sovereignty: Compliance with international regulatory agreements* (Cambridge, MA: Harvard U.P., 1995), esp. 26–8; M.R. Fowler and J.M. Bunck, *Law, Power and the Sovereign State: The evolution and the application of the concept of sovereignty* (University Park, PA: Pennsylvania State University Press, 1995); Robert H. Jackson, *Quasi-States: Sovereignty, international relations and the Third World* (Cambridge: Cambridge U.P., 1993); Peter Malanczuk, *Akehurst's Modern Introduction to International Law*, (7th ed.) (London: Routledge, 1997), at 17–18; Müllerson (2000), n. 69 above, at 118–34, 166; James N. Rosenau, *Turbulence in International Politics: A theory of change and continuity* (Princeton: Princeton U.P., 1990), at 435–40; Janice E. Thomson, 'State Sovereignty in International Relations: Bridging the gap between theory and empirical research' (1995) 39 Int'l Studies Q. 213, at 218–20.

(b) Possible rationales for the core crimes

If the core crimes of international criminal law are seen as a restricted set of prohibitions limiting the legitimate exercise of sovereignty, and whose establishment of direct international responsibility for individuals is justified by the fundamental international interests implicated by the relevant norms, then the question arises: what specifically are those international interests? The answer is largely unclear, at least at present, although increased attention to international criminal law may in future drive efforts to characterize such interests more clearly.

The most frequently cited interests underlying international criminal law are 'international peace and security', 'the collective conscience of humankind', and 'State action or policy'. The first two articulate the interest of the international community in a stable and principled world order, and thus at the end of World War II served to justify what had been seen, at the end of World War I, as an illegitimate intrusion on sovereignty. At the same time, they elude easy and perhaps any definition. In the post-War international system, and more explicitly since the end of the Cold War, these interests have been asserted by some as not incompatible with, but as conditions of State sovereignty. 'State action or policy' has, at most, a supporting role for the other two.

'International peace and security' is perhaps the primary rationale of international criminal law. The early development of the 'core crimes' in the aftermath of the Second World War was part of the general elaboration of new international legal structures to preserve international security and prevent upheavals capable of unleashing the horrors of modern warfare.[75] The stability of the international order—'international peace and security' as it is phrased in the UN Charter—is the most fundamental interest of the post-War international system.[76] It underlies the Charter, including its provisions for sanctions, peaceful settlement, and a role for regional alliances, in essence restricting previously existing sovereign prerogatives in the name of geopolit-

---

[75] Antonio Cassese, *International Law in a Divided World* (Oxford: Clarendon, 1986), at 64–6.

[76] Bruno Simma, ed., *The Charter of the United Nations: A commentary* (Oxford: Oxford U.P., 1995), at 50–2, 74–5, 97–128; *Charter of the United Nations* (26 June 1945), 1 U.N.T.S. xvi, reprinted in Ian Brownlie, ed., *Basic Documents in International Law* (4th ed.) (Oxford: Clarendon, 1995), at 1. The first purpose of the U.N., set down in Art. 1(1), is:

To maintain international peace and security, and to that end: to take effective collective measures for the prevention and removal of threats to the peace, and for the suppression of acts of aggression or other breaches of the peace, and to bring about by peaceful means, and in conformity with principles of justice and international law, adjustment or settlement of international disputes or situations which might lead to a breach of the peace.

This purpose is reinforced by the pledge undertaken by Member States through Art. 2(4):

All Members shall refrain in their international relations from the threat or use of force against the territorial integrity or political independence of any State, or in any other manner inconsistent with the Purposes of the United Nations.

ical stability.[77] In singling out State agents for international responsibility, it was hoped, in the immediate aftermath of Nuremberg, that international criminal law would provide an incentive for the high-ranking to refrain from devising and executing policies promoting atrocities or aggressive war, and for the low-ranking to refuse to obey orders to carry out such policies. It would thereby contribute to preventing violent conflict between and atrocities by States.

A second justifying rationale, the 'conscience of humanity', is a concept that can be linked to the Martens' clause[78] with its reference to the 'laws of humanity', a broad term that in effect encompassed what have since been distinguished as crimes against peace, war crimes and crimes against humanity.[79] While originally linked to the 'peace and security' rationale,

---

[77] To meet the purpose of U.N. Charter Art. 1(1), and against the backdrop of this wide-ranging renunciation of the use of force by individual States, Member States confer on the Council 'primary responsibility for the maintenance of international peace and security' (Art. 24(1)). The delegation of authority is a wide-ranging one, Members acknowledging that 'in carrying out its duties . . . the Security Council acts on their behalf' (Art. 24(1)) and agreeing 'to accept and carry out the decisions of the Security Council in accordance with the present Charter' (Art. 25). The procedures and standards applicable to the Council's actions and decisions are laid out primarily in Chapters VI ('Pacific settlement of disputes') and VII ('Actions with respect to threats to the peace, breaches of the peace, and acts of aggression') of the Charter.

[78] This clause, intended primarily to indicate that much of humanitarian law continued to exist as unwritten custom, was first included in the Preamble to the *Convention with Respect to the Laws and Customs of War on Land*, 29 July 1899, 1 Bevans 247 [*1899 Hague Convention II*]:

Until a more complete code of the laws of war is issued, the high contracting Parties think it right to declare that in cases not included in the Regulations adopted by them, populations and belligerents remain under the protection and empire of the principles of the international law, as they result from the usages established between civilized nations, from the laws of humanity, and the requirements of the public conscience. [Preamble, para. 9]

Similar formulations appeared in the *Convention Respecting the Laws and Customs of War on Land*, 18 October 1907, 1 Bevans 631 [*1907 Hague Convention IV*] (Preamble, para. 8); the *Geneva Convention for the Amelioration of the Condition of the Wounded and Sick in Armed Forces in the Field* (12 August 1949), 75 U.N.T.S. 31 [*Geneva Convention I*], Art. 63; *Geneva Convention for the Amelioration of the Condition of the Wounded, Sick and Shipwrecked Members of the Armed Forces at Sea* (12 August 1949), 75 U.N.T.S. 85 [*Geneva Convention II*], Art. 62; *Geneva Convention Relative to the Treatment of Prisoners of War* (12 August 1949), 75 U.N.T.S. 135 [*Geneva Convention III*], Art. 142; and *Geneva Convention Relative to the Protection of Civilian Persons in Time of War* (12 August 1949), 75 U.N.T.S. 287 [*Geneva Convention IV*], Art. 158; the *Protocol Additional to the Geneva Conventions of 12 August 1949, and Relating to the Protection of Victims of International Armed Conflicts* (8 June 1977), 1125 U.N.T.S. 3 [*1977 Additional Protocol I*] (Art. 1); the *Protocol Additional to the Geneva Conventions of 12 August 1949, and Relating to the Protection of Victims of Non-International Armed Conflicts* (12 December 1977), 1125 U.N.T.S. 609 [*1977 Additional Protocol II*] (Preamble, para. 4); and the *Convention on Prohibitions and Restrictions on the Use of Certain Conventional Weapons Which May Be Deemed to Be Excessively Injurious or to Have Indiscriminate Effects*, 10 October 1980, 1342 U.N.T.S. 137, 19 I.L.M. 127 [*1980 Conventional Weapons Convention*] (Preamble, para. 5). See Helmut Strebel, 'Martens' Clause', in Rudolf Bernhardt, ed., *Encyclopedia of Public International Law*, (2d ed.) (Amsterdam: Elsevier, 1997) (vol. 3) 326.

[79] M. Cherif Bassiouni, *Crimes Against Humanity in International Criminal Law*, (2d ed.) (The Hague: Kluwer, 1999) ['Bassiouni (1999a)'], at 60ff. The 'collective conscience' concept also appears in the Preamble to the Rome Statute (para. 2).

'collective conscience' has since adopted greater conceptual autonomy.[80] This separation, and the more normative (rather than functional) character of the 'collective conscience' rationale, allows it to evolve with the values of the international community.

Turning to the individual crimes, considerations related to peace and security are most apparent with the crime of aggression, where intentionally launching an aggressive armed conflict forms the *gravamen* of the offence itself, reflecting its purpose of contributing to the prevention of such conflicts. In affirming the elevation of aggressive war from an unlawful act of State to a crime of individuals, the Nuremberg Tribunal declared: 'War is essentially an evil thing. Its consequences are not confined to the belligerent states alone, but affect the whole world. To initiate a war of aggression, therefore, is not only an international crime; it is the supreme international crime differing only from other war crimes in that it contains within itself the accumulated evil of the whole.'[81]

Despite the reference to its being 'the supreme international crime', the status of crimes against peace has nevertheless been contested by some on the basis that it remains a victim of the 'enforcement crisis' that until recently afflicted all international crimes.[82] It was nevertheless included within the

---

[80] The separation of the two rationales is apparent not only in the loss of the nexus to armed conflict in the definition of crimes against humanity (text below), but also in the increasing reliance on this rationale by the Security Council, although the Council must, to evoke its Chapter VII powers, maintain a link between any 'conscience of humanity' considerations justifying Council action and the 'international peace and security' limit imposed by the Charter on the Council's mandate. Formulations that might be placed under the rubric of 'shocking the conscience of humanity' have lent support to Security Council jurisdiction where a secessionist regime denies the rights to freedom and independence to the majority of its population (S.C. Res. 232, 16 December 1966, para. 4 (Southern Rhodesia)); where a State commits massive violence constituting the international crime of apartheid against its population (S.C. Res. 418, 4 November 1977, preamble (South Africa)) or severely represses that population (S.C. Res. 688, 5 April 1991, para. 1 (Iraq)); where civil conflict brings with it heavy loss of life and material damage (S.C. Res. 713, 25 September 1991, Preamble (Yugoslavia)); serious or widespread violations of international humanitarian law (S.C. Res. 808, 22 February 1993 (Former Yugoslavia)); or simply a 'human tragedy' of enormous magnitude (S.C. Res. 794, 3 December 1992, Preamble (Somalia)): see Thomas M. Franck, *Fairness in the International Legal and Institutional System* (General Course on Public International Law) (*Recueil des cours*, vol. 240 [1993-III]) (The Hague: Academy for International Law, 1993), at 202–15. The Security Council has declared that 'the policy of *apartheid* is a crime against the conscience and dignity of mankind': S.C. Res. 392 (19 June 1976), para. 3.

[81] IMT Judgment, above, n. 23, at 186, quoted in Dinstein, above, n. 68, at 120.

[82] A definition of 'crimes against peace' was included in Art. 6(a) of the Nuremberg Charter, and repeated (with some variations) in Art. II(1)(a) of Control Council Law No. 10 and in Art. 5(a) of the Charter of the Tokyo Tribunal: Nuremberg Charter, Chapter I, n. 33 above; *Allied Control Council Law No. 10, Punishment of persons guilty of war crimes, crimes against peace and against humanity*, (20 December 1945) 3 *Official Gazette of the Control Council for Germany* (31 January 1946), reprinted in Bassiouni (1992), n. 3 above, at 590; *Charter of the International Military Tribunal for the Far East* (19 January 1946), T.I.A.S. 1589, established by the *Proclamation by the Supreme Commander for the Allied Powers*, Tokyo (19 January 1946), reprinted in Bassiouni (1992), n. 3 above, 604, 606. While the General Assembly adopted a consensus resolution defining the crime in 1974 (GA Res. 3314 (XXIX) (14 December 1974)), n. 17

jurisdiction of the ICC in the negotiation of the Rome Statute, although it remains to be defined and the preconditions to the Court's jurisdiction established before it can become an active part of the ICC's mandate.[83] While this process is likely to revive the crime of aggression as an active part of international criminal law, the conditions imposed by the Rome Statute make it likely that its evolution will be slow.[84] Moreover, the very process of negotiation towards a definition reflects how political is the question of what constitutes a culpable breach of international peace and security, and above all of where the authority to decide this should lie.[85]

above, this instrument is non-binding, has not been relied upon by the Security Council, deals with aggression in more than just a criminal sense, and has been the subjected to criticism on various grounds: Yoram Dinstein, *War, Aggression and Self-Defence* (Cambridge: Grotius, 1988), at 119–26; M. Cherif Bassioiuni and Benjamin B. Ferencz, 'The Crime against peace', in M.C. Bassiouni, ed., *International Criminal Law* (2d ed.) (Ardsley, NY: Transnational, 1999) ['Bassiouni (1999b)'] (vol. III) 313. For a survey of debates about the crime of aggression and its status under international law, see ibid., at 112–19. Dinstein, ibid. at 116, concludes that although 'when the London Charter was concluded, Article 6(a) was not really declaratory of pre-existing international law . . . [I]t is virtually irrefutable that present-day positive international law reflects the Judgment [of the Nuremberg Tribunal].'

[83] Article 5 of the Statute includes the crime of aggression within the jurisdiction of the Court. However, as the Diplomatic Conference was unable to agree on a definition of the crime in the time available, para. 2 adds that:

The Court shall exercise jurisdiction over the crime of aggression once a provision is adopted in accordance with articles 121 [see n. 84 below] and 123 defining the crime and setting out the conditions under which the Court shall exercise jurisdiction with respect to this crime. Such a provision shall be consistent with the relevant provisions of the Charter of the United Nations.

The Final Act, in Resolution F, para. 7, assigns the Preparatory Commission ('PrepCom'; Chapter IV, n. 21 and related text below) to:

prepare proposals for a provision on aggression, including the definition and Elements of Crimes of aggression and the conditions under which the International Criminal Court shall exercise its jurisdiction with regard to this crime. The Commission shall submit such proposals to the Assembly of States Parties at a Review Conference, with a view to arriving at an acceptable provision on the crime of aggression for inclusion in this Statute. The provisions relating to the crime of aggression shall enter into force for the States Parties in accordance with the relevant provisions of this Statute.

Art. 123(1) indicates that the first Review Conference will be convened seven years after the entry into force of the Statute.

[84] The applicable amendment procedure is set out in Art. 121(5): 'Any amendment to articles 5, 6, 7 and 8 of this Statute shall enter into force for those States Parties which have accepted the amendment one year after the deposit of their instruments of ratification or acceptance. In respect of a State Party which has not accepted the amendment, the Court shall not exercise its jurisdiction regarding a crime covered by the amendment when committed by that State Party's nationals or on its territory.' The restricted jurisdiction provided for in this article (compare the regular jurisdiction of the Court, pp. 76–8 and 80–2 below) opens the possibility that the Court will seldom have jurisdiction over the crime of aggression. The degree of acceptability of any eventual definition will therefore be crucial.

[85] The PrepCom established a Working Group on the Crime of Aggression, which has carried out discussions but made slow progress at several sessions of the PrepCom. Discussions reflected a diversity of views as to the definition of the crime, as well as sharply divided opinions on the appropriate role of the Security Council in relation to the jurisdiction of the ICC: Silvia A. Fernández de Gurmendi, 'The Working Group on Aggression at the Preparatory Commission for the International Criminal Court' (2002) 25 Fordham Int'l L.J. 589; *Discussion paper proposed by the Coordinator*, U.N. Doc. PCNICC/1999/WGCA/RT.1 (9 December 1999)

War crimes, like the crime of aggression, contain armed conflict as an intrinsic threshold element of the offence. This is particularly apparent in the case of grave breaches of the 1949 Geneva Conventions, which relate to the persons protected by those Conventions, and whose protected status is predicated on the existence of an international armed conflict.[86] More importantly, however, war crimes combine the normative, 'collective conscience' impetus with the concern about peace and security by punishing acts which deserve condemnation in themselves, and which by exceeding the bounds of conduct acceptable in armed conflict stand to escalate such conflict (by inviting reprisals etc.) and to perpetuate such crimes. The prohibition of war crimes nonetheless aims primarily to ameliorate rather than to prevent armed conflict, placing these crimes under the rubric of the 'collective conscience of mankind', which aims to affirm principles and enforce minimum standards of conduct within the international community. The inclusion of crimes committed in purely internal armed conflict among this category of international crimes underscores this normative impetus.[87]

Crimes against humanity, which include the conduct of a government against its own citizens, were limited at Nuremberg by a required connection to other crimes under the Charter and were thus related to international conflict as well. The connection made in the Nuremberg Charter Article 6(c), requiring that the acts charged as crimes against humanity be performed 'in execution of or in connection with any crime within the jurisdiction of the Tribunal', was apparently inserted to temper the extent of what the authors of the Charter must have known to be a major improvisation in international law. Despite this, as Orentlicher has put it:

(consolidated text of proposals); *Reference document on the crime of aggression, prepared by the Secretariat*, U.N. Doc. PCNICC/2000/WGCA/INF/1 (27 June 2000); *Proposal submitted by Germany*, U.N. Doc. PCNICC/2000/WGCA/DP.4 (13 November 2000) (discussion paper). In essence, the permanent five members of the Security Council insist that a precondition to the Court's exercise of this jurisdiction be a resolution of the Council, acting under Chapter VII of the UN Charter, finding that an act of aggression has occurred; members of the Non-Aligned Movement strongly oppose this: see Herman von Hebel and Darryl Robinson, 'Crimes Within the Jurisdiction of the Court' in R.S. Lee, ed., *The International Criminal Court: Issues negotiations, results* (The Hague: Kluwer, 1999), 79, at 81–5; and Andreas Zimmerman, Commentary on Article 5, in Otto Triffterer, ed., *The Rome Statute of the Itnernational Criminal Court: Observers' notes, article by article* (Baden-Baden: Nomos, 1999), 97, at 103–6. The difficulties involved in reaching agreement on this crime have led some commentators to feel it 'probable that the definition of this crime . . . will not be agreed upon, at least not in the near future': Antonio Cassese, 'The Statute of the International Criminal Court: Some preliminary reflections' (1999) 10 E.J.I.L. 144, at 147. The most recent and thorough review of efforts to define this crime are in *Historical review of developments relating to aggression*, U.N. Doc. PCNICC/2002/WGCA/L.1 (24 January 2002) and the Addendum to the same, U.N. Doc. PCNICC/2002/WGCA/L.1/Add.1 (18 January 2002). For a discussion of the definition prior to the current negotiations, see Dinstein, n. 81 above, at 119–35.

[86] Convention I (Arts. 2, 12); Convention II (Arts. 2, 13); Convention III (Arts. 2, 12); Convention IV (Arts. 2, 13).

[87] See Chapter IV n. 28 and Chapter VI n. 24 below.

To the extent that they reached Nazi offenses against German nationals, the Nuremberg prosecutions represented a radical innovation in international law. With few and limited exceptions, international law had not previously addressed a state's treatment of its own citizens, much less imposed criminal sanctions for such conduct. The Nuremberg prosecutions thus broadened the scope of international law in general, and of international criminal law in particular.[88]

This required 'nexus' to armed conflict no longer applies to crimes against humanity,[89] and has never applied to genocide,[90] giving these two the potential to apply to purely internal matters in the absence even of an internal armed conflict. With this change, the rationale behind these crimes has attenuated its connection to peace and security, affirming that individual responsibility under international law may justifiably rest not on the stability of the international order alone, but on the power of such acts to 'shock the conscience of humanity'. Resting in this way on the protection of fundamental rights and the promotion of common values, which are subject to evolution, crimes against humanity may be expected to develop over time. This has already occurred with the inclusion of apartheid and enumerated crimes of sexual violence within the Rome Statute and previous instruments, and could happen in future with other crimes.[91]

---

[88] D. Orentlicher, 'Settling Accounts: The duty to prosecute human rights violations of a prior regime' (1991) 100 Yale L.J., 2537, at 2555 (footnotes omitted).

[89] The connection to armed conflict was retained in Art. 5 of the Statute of the International Criminal Tribunal for the Former Yugoslavia: Chapter IV n. 10 below. This was done out of an apparent desire to restrict the jurisdiction of the Tribunal, rather than out of a narrow view of the law. As stated by the Appeals Chamber of the ICTY in the *Tadic* jurisdictional decision:

It is by now a settled rule of customary international law that crimes against humanity do not require a connection to international armed conflict. Indeed . . . customary international law may not require a connection between crimes against humanity and any conflict at all [*Prosecutor v. Dusko Tadic, a.k.a. 'Dule', Decision on the Defence Motion for Interlocutory Appeal on Jurisdiction* (ICTY Case No. IT–94-I) (2 October 1995) (Appeals Chamber) ['*Tadic* jurisdictional decision'], at para. 141].

Neither Art. 3 of the Statute of the Rwanda Tribunal, Chapter IV n. 10 below, nor Art. 7 of the Rome Statute require any 'nexus' to armed conflict: see Virginia Morris and Michael P. Scharf, *The International Criminal Tribunal for Rwanda* (2 vols.) (Irvington-on-Hudson, NY: Transnational, 1998) (vol. I), at 202–5; M.C. Bassiouni, *Crimes Against Humanity in International Criminal Law* (2d ed.) (The Hague: Kluwer, 1999) ['Bassiouni (1999a)'] at 193–203; Darryl Robinson, 'Defining "Crimes Against Humanity" at the Rome Conference' (1999) 93 A.J.I.L. 43 at 45–6.

[90] William A. Schabas, *Genocide in International Law: The crime of crimes* (Cambridge: Cambridge U.P., 2000) at 10, 71–2.

[91] The *Apartheid Convention* declares apartheid to be a crime against humanity: *International Convention on the Suppression and Punishment of the Crime of Apartheid*, 30 November 1973, 1015 U.N.T.S. 243, Art. I(1). Apartheid was included in both the 1991 and 1996 Draft Codes as a crime against humanity: 1991 ILC Report, 1996 ILC Report. Crimes of sexual violence could be encompassed by the wording of Art. 6(3) of the Nuremberg Charter by being characterized as 'other inhumane acts', but no charges of rape were brought at Nuremberg: Kelly Dawn Askin, *War Crimes Against Women: Prosecution in international war crimes tribunals* (The Hague: Kluwer, 1997), at 140–2. Rape was expressly mentioned in Control Council Law No. 10, and was included in both draft Codes, as well as in a much more elaborated form in the Rome Statute (which includes '[r]ape, sexual slavery, enforced prostitution, forced pregnancy, enforced

Despite their primary reliance on the 'collective conscience' rationale to justify the international responsibility they impose, it should be noted that atrocities of a magnitude capable of being labelled crimes against humanity, genocide, or violations of the laws and customs applicable in non-international armed conflict have historical and causal links to international conflicts, having the potential in many cases to destabilize both national society and international peace. Conversely, the crime of aggression has clearly been felt to 'shock the conscience of humanity'. These two major rationales therefore overlap in each of the core crimes.

The third potential rationale requires more caution. 'State action or policy' has been put forward as a fundamental rationale of international criminal law, in essence underlying the above two considerations. One major commentator writes:

What makes the specific crimes contained in Article 6(c) [of the Nuremberg Charter] and subsequent formulations part of the international crime category of 'crimes against humanity' is their nexus to one overarching international or jurisdictional element. This element is therefore the indispensable link that warrants inclusion in the international criminal category of that which would otherwise remain within the category of national crimes. And that international element is 'state action or policy'.[92]

Bassiouni also implies that, at least in the case of crimes against humanity, 'State action or policy' is a precondition to the large scale victimization that can result in threats to peace and security and shock the conscience of humanity.[93] Without such a rationale, he argues, international criminal law will be less clearly defined and lose the support of States, undermining its legitimacy.[94] Moreover, the role Bassiouni assigns to 'State action or policy' is not restricted to crimes against humanity, but extends to all crimes which can be characterized as being *jus cogens* (thus, to all the core crimes):

certain crimes affect the interests of the world community as a whole because they threaten the peace and security of human kind and because they shock the conscience of humanity. If both elements are present in a given crime, it can be concluded that the crime is part of *jus cogens*. The argument is less compelling, though still strong enough, if only one of these two elements is present. Implicit in the first, and sometimes the second element, is the fact that the conduct in question is the product of a state-action or a state-favoring policy. Thus, essentially, a *jus cogens* crime is characterized explicitly or implicitly by state policy or conduct, irrespective of whether it is manifested by commission or omission. This is one of the distinctions between *jus cogens* and other international crimes [as broadly conceived], which are not the product of a state-action or a state-favoring policy.[95]

sterilization, or any other form of sexual violence of comparable gravity' as both crimes against humanity, in Art. 7(1)(g), and war crimes, in Art. 8(2)(b)(xxii) and 8(2)(e)(vi)).

[92] Bassiouni (1999a), n. 89 above, 256.
[93] Ibid. at 244 n. 4.
[94] Ibid. at 246.
[95] Bassiouni, 'Sources and Content', in Bassiouni (1999b) vol. 1.

Bassiouni is right to assert the importance of considering State action or policy, and to emphasize its historical importance in the development of international criminal law. Inter-State aggression will no doubt always have an element of State policy, and crimes against humanity, as defined most recently by the Rome Statute, are defined in part by such an element.[96] Nonetheless, this factor should be ascribed a more flexible position than Bassiouni gives to it. While State action or policy may be decisive in causing an abuse to threaten international peace and security, and the abuse of power and authority by State agents may make conduct rise to a level that is deemed to shock the conscience of humanity, this will not always necessarily be the case. For example, war crimes are frequently committed with no policy element,[97] and genocide could conceivably occur without such a policy, even if such an occurrence is rare.[98] The fundamental international interest in peace and security and the ability of international law to respond appropriately to affronts to the public conscience are important enough that the possibility of flexible future development should be not closed off in the name of a conceptually neat but restrictive doctrinal arrangement. Particularly in light of the growing prominence of non-State actors, State action or policy should be seen as relevant, but should not always be read into the crimes themselves or their underlying rationales as Bassiouni suggests.

[96] Art. 7(2)(a) of the Rome Statute defines the threshold of crimes against humanity as including an attack on a civilian population 'pursuant to or in furtherance of a State or organizational policy to commit such attack'.

[97] The Rome Statute states, in Art. 8(1), that the ICC 'shall have jurisdiction in respect of war crimes in particular when committed as part of a plan or policy or as part of a large-scale commission of such crimes'.

[98] The Elements of Crimes, as adopted in draft by the PrepCom on 30 June 2000, require not that genocide be committed pursuant to a plan or policy, but as part of 'a manifest pattern of similar conduct': *Finalized Draft Text of the Elements of Crimes*, U.N. Doc. PCNICC/2000/INF/3/Add.2 (6 July 2000), Element 4 of Art. 6 crimes. Such a pattern will often, but not always amount to the same thing.

III

The Rule of Law and International Accountability

The rationales underlying international criminal law, set out above, posit a relationship between international criminal law and the maintenance of order (or of a certain principled kind of order) in the international system. It must be presumed that these rationales would be best served by the enforcement—and indeed by the sufficiently regular enforcement—of international criminal law. Any attempt to address the regular enforcement of the criminal law, whether national or international, must inevitably evoke the notion of the rule of law.[1] Under its classic conception, the rule of law is an idea that aims to legitimate the internal sovereignty of the State in its claim to an exclusive right to law-making, adjudication, and enforcement within its territory,[2] and

---

[1] Formulations of the 'rule of law' have reflected the diverse use to which the concept has been put. For example, the concept was used during the Cold War as part of a conservative critique of the welfare State: F.A. Hayek, *The Road to Serfdom* (London: Routledge & Kegan Paul, 1944); *The Constitution of Liberty* (London: Routledge & Kegan Paul, 1960). Around the same time, the concept was used to promote the constitutionalism and separation of powers associated with modern capitalist democracies: see International Commission of Jurists, *The Rule of Law in a Free Society: A Report of the International Congress of Jurists, New Delhi, India, January 5–10, 1959* (Geneva: I.C.J., 1959). More broadly, a fundamental debate in the jurisprudential literature has been that between naturalists and positivists, relating to the relationship between law and morality: see in particular H.L.A. Hart, *The Concept of Law* (2d ed.) (Oxford: Clarendon, 1994); and Joseph Raz, 'The Rule of Law and its Virtue' (1977) 93 L.Q.R. 195, at 205–6, for examples of the view that law and morality are distinct, and Lon L. Fuller, *The Morality of Law* (New Haven: Yale U.P., 1964) for a leading exponent of the naturalist position that law inherently involves a moral element. For a dialogue between Hart and Fuller, see H.L.A. Hart, 'Positivism and the Separation of Law and Morals' in Ronald Dworkin, ed., *The Philosophy of Law* (Oxford: Oxford U.P., 1977); and Lon Fuller, 'Positivism and Fidelity to Law: A Reply to Professor Hart' (1958) 71 Harvard L. Rev. 630. A similar debate is between Raz and Weinrib: Joseph Raz, 'Formalism and the rule of law' in Robert P. George, ed., *Natural Law Theory: Contemporary essays* (Oxford: Clarendon, 1992) 309, and Ernest J. Weinrib, 'Why Legal formalism' in ibid., 341; and Ernest J. Weinrib, 'Legal Formalism: On the immanent rationality of law' (1989) 97 Yale L.J. 949. Raz argues that by making the formal characteristics of the law moral aims in themselves, Weinrib's formalism (and by extension, Fuller's and Hayek's) tends to constrain law to pursue only those objectives that can be pursued in a high degree of conformity with the rule of law; in Raz's view, such an approach is too limiting, as the rule of law is simply one objective, and may be derogated from in part in order to pursue other legitimate social aims: ibid., 318.

[2] Dworkin holds that the 'organizing center' of any conception of law is the general justification it offers for the application of coercive force by the State: Dworkin (1986), at 190. This is fundamentally a question of legitimacy and political obligation: ibid., at 190–5. See also Max Weber, 'Politics as a Vocation' in H.H. Gerth and C. Wright Mills, eds., *From Max Weber: Essays in sociology* (New York: Oxford U.P., 1946) 77, at 77–8; see the discussion in Anthony Giddens, *The Nation-State and Violence* (*A Contemporary critique of historical materialism*, vol. II) (Berkeley: U. of California P., 1987), at 18–30. See also Hans Kelsen, 'Sovereignty and International Law' in W.J. Stankiewitz, ed., *In Defense of Sovereignty* (New York: Oxford U.P.,

as such has a key role in the constitutional order of the modern State;[3] it fulfils this role through ensuring the separation of powers, legal controls on the use of power, and the application of laws possessing at least minimal formal qualities.[4] Yet having developed as a normative and explanatory tool in relation to domestic legal systems, the applicability of 'rule of law' standards to the very different system of international law must inevitably be questioned. Such questioning exposes some key assumptions in the literature of international accountability to be if not in theoretical, then at least in practical tension with contemporary manifestations of sovereignty and the way in which the legitimate use of force is distributed in the international system. The very real tension between the principles of international criminal law and the practice of States will be explored in some depth with respect to various key aspects of international criminal law below (pp. 63–6).

When invoked internationally, the 'rule of law' tends to act as an idealized reference point in calling for an international order based on compliance with international law (for example, that related to the use of force in the UN Charter), as opposed to an order determined by power or expediency. The applicability of the doctrine of the rule of law to international law has not

---

1969) 115; Kurt Mills, *Human Rights in the Emerging Global Order: A new sovereignty?* (London: Macmillan, 1998), at 9–53; and David Beetham, *The Legitimation of Power* (London: Macmillan, 1991), at 121–6.

[3] Particularly, the democratic modern State: Joseph Raz, 'The Politics of the Rule of Law' (1990) 3 Ratio Juris 331. Raz is nonetheless critical of attempts to load the concept of 'the rule of law' with detailed and comprehensive implications for the political order: Raz (1977), n. 1 above, at 195–6, 203–4 (criticizing views exemplified by Hayek and the International Congress of Jurists, n. 1 above, and arguing that the rule of law is distinct from substantive values of justice, human rights, etc.). For a nuanced discussion of the place of the rule of law in legitimating the political order of the modern democratic State, see Jürgen Habermas, 'On the Idea of the Rule of Law', (Kenneth Baynes, trans.), *Law and Morality*, in Sterling M. McMurrin, ed., *The Tanner Lectures on Human Values* (vol. VIII) (Cambridge, Mass.: Cambridge U.P., 1988) 217, at 249 ('There can be no autonomous law without the realization of democracy': ibid., at 279); his view of the close interrelationship of the rule of law and democracy is developed at length in Jürgen Habermas (William Rehg, trans.), *Between Facts and Norms: Contributions to a discourse theory of law and democracy* (Cambridge, Mass.: MIT, 1998). See also Beetham (1991), n. 2 above, at 124–5 (emphasizing 'the inadequacy of any purely legal or institutional approach to the "rule of law" ', a point often neglected in the jurisprudential literature), 247 (primacy of the question of democracy).

[4] The latter qualities include non-retroactivity, reasonable clarity and precision, non-discrimination, and knowability. See the discussion in Beetham (1991), n. 2 above, at 121–6. These characteristics are derived from the work of Fuller (1964), n. 1 above, at 33–94, esp. 39. Fuller's principles are broadly confirmed and further elaborated (albeit with significant differences, especially as to the overall aims and framework of the doctrine) by Rawls, Raz, and Finnis: John Rawls, *A Theory of Justice* (Oxford: Oxford U.P., 1972), at 235–43; Raz (1977), at 198–202; John Finnis, *Natural Law and Natural Rights* (Oxford: Clarendon, 1980), at 270–6. The law should also be passed through proper procedures, that is, in accordance with valid 'secondary rules of recognition', the assumption being that these procedures safeguard legitimacy in themselves (as notably through the checks and balances of a democratic system). The concept of a 'rule of recognition' originated with Hart (1994) n. 1 above, at 94–100; for one critique, see Ronald Dworkin, *Law's Empire* (Cambridge, Mass.: Belknap, 1986), at 34–5.

been rigorously analysed as such,[5] although links of greater or lesser clarity can be drawn between the concepts assembled under the 'rule of law' and certain areas of international scholarship (compliance,[6] legitimacy,[7] and some analyses relating to the use of force, the UN system, and the nature of the international order).[8] In attempting to translate the rule of law into the very different order of the international community, there is no great difficulty in judging international criminal law by the rule of law's formal aspects (prospectivity, clarity: see pp. 26–39 above). Yet the rule of law is more than just a bundle of formal qualities. It is also generally understood as a practice, and to call at the international level for the consistent, impartial practice implied by the concept raises profound difficulties, at least as the international system currently exists and is likely to develop. Past failures of enforcement are best explained, and future progress would be best assisted, by firmly conceiving of international criminal law in the context of the sovereignty-based, diffused peace and security system in which it must develop. It will be seen in the following Part that, although the regular enforcement of international criminal law is not in principle inconsistent with the international system, such enforcement encounters deep political and practical problems when invoked in any robust form.

(a) Accountability and the rule of law

As support for the enforcement of international criminal law has grown, a considerable literature dealing with issues of accountability has arisen. Broadly speaking, this literature encompasses not only criminal prosecution, but also post-conflict justice and the legal regulation of major political and social transitions generally. As such, the existence and extent of the duty to prosecute, the place of international tribunals, the role of commissions of inquiry ('truth commissions'), the permissibility of amnesties, principles

---

[5] Ian Brownlie applies the concept of the rule of law to international law (without examining the full implications of so doing) in *The Rule of Law in International Affairs: International law at the fiftieth anniversary of the United Nations* (The Hague: Martinus Nijhoff, 1998), esp. 213ff.; see also Antonio Cassese, 'On the Current Trends towards Criminal Prosecution and Punishment of Breaches of International Humanitarian Law' (1998) 9 E.J.I.L. 2, at 9 ('the rule of international law') and 17 ('international rule of law'). An article dealing with the formal aspects of the rule of law but lacking adequate theoretical support is R. Bhattacharyya, 'Establishing a Rule-of-Law International Criminal Justice System' (1996) 31 Texas Int'l L.J. 57.

[6] Benedict Kingsbury, 'The Concept of compliance as a function of competing conceptions of international law' (1998) 19 Michigan J. of Int'l L. 345; Chayes and Chayes (1995).

[7] See for example Thomas M. Franck, *The Power of Legitimacy Among Nations* (New York: Oxford U.P., 1990).

[8] Antonio Cassese, *International Law in a Divided World* (Oxford: Clarendon, 1986); idem., *Violence and Law in the Modern Age* (Princeton, NJ: Princeton U.P., 1988), esp. ch. 2, 'Why States Use Force with Impunity: The "black holes" in international law', ibid., 30.

applicable to reparations for victims, and the desirability of 'lustration' and similar processes have all been the subject of wide comment.[9]

The accountability literature widely asserts that criminal prosecution should be pursued in the case of certain major crimes. National prosecutions legitimate a new government in a post-transitional situation, being a prime indicator of support for the rule of law:

Any transition from authoritarian rule to greater democracy necessarily involves efforts to establish and promote the rule of law. Societies in which massive human rights violations occur with impunity are by definition lawless societies. The lawlessness of the state itself serves to disempower ordinary citizens, making them fearful to think or speak out and breeding cynicism and passivity. As societies attempt to recover from these periods of lawlessness, one of the first opportunities to reestablish the primacy of law over individuals comes in the treatment of the former rulers, torturers, and jailers. If such people are treated summarily, extracting an eye for an eye, the transition to a society of laws is set back immeasurably. On the other hand, a blanket amnesty and silence from the new government perpetuate the existence of a separate class to whom the rule of law does not apply. Continued impunity equally undermines efforts to reestablish legality. Thus, the need to define legal procedures and criteria for dealing with past abuses takes on a special importance.[10]

The policy benefits attributed to accountability include 'social healing', affirmation of the dignity of the victims, the reclaiming of the political sphere by the majority of society, historical rectification (with the efficient fact-finding that prosecution can bring), deterrence, the reestablishment of the rule of law, and the (re-)embedding of civilian control. The literature also discusses or alludes to potential negative effects or difficulties of a policy of accountability, such as the exacerbation of irreconcilable social divisions, resource constraints (with the related issue of whom to hold to account, through which mechanism), uncertain standards of proof (where lustration or truth commissions rather than trials are pursued), the potentially destabilizing effect of prosecutions, the potential for prosecutions to be used to pursue old grievances or new injustices, and the loss of legitimacy that a fragile new government might suffer through its inability to pursue prosecutions effectively.[11]

---

[9] Valuable sources on these issues include M.C. Bassiouni and Madeline H. Morris, eds., *Accountability for International Crimes and Serious Violations of Fundamental Human Rights* (1996) 59 L. and Contemp. Probs.; Christopher C. Joyner, ed., *Reining in Impunity for International Crimes and Serious Violations of Fundamental Human Rights* (1998) 14 Nouvelles Etudes Pénales; Naomi Roht-Arriaza, ed., *Impunity and Human Rights in International Law and Practice* (New York: Oxford U.P., 1995); and Neil J. Kritz, ed., *Transitional Justice: How emerging democracies reckon with former regimes* (3 vols.) (Washington, D.C.: U.S. Institute of Peace, 1995).

[10] Naomi Roht-Arriaza, 'Introduction', in Roht-Arriaza (1995), n. 9 above, 3, at 4.

[11] Ibid., at 7–9; see also the pieces by Bassiouni and Morris at n. 9 above.

Legally, and in line with the Nuremberg Principles (above, pp. 19–22), the view has gained support that crimes against humanity (including torture) and genocide—which are generally of most immediate concern to this literature, focusing as it frequently does on situations of internal oppression—give rise to a duty to prosecute, not just on the part of the State in question, but on the part of the international community as a whole. This duty gives rise to universal jurisdiction to try offenders in the national court of otherwise uninvolved States, as well as to the possibility of international tribunals. Apart from individual instruments, the legal basis for these assertions is found in the principle that the underlying standards protected by crimes against humanity are peremptory norms of international law, *jus cogens*, and give rise to obligations *erga omnes*, owed to the international community as a whole and to each of its members. This duty to investigate and prosecute is asserted to bring with it the threat of international opprobrium and isolation if it is not complied with, and so transforms into non-negotiable what might otherwise be negotiated away, thus strengthening the position of post-transition administrations.[12] This view is motivated by the fact that crimes such as disappearances and death-squad killings are designed to prevent accountability for the State agents who commit them, so that only by imposing duties to investigate, prosecute, and compensate can the relevant prohibitions and the effort to prevent future abuses be made meaningful. A corollary of this view is that blanket amnesties are impermissible for the most serious offences (roughly speaking, the 'core crimes' of international criminal law) and that, whether trials are held nationally or internationally, their fair conduct holds the potential to promote a lasting peace through reconciliation and 'social healing'.

While these views are generally cogent, two major shortcomings may be highlighted in the accountability literature, both related to the absolute value frequently attributed to prosecution by writers in the area.[13] The first relates to the call for a reduction in sovereignty, and the second to the call for increased use of force in support of international criminal law. The first assumes a greater potential for fundamental change in the international system, and the second a much greater degree of impartiality and legal control over the use of force, than exist at present.

The former President of the International Criminal Tribunal for the Former Yugoslavia, Antonio Cassese, describes the choice in stark terms: either one supports the international rule of law, or one supports State sovereignty. The two are not, in his view, compatible. International criminal law as

---

[12] Naomi Roht-Arriaza, 'Introduction', in Roht-Arriaza (1995), n. 9 above, 3, at 5.

[13] Theo van Boven, 'Accountability for International Crimes: The victim's perspective', Jason Abrams and Madeline Morris, 'Assessing the Efforts to Develop International Principles or Guidelines on Accountability: Report of Rapporteurs' and Madeline Morris, 'International Guidelines against Impunity', all in Joyner (1998), n. 9 above, at 349, 345, and 359 respectively.

a doctrine defines a limit to State sovereignty, but that sovereignty in fact reappears when States fail to cooperate with (in Cassese's experience) the ICTY and when the international community fails to bring force to bear in a concerted way to deal with the non-cooperation.[14] Cassese recognizes the dependence of the international rule of law on the effective deployment of the UN collective security apparatus, but does not assess the conditions for ensuring such deployment:

Judicial reckoning, while necessary in order to uphold and enforce the international rule of law, should run parallel to steps taken on the political level. The prosecution and punishment of war criminals by an international criminal tribunal (whether ad hoc or permanent) cannot be a substitute for robust action by the United Nations where required to restore international peace and security. As long as the ideological, political and military leaders behind the serious violations of international humanitarian law still remain firmly in power, flaunting with impunity their rendezvous with justice, this can only result in discrediting the work of international criminal tribunals. So long as states retain some essential aspects of sovereignty and fail to set up an effective mechanism to enforce arrest warrants and to execute judgments, international criminal tribunals may have little more than normative impact. Thus, we are once again reminded of the limits posed by international politics on international law.[15]

Another advocate of increased use of force in support of prosecution is found in Madeline Morris, who writes:

Political constraints, involving delicate balances of power, often with the specter of war or other violence, frequently prove to be a very real obstacle to the pursuit of accountability. In order to surmount political constraints, a set of facilitative provisions with the Guidelines [against Impunity] might state that member states should provide mediation or even military intervention to foster accountability under some circumstances. Of course, one can readily envision limits to what would be possible in this regard. The mixed results of peacekeeping and related missions trace those limits graphically. Nevertheless, diplomatic and military interventions can be efficacious and could be brought much more to bear in the cause of accountability.[16]

The 'limits' which Morris envisions are evidently logistical and practical ones. She does not address the question whether the process by which the decision to apply force is made will itself be transparent and accountable, nor whether the application of this enforcement power will therefore be impartial and fairly distributed. Such questions are essential when one discusses international enforcement through such mechanisms as the Security Council (see pp. 155–62 below).

[14] Cassese (1998) at 11–17.

[15] Ibid., at 17; see also Antonio Cassese, 'The Statute of the International Criminal Court: Some preliminary reflections' (1999) 10 E.J.I.L. 144, at 170–1 (criticizing the Rome Statute as overly deferential to concerns of sovereignty).

[16] Morris, n. 13 above, at 367.

The stream of scholarship of which the above are examples often implicitly or explicitly presents the use of force and the reduction of sovereignty in the name of enforcement as desirable, without considering adequately the formal and political limits to which the deployment of force is subject in the international system. The implication is that the international system is becoming or should become increasingly unified and increasingly subject to legal regulation, if only 'politics' and the failure of 'political will' did not intervene.[17] The point here is not to disparage such scholarship, which is frequently of very high quality; rather, it is to assert that international criminal law will only move towards more regular enforcement, or only maximize the legitimacy of such enforcement as it does achieve, if the 'real world' conditions in which it operates—including those of a sometimes unsettled and even contradictory international law—are examined more closely than has been done so far. Such pragmatic analysis must be considered a key task for the future, if the effective enforcement of international criminal law is to be secured in even a minimally fair and legitimate manner.

(b) The International rule of law and the State system

The required practice (and consistency of practice) called for by the accountability literature sits uneasily alongside some of the fundamental characteristics of the modern State system. If the international rule of law is to become firmly rooted in practice, it will have to do so against the background of the modified or post-Westphalian system of the post-War international order. This order is characterized by a diffusion or a 'delegation', primarily to individual States, of law-making authority, of interpretive and enforcement power, and of monopolies on legitimate force.[18] Were the enforcement of international criminal law to imply the revision of these characteristics, it would require a deep change in the international order, either through a marked decline in (or delegation of) sovereignty, or through a substantial convergence of interests among States (giving rise, for example, to an international police authority). Yet there are few signs that the tension between the 'international order' rationale of international criminal law and the State-centric character of the 'Westphalian' system is likely to abate in the foreseeable future (see pp. 185–92 below). In light of this, the achievement of the highest possible degree of regular enforcement for international criminal law depends on a realistic appraisal of the character of the international system and of its developing trends.

---

[17] 'What is needed . . . is the uniform application of these norms to the same types of victimization irrespective of the contexts in which they occur and regardless of how they are legally characterized, but the enforcement of these norms requires their non-derogation through political settlements and peace arrangements': M. Cherif Bassiouni, 'Searching for Peace and Achieving Justice: The need for Accountability', in Bassiouni and Morris, n. 9 above.

[18] Cassese (1986), n. 8 above, at 13–14.

The sovereignty of States and the role of international law in their interaction has been at the heart of the Westphalian system from its inception.[19] Sovereignty, however, is not always adequately characterized. First, sovereignty is often implicitly understood as arising apart from and prior to its existence as part of an international system. As indicated,[20] sovereignty is increasingly seen as a product of the recognition conferred by the international system itself, rather than as a pre-existing trait inherent in States. Secondly, it is sometimes assumed that sovereignty is synonymous with control or autonomy. It is important, in this context, that the *authority* to rule over a territory be distinguished from behavioural *autonomy* inside or outside that territory, and that the complex and unstable relationship of the former to the latter be recognized.[21]

Because authority and control are not coextensive, a sovereign State may delegate aspects of its decision-making power without eroding its sovereignty as such. It will be argued in connection with the phenomenon of 'globalization' (see pp. 185–92 below) that precisely such a development is an increasingly prevalent characteristic of the present system, in which sovereignty appears to be more diffused than in previous eras. The derivation of sovereignty from the inter-subjective recognition of States also leads to its character as contingent and changeable. The 'terms and conditions' imposed by the international community on those recognized as participants are variable over time.[22] Qualities that are constitutive of sovereignty, and functional limits to which the exercise of sovereignty is subject, may occasionally appear or disappear, and certainly change their emphasis. Thus it has been argued that territorial integrity has shifted from being a virtually sacred principle to one which is subject to greater flexibility in the wake of the Cold War's end, even as human rights and humanitarian standards have gained new importance as functional limits over the same period.

Even if these arguments support the conclusion that international criminal law is capable of being strenuously enforced by the international community without diminishing the institution of sovereignty, it is equally true that there remains a tension—if not a contradiction—between the rule of law for the 'vertical' order of international criminal law and the maintenance of the international system through the 'horizontal', auto-interpretive, auto-enforcing regime of international law.

---

[19] Ibid., at 34–8.

[20] See Chapter II, n. 74 and related text above.

[21] David Held, David Goldblatt, Anthony McGrew, and Jonathan Perraton, *Global Transformations: Politics, economics and culture* (Cambridge: Polity, 1999), at 52; Janice E. Thomson, 'State Sovereignty in International Relations: Bridging the gap between theory and empirical research' (1995) 39 Int'l Studies Q. 213, at 214, 216; and David Beetham, *The Legitimation of Power* (London: Macmillan, 1991), at 122–3.

[22] Cassese (1986), n. 8 above, at 22–6; J. Samuel Barkin, 'The Evolution of the Constitution of Sovereignty and the Emergence of Human Rights Norms' (1998) 27 Millennium 229.

In fact, significant delegations of decision-making authority in vital areas of the policing, security, and military functions of States are not typically made in international law. For all the international regulation to which the discretion of States was subject in the twentieth century, it remains true that decisions regarding the actual deployment of force are highly devolved in the international system. This is true, even given the 'monopoly on legitimate force' represented by Chapter VII of the United Nations Charter.[23] While the establishment of the UN (and of NATO around the same time) imposed significant restrictions on States with respect to the use of their militaries, the actual exercise of the nominal monopoly of Chapter VII remains subject (against the apparent wishes of the Charter's drafters) to the discretion of individual Member States, who exercise a political and diplomatic logic in deciding whether to contribute to a given operation.[24] While legal factors and international considerations play an increasing role in State decision-making, the very fact that key decision-making powers remain in State hands ensures an ongoing role for a range of extra-legal (diplomatic, economic, strategic, and 'purely political') considerations.[25] Despite the tremendous development in the scope and efficacy of international law in the twentieth century, it remains, to borrow Niemeyer's dramatic formulation, 'an edifice built on a *volcano*—state sovereignty'.[26]

The continuing role of a 'political' decision-making discretion in State hands has led to an international system in which any international equivalent of a division of powers has not been institutionalized. This is particularly true in the area of peace and security. Legislative, executive, and adjudicative functions all combine in the discretion of States. The existence of an international 'constitution' entailing a sustained division of powers therefore remains at best contestable.[27] A consequence of this is that the responses of

[23] The combined effect of the relevant provisions of the UN Charter (Chapter 2, nn. 76–7 above) is to confer on the Security Council as custodian of the primary purpose of the United Nations (to maintain international peace and security) an effective monopoly on the legitimate use of force under the Charter system. The only use of force expressly recognized under the Charter—apart from that under Chapter VII—is that of Art. 51, which reads in part: 'Nothing in the present Charter shall impair the inherent right of individual or collective self-defence if an armed attack occurs against a Member of the United Nations, until the Security Council has taken measures necessary to maintain international peace and security'. Even here, the use of force is conditioned upon the inaction of the Security Council.

[24] See Part III, n. 6 and related discussion below.

[25] 'Transformations in international law and human rights regimes impinge on the sovereignty of states but not yet, at least in terms of consistency of application, on the autonomy of all states. The *de jure* entitlement to rule may to an extent be transformed, but the *de facto* autonomy of the state may not yet be radically affected, due, of course, to weaknesses in enforcement mechanisms': Held, et al., n. 21 above, at 442.

[26] H.G. Niemeyer, *Einstweilige Verfügungen des Weltgerichtshofs, ihr Wesen und ihre Grenzen* (1932), at 3; paraphrased by Cassese (1998), n. 5 above, at 11.

[27] Colin Warbrick, 'The United Nations System: A place for criminal courts?' (1995) 5 Transnat'l L. & Contemp. Probs. 237; M. Weller, 'The Reality of the Emerging Universal Constitutional Order: Putting the pieces together' (1997) Cambridge Rev. Int'l Studies; Bardo

other States to a given violation of international law will be determined by a series of factors, some related to the political and legal context in which the violation takes place, others related solely to the national interests of the States deciding how to respond. Such a state of affairs is unlikely to result in the entrenchment of the rule of (criminal) law in any robust sense. The normative infrastructure of duties to prosecute, to cooperate with other States and with international tribunals, to apply no official immunities, etc. can only strengthen, but cannot replace, the multiple pressures that lead to compliance in the international system and contribute to that system's legitimacy (see pp. 185–92 below).

In light of the ongoing fact of autonomous State decision-making (especially with regard to the use of force) and the limited potential of the Security Council to act with regularity, it can be seen that the internal doctrinal imperatives of international criminal law—notwithstanding its justifying rationale of international order—are in tension with how coercive power is managed in practice. Insofar as international criminal law both *justifies* a limiting of sovereignty and *urges* it (through the discourse of enforcement and of the rule of law that it encourages), and insofar as its regular enforcement would require the use of force, the core doctrines of international criminal law assume a dramatic rationalization of international sanctioning power and of the use of force beyond that which currently exists. Moreover, the view that the contemporary world order is capable of or is even approaching such rationalization appears to be implicit in at least some calls for accountability for violations of international criminal law and for the use of international police or military powers to this end. Yet because regular enforcement assumes impartiality in the use of force, while in reality a carefully guarded residue of political discretion continues to play a decisive role, one could argue that in its strongest form, 'accountability' advocacy may indirectly lend support to a highly selective and imperfect form of justice by promoting (irregular) intervention by the Security Council or by individual States.

From this conclusion it may be seen that the rule of law, whether national or international, intrinsically involves some redistribution of power as a result of the formal equality it presupposes and which, when properly functioning, it reinforces. To call for the international rule of law to be fully or formally realized in practice is therefore to ask States to agree to a redistribution of power in a crucial area. Leading States, including in particular the United States, have recognized this impetus and have acted to ensure that developments in this area are compatible with their own interests (see pp. 163–84 below). Whatever the prospects for the rule of law in the international system at present, understanding the sometimes complementary, sometimes

Fassbender, 'The United Nations Charter as a Constitution of the International Community' (1998) 36 Columbia J. Transnat'l L. 529.

contradictory connection between individual responsibility and the basic structures of the international community is crucial to any attempt either to explain the weaknesses of the pre-ICC system of enforcement or to sustain more effective enforcement in future.

Part II

Practice

The last decade of the twentieth century saw an unprecedented acceleration in the development of international criminal law. Not since the Second World War and its aftermath, with the formulation of the Nuremberg Charter and related prosecutions,[1] have events moved as quickly as since the start of the 1990s. A core of norms and principles, preserved essentially intact from the 1940s, has taken on new significance as efforts have revived to put them into practice. In particular, the Rome Statute of the International Criminal Court[2] aims to entrench an effectively enforced international criminal law as an integral part of both national and international life.

This renewal takes place against a historical background of lassitude, even failure. The market expansion, industrialization, and nationalism character-istic of modernity have seen both endemic atrocities and the emergence of liberal doctrines of human rights underpinning the Nuremberg principles. Yet efforts to give international criminal law the sort of effective enforcement implicit in the idea of the rule of law, whether nationally or internationally, were noticeably unsuccessful in the half-century following Nuremberg. Global strategic dynamics, a lack of political will, and absence of the neces-sary legal framework conspired to reduce the 'Nuremberg precedent' to an anomaly of fragmentary effects and often of little more than hortatory force.

---

[1] See Chapter I, n. 33 above and accompanying text. The Nuremberg and Tokyo Tribunals were established to try major war criminals, while trials by national occupation authorities dealt with lesser offenders (see pp. 84–5 below). At Nuremberg, 12 defendants were sentenced to death (1 *in absentia*), 7 to terms of imprisonment (3 for life, 2 for 20 years, 1 for 15 years, 1 for 10 years), and 3 were acquitted: see M.C. Bassiouni, *Crimes Against Humanity under International Law* (Dordrecht: Martinus Nijhoff, 1992) at 208–10 and 586–9. For an even-handed review of the fair-ness of the Nuremberg trials by a former member of the American prosecution team, see Telford Taylor, *The Anatomy of the Nuremberg Trials* (New York: Alfred A. Knopf, 1992), at 626–49. The Tokyo Tribunal stood largely for the same principles but has been more widely criticised for unfairness. Of 28 defendants, 2 died during trial, 1 was unable to plead and was assigned to a psy-chiatric ward, while, in its judgment of 4 November 1948, the Tribunal sentenced 7 to death and the remaining 18 to terms of imprisonment (16 for life, 1 for 20 years and 1 for 7 years): see Bassiouni, ibid. at 211–12 and 619–21; A.C. Brackman, *The Other Nuremberg: The untold story of the Tokyo war crimes trials* (London: Collins, 1989), at 422ff. and 454–62; R.S. Clark, 'Nuremberg and Tokyo in Contemporary Perspective', in T.L.H McCormack and G.J. Simpson, eds., *The Law of War Crimes: National and international approaches* (The Hague: Kluwer, 1997) 171, at 179ff.; and R.H. Minear, *Victors' Justice: The Tokyo war crimes trial* (Princeton, NJ: Princeton U.P., 1971), esp. chs. 3 and 4.

[2] See Introduction, n. 1, above.

Once the Nuremberg and Tokyo Tribunals had completed their task, initial moves to establish a permanent international jurisdiction to succeed them faltered and died in the rising tide of the Cold War. After affirming the Nuremberg Principles (without describing their content), the General Assembly instructed the newly established International Law Commission to formulate those same principles.[3] The Assembly, rather than adopting the text subsequently submitted to it,[4] returned it to the ILC for further consideration.[5] Meanwhile, the 1948 Genocide Convention was adopted, which contemplates trial 'by such international penal tribunal as may have jurisdiction with respect to those contracting parties which shall have accepted its jurisdiction'.[6] The General Assembly asked the ILC to incorporate the Nuremberg Principles into a Draft Code of Offenses Against the Peace and Security of Mankind,[7] as well as to study the desirability and possibility of establishing a permanent International Criminal Court.[8] The ILC considered that the establishment of a Court was both desirable and possible.[9] The General Assembly then established a Committee on International Criminal Jurisdiction,[10] which submitted draft statutes in 1951 and 1953.[11] Under the pretext of a temporary delay pending completion of a definition of aggression under consideration by a Special Committee, the Assembly instructed the ILC to halt its work on the Draft Code in 1954.[12] The Court followed the Draft Code into oblivion.

In the atmosphere of suspicion and obstructionism brought on by the Cold War, enforcement was left to national systems (as through the Genocide and Geneva Conventions) and proved ineffective. Conflicts continued and atrocities took place (mostly within the borders of individual States) not infrequently with the acquiescence, connivance, or direct involvement of one of the superpowers. In spite of this, efforts to bring Nazi perpetrators of genocide and crimes against humanity to justice kept issues of accountability in the

---

[3] G.A. Res. 177(II) (21 November 1947), Chapter II, n. 62 above.

[4] *Report of the International Law Commission Covering its Second Session,* (1950) 5 U.N. G.A.O.R. Supp. No.12, U.N. Doc. A/1316 ['1950 ILC Report'], at 11.

[5] G.A. Res. 488(V) (12 December 1950), U.N. Doc. A/1775, G.A.O.R., 5th Sess., Supp. No. 20, at 77.

[6] *Convention on the Prevention and Punishment of the Crime of Genocide,* 9 December 1948, 78 U.N.T.S. 277, Art. 6.

[7] In G.A. Res. 177(II): see pp. 28–9 above.

[8] G.A. Res. 260B(III) (9 December 1948), U.N. Doc. A/810 (1948), G.A.O.R., 3rd Sess., Pt. 1, at 177.

[9] 1950 ILC Report, n. 4 above, at 16.

[10] G.A. Res. 489(V) (12 December 1950), U.N. Doc. A/810 (1948), G.A.O.R., 3rd Sess., Pt. 1, at 177.

[11] (1952) 7 U.N. G.A.O.R. Supp. No. 11, U.N. Doc. A/2136 and (1953) 9 U.N. G.A.O.R. Supp. No. 12, U.N. Doc. A/2645: the latter is reprinted in M.C. Bassiouni, ed., *The Statute of the International Criminal Court: A documentary history* (Ardsley, N.Y.: Transnational, 1998).

[12] G.A. Res. 897(IX) (4 December 1954), U.N. Doc. A/2890, G.A.O.R., 9th Sess., Supp. No. 21, at 50.

spotlight, at least to some extent, from the 1960s through the 1980s (see Chapter V, n. 6). Then, in a unique convergence of opportunity, will, and events, the International Criminal Tribunals for the Former Yugoslavia and for Rwanda were established (Chapter IV, n. 10 below), while renewed efforts to develop a permanent international criminal jurisdiction gathered momentum. The adoption of the Rome Statute in July 1998 and its entry into force on 1 July 2002 have set the stage for a new, pragmatic phase in international criminal law, one in which the practicality and the aspirations of this law will be tested and refined in the political, financial, and legal environment of the early twenty-first century.

This Part examines a number of areas crucial to the effectiveness and legitimacy of international criminal law, by exploring how the centralizing, 'vertical' order of international criminal justice has emerged or may emerge within the framework of the decentralizing, 'horizontal' order of inter-State relations. It begins with an overview of the outcome of the negotiations towards a permanent International Criminal Court (Chapter IV) examining the balance that was struck between State interests and the need for a credible system of international justice. As the ICC is conceived of under the principle of 'complementarity' as a court of last resort, deferring to good faith national processes, the following Chapters deal with investigations and prosecutions by the State on the territory of which or by the national of which the alleged crime was committed (Chapter V below), and with processes undertaken by States on the basis of universal jurisdiction (Chapter VI below). A very real barrier to accountability—at least at the national level—lies in doctrines of immunity, which are dealt with in Chapter VII. Should national authorities fail to take adequate steps to see justice done, the ICC will then have the potential to exercise jurisdiction, in which case States Parties will be under an obligation to cooperate with it. An examination of this obligation to cooperate therefore follows in Chapter VIII, revealing critical issues for the future effectiveness of the Court. In particular, it will be seen that, even with a permanent International Criminal Court, regular enforcement of international criminal law will be impossible without adequate national legislation and effective action by national authorities, given the absence of the overwhelming international police and military support that was available to the prosecution at Nuremberg. Because the support, or at least the acquiescence, of the United States is essential in mobilizing the Security Council, and because Security Council action will be indispensable where national authorities are weak or intransigent, Chapter IX reviews the evolving stance of the United States towards the ICC.

Emphasis is placed throughout this Part on the tension between the rationales that push towards the regular enforcement of international criminal law and the State interests that seek to retain critical discretion in State hands. This tension has an important role in determining the pace and course of development in this law, while its study reveals much about the factors that promote or hinder the development of the international rule of law with respect to the worst crimes.

IV

The International Criminal Court

1. BASIC SCHEME OF THE ROME STATUTE

The International Criminal Court must ultimately be the foundation stone of any claim that international criminal law is moving towards effective enforcement, that is, towards the rule of law. Only the ICC will have the jurisdictional reach as well as the potential resources and legitimacy to secure, with any regularity, a meaningful degree of accountability for the politically sensitive and politically motivated crimes that lie at the heart of the Rome Statute. More than this, the ICC's own effectiveness will afford the best guarantee that domestic legal systems will have an incentive to take genuine action against international crimes. A survey of the Court's design, history, and probable effects is therefore essential in order to assess how far it is likely to contribute to such results, what impediments it may meet, and what assistance it may need along the way. The analysis here is brief, focusing on key aspects that affect the prospects for the Statute's effective and impartial enforcement.

In seeking to clarify its likely effects, continual emphasis should be laid on two all-pervading and sometimes incompatible aspects of the Statute. These are, first, the way in which the Statute is designed to attract signatories and encourage cooperation with the Court by providing broad recognition of the authority, discretion, and sovereignty of States (both parties and non-parties); and secondly, those features of the Statute that aim to secure the Court's viability and authority through safeguards of its independence, impartiality, and effectiveness. The latter aspects of the Statute result from a tacit recognition that the Court will inevitably be judged by 'rule of law' standards, and that its long-term credibility depends ultimately on its performance in this regard. The tension, inscribed in the Statute, between the particular interests of States and the normative interest of the international community as a whole in repressing crimes under international law lies at the heart of the ICC system. How successfully the drafters of the Statute struck the balance between these two competing impulses will ultimately determine the effectiveness and legitimacy of the Court.

It is worth emphasizing that this tension or dichotomy is itself the product of the fact that the Statute is a treaty, and not some other form of instrument. It was recognized from the outset that establishment through a multilateral convention was the only means that combined viability with legitimacy for the Court.[1] That its establishment through a Security Council resolution—one of the available options—was rejected reflects in part the awareness of States, first, that the Council is not structurally suited to provide the sort of regularity that legitimacy and the rule of law demand, and secondly, that the mandate of the Council to take action to maintain and restore international peace and security does not necessarily overlap neatly with the need to address occurrences of the 'core crimes' of international criminal law. A gap between the rationales for imposing international responsibility under international criminal law and those for taking action under Chapter VII persists, notwithstanding some common principles.

As a multilateral convention, the Statute must be able to attract the broad signature and ratification that will give the ICC the authority, profile, and resource base necessary to make it viable.[2] At the same time, the Court as an institution, capable of imposing criminal responsibility, and that potentially of high government officials, finds itself within the most jealously guarded precinct of State sovereignty. To have deferred to State concerns at every step would have rid the Court of its effectiveness and tarnished its legitimacy. Yet to have demanded of States Parties complete submission to the Court would have ensured that the Statute attracted few—and geographically limited—ratifications, undermining the purpose and perhaps the very existence of the Court. The drafters of the Statute thus found themselves in a delicate balancing act between ensuring the Court's effectiveness and accommodating State sensitivities. The final text reflects this throughout, for example by disallowing reservations (Article 120) and giving the Court inherent jurisdiction (Article 12(1)), on one hand, while requiring deferral to national proceedings (Article 18) and allowing a seven-year 'opt-out' from the Court's jurisdiction over war crimes (Article 124), on the other.

A more complete study of how 'sovereignty' and 'effectiveness' came to be embedded in the Statute in the way that they were would necessarily be an interdisciplinary one. Such a study would involve examination of the role of NGOs and of the extent to which the decision-making procedures of various countries or political systems were susceptible to their influence. It would also

---

[1] 1994 ILC Report, at 32–4. The other options mentioned in the 1994 ILC Report were establishment by resolutions of the Security Council and even of the General Assembly. Like other NGOs, Amnesty International supported the establishment of the Court through amendment of the UN Charter, but recognized that this was not presently realistic: Amnesty International, *Establishing a Just, Fair and Effective International Criminal Court* (AI Index No. IOR 40/05/94) (London: AI, 1994), at 22–4; see also Roger S. Clark, 'The Proposed International Criminal Court: Its establishment and its relationship with the United Nations' (1997) 8 Crim. L. Forum 1, at 5–11.

[2] Philippe Kirsch and John T. Holmes, 'The Rome Conference on an International Court: The negotiating process' (1999) 93 A.J.I.L. 2, at 10. Not insignificantly, the ICC will be funded by its States Parties (Art. 117) on a scale of assessment not unlike that of the UN, at least until sufficiently broad support (including that of the United States: see Chapter IX, n. 7 below) becomes available to justify funding out of the General Assembly budget.

consider in detail the policy aims and relative positions of particular participants in the negotiations (notably the United States, Arab or Islamic States, the Like-Minded Group, and so on). Such a textured treatment of the negotiations and their outcomes will not be attempted here, although some major dynamics are outlined in the historical sketch below (at pp. 70–6).

Any full review of the Rome Statute would also have to treat those provisions promoting the Court's effectiveness with respect to sexual and gender-based crimes,[3] protecting victims and witnesses,[4] ensuring fairness and independence,[5] etc. These are not treated here. Rather, six features of the Statute are outlined, with emphasis on the interplay between safeguards for the fairness and basic effectiveness of the Court and features promoting broad State support and the prospect of relatively early entry into force. These features are jurisdiction (personal, subject-matter, and temporal), trigger mechanisms, preconditions to the exercise of jurisdiction, the relationship to national proceedings ('complementarity'), the system for State cooperation, and the role of the Security Council. The first three are treated in this Chapter (after a brief sketch of the main events in the development of the Statute). Because complementarity and cooperation are central to the effectiveness of the regime envisioned by the Rome Statute, and will be responsible for its greatest direct effects in securing regular enforcement, they are treated in separate Chapters (pp. 84–104, and 151–62 below). The role of the Security Council is also addressed Chapter VIII on cooperation (pp. 160–1 below). Regarding other aspects, prospectivity and clarity have been dealt with above (pp. 30–9) and those aspects of the Statute relevant to universal jurisdiction and immunities are dealt with below (at pp. 112–18 and

---

[3] These include the provision of sexual offences under crimes against humanity (Art. 7(1)(g)) and war crimes in both international (Art. 8(2)(b)(xxii)) and non-international (Art. 8(2)(e)(vi)) armed conflict, the appointment of a gender adviser to the Prosecutor's office (Art. 42(9)), recognition of the need for male and female judges (Art. 36(8)(a)(iii)), witness protection provisions (Art. 68(2)), etc. See Barbara Bedont, 'Gender-Specific Provisions in the Statute of the International Criminal Court', in Flavia Lattanzi and William A. Schabas, eds., *Essays on the Rome Statute of the International Criminal Court* (vol. 1) (Ripa Fagnano Alto: Il Sirente, 1999) 183; and Cate Steains, 'Gender Issues', in Roy S. Lee, ed., *The International Criminal Court: Issues, negotiations, results* (The Hague: Kluwer, 1999), 357.

[4] Such provisions include the establishment of a Victims and Witnesses Unit under the care of the Registry (Art. 43(6)), protection for witnesses and for participation of victims in proceedings (Art. 68), the establishment of a Trust Fund (Art. 79), and the power to assess and award reparations (Art. 75): see David Donat-Cattin, 'The Role of Victims in ICC proceedings', in Lattanzi & Schabas (1999), n. 3 above, 251; Christopher Muttukumaru, 'Reparation to Victims', in Lee (1999), n. 3 above, 262.

[5] In particular, broad protections are offered to suspects and the accused at the investigation (Art. 55) and prosecution (Arts. 63, 66, 67) stages of proceedings. The qualifications of the Court's elected officials (Arts. 36 and 42), their duties of impartiality (Arts. 40 and 42), and the powers of disqualification and removal from office (Arts. 41, 42, 46, and 47) further ensure this. See Silvia A. Fernández de Gurmendi, 'The Process of Negotiation', Fabricio Guariglia, 'Investigation and Prosecution', Hans-Jörg Behrens, 'The Trial Proceedings', Hakan Friman, 'Rights of Persons Suspected or Accused of a Crime', and Helen Brady and Mark Jennings, 'Appeal and Revision', in Lee (1999), n. 3 above, 217, 227, 238, 247, and 294.

136–46 respectively). Taken as a whole, these features seek to secure the maximum possible effectiveness of the Court in the context of the present international system, where the good will and cooperation of States is essential. As will be seen, however, serious questions arise as to the prospects for securing the effectiveness of the emerging system of international justice in the State system, as it exists.

(a) Development of the Rome Statute: General remarks[6]

The current momentum towards the establishment of a permanent international criminal jurisdiction began in 1989 when the Prime Minister of Trinidad and Tobago suggested to the UN General Assembly that an international court be established to try individuals accused of major drug trafficking offenses.[7] With this renewed international attention to what was to become the broader initiative of the ICC, an 'expert phase' began as the General Assembly asked the International Law Commission to resume its consideration of the issue.[8] The ILC over the next four years formulated principles, institutional outlines, and draft texts. At the request of the General Assembly, the ILC produced its final Draft Statute in 1994.[9] Although rudimentary in some respects, the ILC Draft rested upon a base of principles that continues to underlie the Rome Statute. It proposed the establishment of the Court by treaty and, recognizing that the widespread support of States would be essential, proposed a scheme based on respect for State consent, a complementary relationship between the ICC and national justice systems, and cooperation between States and the Court.

The movement from the scheme reflected in the Draft Statute of the International Law Commission to that embodied in the Rome Statute involved a shift from a markedly State-controlled and largely procedural instrument using 'opt-in' jurisdiction to a substantive one offering a virtual code of the applicable law, as well as inherent jurisdiction and a core of powers necessary for the effectiveness of an ICC. At the same time, the Court's powers remain entrenched in an overall framework that recognizes the primacy of States and national legal systems and provides for a flexible accommodation of their interests in a variety of ways. Negotiations entrenched guarantees of effectiveness even as they elaborated mechanisms for flexibility, discretion, and deferral. As a result the Statute alters but does not remove the

---

[6] For a more thorough history, see M. Cherif Bassiouni, 'Historical survey: 1919–1998' in Bassiouni, ed., *The Statute of the International Criminal Court: A documentary history* (Ardsley, N.Y.: Transnational, 1998) 1; Kirsch and Holmes (1999), n. 2 above, and Lee (1999), n. 3 above.

[7] Bassiouni (1998), n. 6 above, at 16.

[8] GA Res. 45/41 (28 November 1990), U.N. Doc. A/45/49, G.A.O.R., 45th Sess., Supp. No. 49A 363, para. 3 at 364. The original consideration of an international criminal jurisdiction was suspended in the 1950s: see Part II, nn. 8–12 and related text above.

[9] See Chapter II, n. 24 above.

tension present in the ILC Draft between the rule of law and the room for political calculation that the Westphalian conception of sovereignty makes available to States.

When the ILC delivered its Draft Statute to the General Assembly, the process of creating a permanent Court entered its 'diplomatic phase'. This phase took on unexpected momentum as the international community, galvanized by widespread revulsion at the brutal atrocities being carried out, witnessed the establishment of International Criminal Tribunals for the Former Yugoslavia and for Rwanda.[10] The example of these institutions, their contribution to the clarification of international criminal law, their detailed Rules of Procedure and Evidence, and above all the way in which they highlighted the need for State cooperation, gave both substance and urgency to the ICC talks. The General Assembly handed the ILC Draft over to an *Ad Hoc* Committee in 1995,[11] which the Preparatory Committee of 1996 and 1997 succeeded with further debate and exploration of issues.[12] As more States joined the process and an array of non-governmental organizations and academics took interest, new options were introduced, refinements proposed, and procedural mechanisms elaborated. In particular, agreement emerged that the principle of legality made it appropriate for the Statute to contain exhaustive definitions of crimes, general principles of criminal law, and applicable defences (see pp. 30–4 above). It became apparent that the instrument establishing the ICC would resemble an international criminal and procedural code much more closely than the ILC had anticipated. Finally, in March and April of 1998 the Preparatory Committee prepared a consolidated text of its Draft Statute and Draft Final Act for presentation to the Diplomatic Conference.[13] In it, the ILC foundation was overlaid with much detail and bracketed text indicating differing approaches. New options included a Prosecutor empowered to initiate investigations *ex officio*, reduced possibilities to opt in or opt out of ICC jurisdiction, and extensive State obligations to cooperate.

---

[10] *Statute of the International Tribunal for the Prosecution of Persons Responsible for Serious Violations of International Humanitarian Law Committed in the Territory of the Former Yugoslavia since 1991*, adopted by Security Council on 25 May 1993, U.N. Doc. S/Res/827 (1993), Annex, adopting the Statute proposed by the Secretary-General in the *Report of the Secretary-General pursuant to paragraph 2 of Security Council Resolution 808* (1993), U.N. Doc. S/25704 at 36 ['ICTY Statute']. *International Criminal Tribunal for the Prosecution of Persons Responsible for Genocide and Other Serious Violations of International Humanitarian Law Committed in the Territory of Rwanda and Rwandan Citizens Responsible for Genocide and Other Such Violations Committed in the Territory of Neighbouring States, between 1 January 1994 and 31 December 1994*, adopted by Security Council on 8 November 1994, U.N. Doc. S/Res/955 (1994), Annex ['ICTR Statute'].

[11] See Chapter II, n. 32 above.

[12] See Chapter III, n. 33 above.

[13] See Chapter II, n. 39 above. General Assembly Resolution 52/160 (15 December 1997) formally called for the convening of the Diplomatic Conference.

The United Nations Diplomatic Conference of Plenipotentiaries on the Establishment of an International Criminal Court ('DipCon') was opened by Secretary General Kofi Annan on the morning of Monday 15 June 1998 at the headquarters of the UN Food and Agriculture Organization in Rome. Delegations from 160 States along with hundreds of NGOs and numerous Inter-Governmental Organizations participated over five weeks of intensive discussions. The Conference was presided over by Mr Giovanni Conso of Italy, while its negotiations were in the care of the Committee of the Whole, chaired by Canada's Philippe Kirsch. This Committee oversaw a number of Working Groups and informal meetings. As texts were prepared, they were handed to a Drafting Committee chaired by Professor Cherif Bassiouni (Egypt).

State participants fell into a number of significant groupings that affected the course of negotiations. The Like-Minded Group of countries[14] promoted the early establishment of an effective ICC, and its members sponsored some of the most progressive proposals to appear at both the Preparatory Committee and the DipCon. While a range of views characterized the Group, it was the single most effective State grouping in establishing, not just an ICC, but an independent and relatively effective one. Not insignificantly, the Chair of the Committee of the Whole and the Coordinators of a number of key Working Groups (including those on General Principles, International Cooperation, and Penalties) were delegates of Like-Minded countries. The dozen or so States present from the Southern African Development Community (SADC) frequently spoke with one voice through the delegation of South Africa, and were also significant and largely unified supporters of an effective Court. The EU countries issued joint statements on framework issues through Austria, the holder of the EU Presidency. Also, the Arab block and the Non-Aligned Movement (NAM) each provided a strong and relatively coherent front on at least certain issues (including the role of the Security Council, the regulation of crimes committed during internal armed conflict, and the powers of the Prosecutor). The permanent five (P5) members of the Security Council shared key positions and held some common perspectives. They were not of one view, however, and each took its own position in certain respects, with Britain, France, and the United States being particularly active. The impact of these three delegations on the proceedings can hardly be exaggerated, although the US occupies a category of its own (see Chapter IX). Its large and well prepared delegation, led by David Scheffer (Ambassador at Large for War Crimes Issues) presented many and strongly held views, often in isolation from other delegations. In adhering

---

[14] The LMG consists of approximately 60 States. Long-time members include Argentina, Australia, Canada, Costa Rica, Germany, the Netherlands, and South Africa. Jordan, Sierra Leone, and others declared their affiliation with the Group in the course of the Diplomatic Conference.

firmly to its carefully articulated vision of a narrow ICC, and reminding delegates of its power to 'make or break' the Court through its role on the Security Council and in peace-keeping and enforcement actions, its concerns affected the Statute in fundamental ways.

Some have claimed, not implausibly, that the NGO Coalition for an International Criminal Court ('CICC') was the most influential single player in the DipCon.[15] The Coalition was coordinated by a Steering Committee consisting of representatives of the major human rights NGOs and chaired by the World Federalist Movement. The Coalition divided itself at Rome into thirteen teams covering thematic areas, as well as issue caucuses (Women's Caucus, Victims' Caucus, etc.) and regional groupings. Through its daily newsletters and direct communications with delegates, its access to domestic constituencies and skill in media relations, the CICC proved to be a leading force at the Conference in terms of size, information gathering and distribution potential, and overall effectiveness in meeting its goals. NGO representatives found solutions to impasses that arose between States or State groupings, suggested text, made major proposals, and generally supported options that would lead to an effective Court. Being without the formal negotiating role of governments, the Coalition struggled to keep up with behind-the-scenes negotiations and to gain access to closed meetings. NGOs also had different levels of expertise and diplomatic ability, different and sometimes incompatible agendas, and a variety of working methods. Overall the Conference displayed an unprecedented level of integration of NGOs into the process of negotiations.

In essence, there were three fundamental perspectives on the core issues touching on the balance between effectiveness and sovereignty. The first was that State consent should be the overriding principle upheld by all aspects of the Statute. India, backed sometimes by the Non-Aligned Movement, Pakistan, Indonesia, China, and others, exemplified this view. This perspective emphasized maximum protection of State prerogatives, objecting to a broad role for the Security Council, to an *ex officio* Prosecutor, and to arrangements for complementarity or jurisdiction that would limit the options available to States, for example by providing for automatic and universal jurisdiction over all core crimes (which furthermore should be defined narrowly). The second was that endorsed by the United States (and to a lesser extent by other P5 States). It raised the importance of the role of the UN Security Council in maintaining peace and security as an objection to any attempt either to limit the Council's prerogatives in the exercise of this function or to give the Court the ability to prosecute military personnel and other officials from non-party States. This view emphasized the principle of State

---

[15] William Pace and Mark Thieroff, 'Participation of Non-Governmental Organizations' in Lee (1999), n. 3 above, 391.

consent (making the ICC a court of last resort for parties only) while allowing a departure from this principle where the Security Council was active, underscoring also the need of the Council to be free to execute its Charter mandate without unlimited scrutiny by the ICC. The third perspective, upheld by the progressive 'vanguard' of the Like-Minded Group of States (Argentina, Australia, Belgium, Canada, Germany, the Netherlands, and others) was that of promoting a 'just, fair and effective' ICC. Among the State perspectives, this was the closest to, and most informed by, NGO positions. It put its weight on the need for the Court to have genuine powers if it was to fulfil its mandates of ending impunity and deterring abuses. This included providing for an *ex officio* Prosecutor, giving the Court inherent jurisdiction over core crimes (broadly defined to include war crimes arising in internal armed conflict and excluding any armed conflict nexus from crimes against humanity), and crafting the complementarity provisions in such a way that States would have a real incentive to conduct national proceedings in a proper manner. It was this perspective, supported and deeply influenced in its development by NGOs, which ultimately formed the basic shape of the ICC, although significant steps were taken to achieve consensus by including elements of the other two.

Over the course of the Conference many differences emerged and irreconcilable proposals were made, while many more were overcome or reconciled. Contentious issues seemed to offer no hope of a solution, only to be resolved by hard bargaining at the last moment. Recognizing that agreement would not be reached by formal process in the time available, the Bureau pre-empted matters by coordinating, first, production of a Discussion Paper,[16] and then of a Bureau Proposal (a refinement of this crafted on the basis of extensive input on the previous document).[17] This evolving 'package' quickly focused the discussion. It incorporated aspects of competing concerns while proposing imaginative solutions to thorny problems such as the death penalty or the crime of aggression. It was able to provide face-saving solutions that accommodated the interests of various players and moved the Conference to the point at which agreement became possible on the overall shape and mechanics of the Court. The basis of agreement was the proposed text presented without options on an 'all or nothing' basis on the eve of 17 July, the last scheduled day of the Conference.[18] This package was voted on and supported by a majority of over two-thirds (120 States in favour, seven against, and twenty-one abstaining in an unrecorded vote, with the Non-Aligned Movement and the P5 being, significantly, split),[19] and the Rome Statute of the International Criminal Court was adopted. The Statute and Final Act of

---

[16] Discussion Paper, U.N. Doc. A/Conf.183/C.1/L.53 (6 July 1998).
[17] Bureau Proposal, U.N. Doc. A/Conf.183/C.1/L.59 (10 July 1998).
[18] Chapter II, n. 45 above.
[19] Kirsch and Holmes (1999), n. 2 above, at 11.

the Conference[20] were then opened for signature, and by the late afternoon of Saturday 18 July, following a ceremony presided over by the Secretary General, twenty-six States had signed.

The Final Act of the Rome Conference provides for the establishment of a Preparatory Commission ('PrepCom') consisting of all States invited to participate in the Rome Conference, and charged with proposing practical arrangements for bringing the Court into operation, including the preparation of draft texts of the additional instruments needed for the Court to function.[21] The General Assembly called for three sessions in 1999[22] and 2000,[23] and for two sessions in 2001[24] and 2002.[25] The Commission finalized its most demanding task with adoption of draft texts of the Rules of Procedure and Evidence and Elements of Crimes on 30 June 2000.[26] In addition to the Rules and Elements, which will be of immediate importance before the Chambers of the Court itself, the Commission prepared draft texts of an agreement between the Court and the UN and of basic principles of an agreement between the Court and the host country (the Netherlands), as well as of rules for the Assembly of States Parties, financial regulations and rules, an agreement on the privileges and immunities of the Court, and a budget for the first financial year.[27] The Preparatory Commission was also charged with preparing proposals on the crime of aggression[28] for consideration and possible adoption under the Statute's amendment procedures (Article 121(5)) at the Statute's first Review Conference, to be held seven years after entry into force (Article 123). Such proposals would include the crime's definition, its Elements, and the conditions under which the ICC would be able to exercise its jurisdiction (bearing in mind, significantly, the powers of the Security Council under the UN Charter). The draft instruments would be presented to the Statute's first Review Conference, to be held seven years after its entry into force (Article 123), for consideration and possible adoption under the Statute's amendment procedures (Article 121(5)). The draft instruments prepared by the PrepCom were placed before the first session of the Assembly of States Parties ('ASP') for it to consider and (as appropriate) adopt. The Preparatory Commission was to be formally dissolved at the conclusion of that first ASP session.[29]

---

[20] Final Act, Chapter II, n. 62 above.

[21] Resolution F, Annex I to the Final Act.

[22] U.N. Doc. A/Res/53/105 (8 December 1998).

[23] U.N. Doc. A/Res/54/105 (9 December 1999).

[24] U.N. Doc. A/Res/55/155 (12 December 2000).

[25] U.N. Doc. A/Res/56/85 (12 December 2001).

[26] *Finalized Draft Rules of Procedure and Evidence,* U.N. Doc. PCNICC/2000/1/Add.1 (2 November 2000); *Finalized Draft Text of the Elements of Crime,* Chapter II, n. 98 above.

[27] These documents are available online at the web-page of the ICC Preparatory Commission: http://www.un.org/law/icc/prepcomm/prepfra.htm (site last visited on 21 July 2002).

[28] See Chapter II, nn. 83–5 and related text above.

[29] Final Act, Resolution F, Chapter II, n. 52 above, para. 8.

By 31 December 2000, the deadline for signature set down in Article 125 of the Statute, 139 States had signed the Rome Statute, while twenty-seven had ratified. According to its (rather complicated) terms (Article 126), the Statute 'shall enter into force on the first day of the month after the 60th day following the date of the deposit of the 60th instrument of ratification, acceptance, approval or accession with the Secretary-General of the United Nations' (Article 126(1)). With the simultaneous deposit of ten instruments of ratification at the United Nations on 11 April 2002, the number of ratifications rose to sixty-six, triggering the entry into force of the Rome Statute on 1 July 2002,[30] and the convening of the inaugural session of the Assembly of States Parties in early September, to adopt draft PrepCom documents and initiate the nomination and election of the Court's key officials. The oversight of the Court will henceforth be in the hands of States Parties acting in accordance with the Statute through the Assembly of States Parties, although non-States Parties will still be able to sit in the Assembly as observers (Article 112(1)).

(b) Jurisdiction

A limited set of crimes, precisely defined and subject to clear (and relatively high) thresholds, alongside clear principles of jurisdiction *ratione personae* and *ratione temporis*, played a significant part in winning agreement to guarantees of effectiveness elsewhere in the Statute, as for example in the preconditions for the exercise of jurisdiction and the trigger mechanisms (below).[31]

The subject-matter jurisdiction of the Court is limited to 'the most serious crimes of concern to the international community as a whole' and will consist initially only of genocide, crimes against humanity, and war crimes (Article 5).[32] The limiting of the Court's jurisdiction to the crimes as defined in the Statute (in Articles 6, 7, and 8 respectively) and as strictly construed, is the result of the formulation of the principle of *nullum crimen sine lege* in Article 22 (see pp. 34–5 above). More importantly, it ensures that States Parties are certain as to the scope of their officials' vulnerability to prosecution, rather than having judges make recourse to the more debatable content of general

[30] 'Ratification Ceremony at UN Paves Way for International Criminal Court', UN Press Release (11 April 2002); Barbara Crosette, 'War Crimes Tribunal Becomes Reality, Without U.S. role' New York Times (12 April 2002). The 10 States were Bosnia-Herzegovina, Bulgaria, Cambodia, Democratic Republic of the Congo, Ireland, Jordan, Mongolia, Niger, Romania, and Slovakia. By 1 July 2002 76 States had become Parties to the Statute.

[31] 'Delegations were prepared to consider the inclusion of a broad range of crimes, if the jurisdiction of the court was limited, for example, by requiring state consent on a case-by-case basis or by permitting states to opt in or opt out of certain crimes. Conversely, the possibility of automatic jurisdiction upon ratification, or of a system close to universal jurisdiction, provoked some delegations to argue for a limited range of crimes, narrower definitions and higher thresholds': Kirsch and Holmes (1999), n. 2 above at 5.

[32] For the crime of aggression, see Chapter II, nn. 83–5 and related text above.

international law. The Court's power to oblige States Parties to cooperate in the prosecution of their own officials (among others) (see pp. 155–9 below), and the resulting incentive of States to take action through national courts (pp. 86–93 below) are circumscribed by the scope of these definitions. The definitions in the Statute are further refined by the Elements of Crimes adopted in draft by the PrepCom; although intended only to 'assist' and not to bind the Court (art. 9(1)), the Elements will be influential in the interpretation of Articles 6, 7, and 8.[33]

The crime of genocide, defined in the Statute to reflect the 1948 Genocide Convention, can be committed either in time of armed conflict or in time of peace (like crimes against humanity) and would be quite broad were it not for its characteristic special intent requirement (that the enumerated acts be committed 'with intent to destroy, in whole or in part, a national, ethnical, racial or religious group, as such').[34] Genocide does not call for a State or organizational plan or policy to commit the crime; this sets it apart from crimes against humanity, which requires acts committed 'as part of a widespread or systematic attack directed against any civilian population, with knowledge of the attack.'[35] Nor does genocide call for large numbers of acts or a specified number of victims, although the reference in the listed acts to 'members of the group', 'the group', or 'children of the group', and the inadmissibility before the Court of cases of insufficient gravity (Article 17(1)(d)) in effect ensures that scale (and with it, plan or policy) will be an important consideration.[36] The latter point is also true of war crimes, which do not in all circumstances require a 'large-scale commission' or a 'plan or policy' to commit them, although the Court will have jurisdiction 'in particular' in such situations

[33] Erkin Gadirov, 'Commentary on Article 9', in Otto Triffterer, ed., *The Rome Statute of the International Criminal Court: Observers' notes, article by article* (Baden-Baden, Nomos, 1999), 289.

[34] See William Schabas, 'Commentary on Article 6' in Triffterer (1999), n. 33 above, 107; see also Amnesty International, *The International Criminal Court: Fundamental principles concerning the elements of genocide* (AI Index: IOR 40/01/99) (London: AI, 1999).

[35] These words are from the introductory 'chapeau' to the definition of crimes against humanity (Art. 7), which was the focus of critical struggle over the scope of the Court's jurisdiction, outlining as it does the Court's authority to scrutinize the internal situations of States. Whether a link to armed conflict would be required, and whether the attack should be described as 'widespread *and* systematic' or 'widespread *or* systematic' were particularly controversial: Darryl Robinson, 'Defining "Crimes Against Humanity" at the Rome Conference' (1999) 93 A.J.I.L. 43; also von Hebel and Robinson, in R.S. Lee, ed., *The International Criminal Court: Issues, negotiations, results* (The Hague: Kluwer, 1999) at 92–8. The required attack is defined as 'a course of conduct involving the multiple commission of acts . . . pursuant to or in furtherance of a State or organizational plan or policy': Art. 7(2)(a). When the Rome Statute was first adopted, this phrase was criticized for raising the threshold of crimes against humanity beyond that required under customary law: see Machteld Boot, Rodney Dixon, and Christopher K. Hall, 'Commentary on Article 7', in Triffterer (1999), n. 33 above, 117. See also Theodor Meron, 'International Criminalization of Internal Atrocities', in Theodor Meron, *War Crimes Law Comes of Age* (Oxford: Clarendon, 1998), 228 at 233.

[36] See also the requirement of a 'manifest pattern' introduced during the PrepCom: Chapter II, n. 98 above.

(Article 8(1)). Article 8 lists a wide range of crimes in both international and internal armed conflict. The inclusion of any prohibitions relating to internal conflicts was strongly resisted by a number of States and the crimes adopted, although limited in comparison to those relating to international conflicts, were considered a victory by many and represent a confirmation of the precedents set by the *ad hoc* tribunals for Rwanda and the Former Yugoslavia.[37]

The jurisdiction of the ICC is subject to the limitations imposed by the preconditions to the exercise of jurisdiction, including those applicable to any additional crimes (particularly treaty crimes) incorporated into the Statute in the future (see pp. 80–2 below and 34–9 above). The scope of jurisdiction is also restricted to natural persons over eighteen years of age (Article 26) for acts committed after the entry into force of the Statute (either generally, or with regard to a particular State Party (Articles 11, 24)), where the *mens rea* and the forms of participation set out in the Statute are proven (Articles 25, 28, 30, 33), and where the particular grounds for excluding responsibility (Article 31) are not made out.[38]

(c) Trigger mechanisms

Investigations may be initiated where a State Party refers a situation to the Court, where the Security Council does so acting under Chapter VII of the UN Charter, or where the Prosecutor begins an investigation *proprio motu* (on his or her own motion) (Article 13).[39]

---

[37] One eminent jurist has described the manner of this inclusion as 'somewhat *retrograde*, as the current trend has been to abolish this distinction and to have simply one *corpus* of law applicable to *all* armed conflicts': Antonio Cassese, 'The Statute of the International Criminal Court: Some preliminary reflections' (1999) 10 E.J.I.L. 144, at 150. Theodor Meron, however, better reflects the majority of commentators when he describes the Rome Statute provisions as 'a significant advance': 'Epilogue', in Meron, n. 35 above, 305 at 308. The provisions on war crimes generally were made more palatable to delegates both by the 'plan or policy' words of Art. 8(1) and by the availability in Art. 124 of a voluntary seven-year 'opt-out' from the Court's jurisdiction over these crimes (see Chapter VIII, n. 42 below). The provisions on crimes committed in non-international armed conflict, in particular, were rendered more acceptable, first by the provisions of Art. 8(2)(d) and (f), which indicate that these crimes 'do not apply to situations of internal disturbances and tensions, such as riots, isolated and sporadic acts of violence or other acts of a similar nature', secondly, in the case of Art. 8(2)(f), by the requirement that the armed conflict be 'protracted', and thirdly, by the stipulation that '[n]othing in paragraph [8](2)(c) and (e) [setting out crimes in internal armed conflict] shall affect the responsibility of a Government to maintain or re-establish law and order in the State or to defend the unity and territorial integrity of the State, by all legitimate means' (Art. 8(3)): Kirsch and Holmes (1999), n. 2 above, at 7; von Hebel and Robinson, n. 35 above, at 103–22; Michael Cottier *et al.*, 'Commentary on Article 8', in Triffterer (1999), n. 33 above, 173; see also Chapter VI, n. 24 below.

[38] Per Saland, 'International Criminal Law Principles', in Lee (1999) 189; see also the relevant commentaries in Triffterer (1999), n. 33 above.

[39] Elizabeth Wilmshurst, 'The Jurisdiction of the Court', in Lee (1999), n. 3 above, 127; Sharon A. Williams, 'Commentary on Article 13', Antonio Marchese, 'Commentary on Article 14', Morten Bergsmo and Jelena Pejic, 'Commentary on Article 15', in Triffterer (1999), n. 33 above, 343, 353, and 359.

That States Parties would have the power to refer a situation to the Court was uncontroversial, although some States (such as India) wished this to be the only means of triggering jurisdiction. That the Security Council should have the power of referral to the Court when exercising its Chapter VII powers was all but universally supported. India and some others objected that a political body such as the Council could have no legitimate role in an independent Court, while the U.S. sought a referral power extended to encompass situations involving the exercise of any powers of the Council (and not just those under Chapter VII). The inclusion of the referral power (limited to Chapter VII activity) was supported in the name of allowing the ICC to act in lieu of any future *ad hoc* tribunals (although this prospect has been thrown into doubt by the stance of the United States: see Chapter IX). Referrals by both States and the Security Council are of 'situations', not 'cases', in order to protect the Prosecutor's power to select suspects impartially and, with this, to protect the reputation of the Court.

The provision granting the Prosecutor power to initiate investigations *proprio motu* on the basis of information from any source (Article 15) was one of the most controversial of the entire Diplomatic Conference.[40] The *proprio motu* power became acceptable only in light of the rest of the Statute. It was a combination of limited and express jurisdiction, of strict preconditions to that jurisdiction, of stringent admissibility requirements, and much else that made possible the incorporation of this power. The power is also subject to significant safeguards on the Prosecutor's exercise of it, including the required authorization by the Pre-Trial Chamber of a proposed investigation (Article 15(3)) and the duty on the Prosecutor to notify governments of proposed investigations and to defer to any national proceedings except in limited circumstances (Article 18).[41] Also indispensable are the guarantees of competence, independence, and accountability to which both the Prosecutor and the judges of the Court are subject (Articles 36, 40, 42, 43, 46, 47). The *proprio motu* power ensures the potential effectiveness of the ICC where States or the Security Council, for political or other reasons, choose not to refer a situation

---

[40] See Silvia A. Fernández di Gurmendi, 'The Role of the International Prosecutor' in Lee (1999), n. 3 above, 175.

[41] The key point of procedural divergence in initiating investigations under the different trigger mechanisms is that of the 'reasonable basis' finding. Where the Prosecutor receives a referral from a State or from the Security Council, she or he considers, *inter alia*, whether there is 'a reasonable basis to believe that a crime within the jurisdiction of the Court has been or is being committed' and if so, and if the other considerations are met, she or he is obliged to initiate an investigation (Art. 53(1)). This initiation then makes available the Prosecutor's investigative powers, including the power to make cooperation requests, which are binding on States Parties under Part 9 of the Statute (Art. 54). On the other hand, when the Prosecutor receives information from any source under her or his *proprio motu* power, she or he then considers whether it discloses a 'reasonable basis to proceed with an investigation', and if so, she or he must then apply to the Pre-Trial Chamber for authorization to investigate. It is the authorization of the Pre-Trial Chamber that makes available the investigative powers of Art. 54, giving rise to the obligation to cooperate under Part 9.

to the Court. Because the power is not restricted to 'situations', it allows families of victims and others interested in a specific case to avail themselves of the Court. As States will have to take action through national courts if they do not wish the ICC to exercise jurisdiction, the *proprio motu* power substantially enhances States' incentive to ensure accountability through their national legal systems. Without this power, the potential effectiveness of the Court would have been seriously diminished.

The *proprio motu* power of the Prosecutor is no guarantor of the ICC's effectiveness in the broadest sense, however. The limited preconditions to the Court's exercise of jurisdiction (below) render the role of the Security Council essential if the Court is to have a worldwide impact. While the Council may therefore be appropriately characterized as the 'sledge-hammer' of the ICC,[42] the stance of the United States (Chapter IX) opens to question the likelihood that the Council will fulfil its potential role.

(d) Preconditions for the exercise of jurisdiction

Through ratification, States accept the jurisdiction of the Court over the crimes in the Statute (Article 12(1)). However, the Court will not exercise its jurisdiction over a crime unless at least one of two States is a party to the Statute (Article 12(2)) or has consented *ad hoc* to the Court's jurisdiction (Article 12(3)).[43] These are the State on the territory of which the conduct occurred and the State of whom the accused is a national.[44] Advocates of a broader Court called for the addition of the custodial State or the national State of the victim,[45] and would have preferred simple universal jurisdiction.[46] The Conference Bureau, in its final 'take it or leave it' proposal,[47] narrowed the list to the territorial and national State of the accused to make the final Statute more broadly acceptable, taking a cautious approach that aimed at increasing the legitimacy and authority of the Court by closely linking its jurisdiction to that of its States Parties. The underlying principle is that territorial and national jurisdiction are the two most deeply rooted, universally

---

[42] Cassese (1999), n. 37 above, at 161.

[43] The Court will also be able to act in the event that the Security Council referred a situation to the Court (Art. 13(b)), enabling the Court to contribute to the maintenance or restoration of international peace and security in the same manner as the ICTY and ICTR.

[44] Both 'automatic jurisdiction' under Art. 12(1) and the requirement of a territorial or national nexus under Art. 12(2) were extremely contentious in the process leading to the adoption of the Statute. See Wilmshurst, n. 39 above; also Sharon A. Williams, 'Commentary on Article 12', Triffterer (1999), n. 33 above, 329.

[45] A widely supported Korean proposal would have ratification or consent of any of four States (territorial, national of accused or victim, and custodial) sufficient for the Court's exercise of jurisdiction: U.N. Doc. A/Conf.183/C.1/L.6 (18 June 1998).

[46] *Proposal of Germany*, U.N. Doc. A/AC.249/1998/DP.2 (1998); see Kirsch and Holmes (1999), n. 2 above, at 8–9.

[47] See Chapter 2, n. 93 above.

respected, and uncontroversial grounds of jurisdiction known to criminal law.[48] The result is to maximize the importance of broad signature and ratification of the Rome Statute: genocide and crimes against humanity are typically committed internally by State officials or their proxies, and if these States do not ratify the Statute the Court will be reliant on the Security Council to trigger its jurisdiction (see above).

The Court's ability to exercise jurisdiction when *either* the territorial State *or* the State of nationality of the accused is a Party (or has consented *ad hoc* through Article 12(3)) gives rise to the possibility that the Court may be able to exercise jurisdiction over the nationals of non-States Parties when such nationals stand accused on reasonable grounds of committing genocide, crimes against humanity, or war crimes on the territory of a State Party (or of a non-State Party which has consented *ad hoc*). However, in the event of such an exercise of jurisdiction the ICC would merely be exercising a jurisdiction indisputably available to its States Parties in circumstances anticipated by the Statute's admissibility provisions (typically, where a State Party was unable or unwilling to proceed). Moreover, the Statute would be addressing the responsibility of individuals, and would not be imposing obligations on States as such. The non-State Party of which the accused was a national could not, for example, be required to cooperate with the Court unless it consented to be so obligated. These arguments have not persuaded the United States, however, which worked strenuously against such jurisdiction at the Diplomatic Conference (see pp. 164–8 below).

The conditioning of the Court's jurisdiction on the participation of the territorial State or the national State of the accused defines the scope of the incentive the Court provides to States Parties to exercise jurisdiction through their own Courts. The fact that the acceptance of this jurisdiction by States Parties is automatic upon their ratification, that the crimes are defined explicitly in the Statute, and that no reservations are allowed (Article 120) are indispensable to this effect. Ultimately, given the importance that national proceedings will have in the regime established through the ICC (Chapter V), this result will have a significant role to play in the ICC's contribution to the rule of law.

Another matter—the power of the Security Council to suspend proceedings of the ICC—might for convenience be treated here as a precondition to the Court's exercise of jurisdiction. Starting from the position that the ICC should seek Security Council approval as a precondition to any exercise of its jurisdiction in a situation being dealt with by the Council under Chapter VIII, the United States agreed late in the Rome Conference to accept the 'Singapore proposal' on Security Council suspension of ICC proceedings. As a result, the Statute provides (in Article 16) that no investigation or prosecution may be

---

[48] See Chapter IX, n. 10 and related text below.

commenced or proceeded with for a period of twelve months after the Council, acting under Chapter VII of the Charter, has so requested the Court; such request is renewable.[49]

This arrangement represents one of the real strengths in the final draft. All permanent members of the Security Council emphasized the need to respect the primary responsibility of the Council under the UN Charter for maintaining international peace and security. In particular, they were concerned that the Council's exercise of its Chapter VII powers not be impaired by the work of the ICC. The US stridently repeated its position, the strongest of the P5, that the Court should have to seek authorization from the Council before it could proceed in relation to any situation being dealt with by that body under its Chapter VII powers. This would have given any of the P5 a veto over ICC proceedings (where they related to Chapter VII situations being dealt with by the Council). At the other extreme, States such as India, Iran, and other members of the Non-Aligned Movement, drawing attention to the political character of Security Council decisions and the unrepresentative distribution of its permanent members, objected to any Council power to suspend or delay Court action. To this it was objected that Charter Article 103 gives primacy to Charter obligations over any conflicting treaty obligation, in which case the Council arguably has power to suspend proceedings in any event.

The Singapore compromise, tabled during the work of the Preparatory Committee, charts a course between these two extremes. By requiring positive action from the Security Council before Court proceedings can be suspended, it effectively reverses the situation with respect to the veto from that proposed by the United States. Instead of enabling any P5 member to block the Court from proceeding by vetoing an authorization, the provision allows the Court to proceed until the Council passes a resolution requesting otherwise, and no such resolution could pass so long as any P5 member objected. Thus, although the request is renewable, it is entirely possible that changing political circumstances and loss of unanimity among the P5 will frequently make such renewals unobtainable. The ICC will only be interfered with where all of the P5 agree that Court action would harm rather than help its peace-making efforts.

The use of this relatively narrow, pragmatic compromise provision as a platform for exempting the personnel of non-States Parties from potential exposure to ICC jurisdiction was, of course, unforeseen until the United States proposed exactly this in mid-2002, as the Statute approached entry into force.[50]

[49] Morton Bergsmo and Jelena Pejic, 'Commentary on Article 16', in Triffterer (1999), n. 33 above, 373; Lionel Yee, 'The International Criminal Court and the Security Council' in Lee (1999), n. 3 above, 143, at 149–52.

[50] On the United States' use of Art. 16 to obtain a Security Council resolution purporting to exempt non-State Party peace-keeping personnel from ICC jurisdiction, see Chapter IX below, p. 180.

2. CONCLUSION

The basic jurisdictional features of the Rome Statute outlined in this Chapter will have a direct effect on the ability of the Court to promote effective, regular accountability for the core crimes of international criminal law. To assess this potential ability it is necessary to examine in some detail two further fundamental aspects of the Statute, namely the 'complementarity' mechanism and the system for cooperation with the ICC by national authorities and by the Security Council. The direct effects of these on national practice will be twofold. First, complementarity will, if it works as envisioned, provide States Parties with an incentive to mobilize national authorities to investigate and try alleged crimes when committed on their territory or by their nationals, and to do so in a sufficiently fair and impartial manner (see pp. 86–93 below). To a lesser extent, even non-States Parties will have the incentive to do the same with respect to crimes allegedly committed by their nationals on the territory of States Parties. Secondly, States Parties will have wide-ranging obligations to cooperate with the Court in the conduct of its own proceedings. These effects may lead to considerable amendments to national law and changes to national practice (see pp. 155–9 below). The national rule of law may ultimately be reinforced by the incentive that is provided to ensure the independence of the judiciary, while the international rule of law may be promoted by the cooperation regime. As will be seen, however, neither of these effects is likely to be unequivocal, and both are contingent on a number of legal and political factors.

The overall design of the ICC, despite some lack of clarity in the grounds on which it will defer to (Article 18) or take jurisdiction from (Article 17(2)) national courts, is one that does promise a considerable degree of effectiveness within its sphere of operation. Such a result came as a surprise to many at the Diplomatic Conference, given the level of resistance shown to an *ex officio* role for the Prosecutor and to other guarantors of effectiveness by some States, and is in large measure a mark of the coordination between NGOs and Like Minded delegations. However, this effectiveness was bought at the price of a careful narrowing of the scope of the ICC's powers, by imposing high definitional thresholds to the three included crimes, strict preconditions to the exercise of jurisdiction, and admissibility and cooperation procedures that are quite deferential to States. Nevertheless, the Statute shows a greater potential for effectiveness than many predicted. This potential is essentially a formal one; at the practical level, the formal potential for effectiveness meets a crucial limit in the diplomatic (and political) processes that will control both budget-making (n. 2 above) and enforcement (pp. 161–2 below).

V

National Proceedings (Including Amnesties)

1. INTRODUCTION

There are a number of advantages to holding trials in the State on whose territory, or by whose nationals an alleged crime was committed. Evidence is typically more easily available, the costs of investigation and of transporting witnesses to the trial are minimized, and above all, the proceedings have the greatest legitimacy and the greatest impact in the eyes of the society most immediately interested in them. They thus have the greatest potential for promoting reconciliation and restoring the social balance in a transitional situation. For this reason, perhaps the greatest contribution that an international system of justice could make would be to encourage the regular and effective enforcement of international criminal law by the jurisdictions closest to the events. Whether and how the ICC might act as such a spur, and the possible effects of this are considered in this Chapter.

In spite of the apparent advantages to victims and society, the historical record is not strong with respect to trials by 'front line' States of crimes under international law. Competition for resources, weakness of governmental institutions, the fact that the perpetrators have often been State agents acting to advance their ideology or to enhance what they view as order and security, as well as an absence of political will have all frustrated efforts to ensure accountability.[1] Not unrelated to the problem of political will, States often have inadequate domestic laws to try all of the relevant crimes effectively.[2]

Efforts by the Allies to pressure Germany into prosecuting war criminals in the wake of World War I were undermined by German authorities (including judges) who perceived the project as illegitimate.[3] In the period following World War II and the trial of Nazi leaders before the Nuremberg Tribunal, many mostly lower-ranking defendants were punished by various national

---

[1] For an impressionistic survey, see 'Doing Justice Abroad and At Home', chapter 6 of Aryeh Neier, *War Crimes: Brutality, genocide, terror, and the struggle for justice* (New York: Random House, 1998) 75.

[2] Christine Van den Wyngaert, 'War Crimes, Genocide and Crimes Against Humanity: Are States taking national prosecutions seriously?' in M.C. Bassiouni, ed., *International Criminal Law*, (2d ed., 3 vols.) (Ardsley, N.Y.: Transnational, 1999) ['Bassiouni 1999b'] (vol. III) 227.

[3] In 1921 the German Supreme Court, sitting at Leipzig, acquitted 6 of 12 accused selected from a list of 45 suspects agreed upon with the Allies; this latter list was itself a compromise from an original list of over 800 names submitted by the Allies: see Gary Jonathan Bass, *Stay the Hand of Vengeance: The politics of war crimes tribunals* (Princeton: Princeton U.P., 2000), at 58–105; M.C. Bassiouni, *Crimes Against Humanity in International Criminal Law* (2d ed.) (The Hague: Kluwer, 1999) ['Bassiouni 1999a'], at 519–23; James F. Willis, *Prologue to Nuremberg: The politics and diplomacy of punishing war criminals of the First World War* (Westport, CN: Greenwood, 1982).

courts and by tribunals set up by the Allies in their occupation zones. Owing to the fact that the victors conducted the prosecutions over their former opponents in a context of complete territorial supremacy, convictions were more plentiful than after the previous conflict.[4] These processes remain the historical exception, however, in the degree of control that was placed in the hands of those most willing to prosecute. When justice relied subsequently on the governments whose agents were responsible for the alleged crimes, much less zeal was generally apparent. There is little practice to point to during the Cold War,[5] although a willingness to make some efforts to hold perpetrators to justice emerged in the 1980s and 1990s in both stable 'Western' countries[6] and transitional Central and South American jurisdictions, notably Argentina.[7] This trend has continued in the wake of transitions in Rwanda, Sierra Leone, East Timor, and Cambodia,[8] where further willingness to undertake prosecutions (at least in principle) has been shown.

---

[4] Control Council Law No. 10, Chapter II, n. 82 above. Reports indicate that in Europe alone the United States convicted 1,814 individuals while Britain convicted 1,085, France 2,107, and the Soviet Union an unknown (but undoubtedly high) number; trials in the Pacific by American, Australian, British, Dutch, and Nationalist Chinese authorities also resulted in many convictions: Bassiouni (1999a), at 531–5; see also I.A. Lediakh, 'The Application of the Nuremberg Principles by Other Military Tribunals and National Courts', in George Ginsburgs and V.N. Kudriavtsev, eds., *The Nuremberg Trial and International Law* (Dordrecht: Martinus Nijhoff, 1990), at 263.

[5] An exception being the United States' prosecutions in connection with the Mi Lai massacre: see *United States* v. *Calley*, (1973) 46 C.M.R. 1131, *aff'd* (1973) 22 U.S.C.M.A. 534, 48 C.M.R.

[6] Australia, Canada, and the passed legislation aimed primarily at crimes committed by the National Socialists during World War II (although Canada's law went farther than this): see Chapter VI, n. 32 below. Klaus Barbie, Paul Touvier, and Maurice Papon were all convicted by French courts (in 1987, 1994, and 1998 respectively) for their activities in connection with the Nazi occupation of France or with the collaborationist Vichy regime: see Nicholas R. Doman, 'Aftermath of Nuremberg: The trial of Klaus Barbie' (1989) 60 Colo. L. Rev. 449; Leila Sadat Wexler, 'The French Experience', in Bassiouni (1999b), see n. 2 above, (vol. III) 273; ead., 'The Interpretation of the Nuremberg Principles by the French Court of Cassation: From Touvier to Barbie and back again' (1994) 32 Colum. J. Transnat'l L. 289; ead., 'Reflections on the Trial of Vichy Collaborator Paul Touvier for Crimes Against Humanity in France' (1995) 20 J.L. & Soc. Inq. 191. It is reported that between the end of World War II and 1988, the Federal Republic and the Democratic Republic of Germany together tried over 91,000 individuals for crimes committed under Nazism: Axel Marschik, 'The Politics of Prosecution: European national approaches to war crimes', in T.L.H. McCormack and G.J. Simpson, eds., *The Law of War Crimes: National and International Approaches* (The Hague: Kluwer, 1997) 65, at 74. The United States passed its own War Crimes Act in 1996, which prohibits acts committed on US territory or by or against US nationals: Mark S. Zaid, 'The U.S. War Crimes Act of 1996', in Bassiouni (1999b), n. 2 above, (vol. III) 331.

[7] Juan E. Méndez, *Truth and Partial Justice in Argentina* (New York: America's Watch, 1987); Anne Marie Latcham, 'Duty to Punish: International law and the human rights policy of Argentina' (1989) 7 Boston U. Int'l L.J. 355; see also Jaime Malamud-Goti, 'Punishing Human Rights Abuses in Fledgling Democracies: The case of Argentina', Jorge Mera, 'Chile: Truth and justice under the democratic government', Irwin P. Stotzky, 'Haiti: Searching for alternatives', and Margaret Popkin, 'El Salvador: A negotiated end to impunity?', all in Naomi Roht-Arriaza, ed., *Impunity and Human Rights in International Law and Practice* (New York: Oxford University Press, 1995) 160, 171, 185, and 198.

[8] See pp. 102–4 below.

2. THE ROME STATUTE INCENTIVE

The Preamble and Article 1 of the Rome Statute declare that the ICC is to be 'complementary' to national jurisdictions. The notion of 'complementarity' was overwhelmingly agreed upon at every stage of the negotiations from the ILC Draft to the Rome Statute, thus ensuring that the ICC would not supersede national courts, which are to retain primary responsibility for investigating and prosecuting international crimes. Yet even with agreement to complementarity in principle, the questions of whether national authorities or the ICC should decide the admissibility of a case before the Court, and of the criteria to be applied, remained contentious. In the end, and crucially for the Court's effectiveness, the ICC was given authority to decide the admissibility of cases before it, although the criteria of admissibility are carefully circumscribed to make them acceptable to States. The resulting balance has made the complementarity regime 'one of the cornerstones on which the future International Criminal Court will be built'.[9]

The Preamble of the Statute 'recall[s] that it is the duty of every State to exercise its criminal jurisdiction over those responsible for international crimes'. The question of *which* State has the duty to prosecute a given crime, i.e. the question of universal jurisdiction, remains ambiguous in this formulation (see pp. 109–12 below). Moreover, unlike e.g. the Convention Against Torture,[10] neither in the Preamble nor elsewhere does the Statute call on States to prohibit the crimes under the Statute or oblige them to extradite or prosecute suspects. Nonetheless, although the Statute imposes no direct duty, it is likely to have an indirect effect on State practice. Because the Court has the power to make the final decisions on the admissibility of cases before it, States that wish to avoid the adverse attention, the diplomatic entanglements, the duty to cooperate and other consequences of ICC activity have a real incentive to take action against crimes under the Statute. The preconditions to the Court's exercise of jurisdiction limit this incentive primarily to the States on the territory or by the nationals of which the alleged conduct was committed (pp. 80–2 above). Crucially, the effectiveness of this incentive is dependent on the provisions of the Statute as well as on the future jurisprudence and practice of the Court.

---

[9] John T. Holmes, 'The Principle of Complementarity', in Roy S. Lee, ed., *The International Criminal Court: Issues, negotiation, results* (The Hague, Kluwer, 1999) 41, at 73. See also Sharon A. Williams, 'Commentary on Article 17', in Otto Triffterer, ed., *The Rome Statute of the International Criminal Court: Observers' notes, article by article* (Baden-Baden: Nomos, 1999) 383, at 385–92; Jeffrey L. Bleich, 'Complementarity', in M.C. Bassiouni, *International Criminal Law Conventions and Their Penal Provisions* (Irvington-on-Hudson, N.Y.: Transnational, 1997) 231.

[10] See n. 20 below.

The complementarity regime is regulated through the admissibility provisions of the Statute (Articles 17–20). Articles 18 and 19 govern procedure, while Articles 17 and 20 set out substantive criteria. Article 18(1) requires that, with respect to situations referred by States Parties or investigations commenced *proprio motu* (but not those referred by the Security Council), the Prosecutor, on determining that there would be a 'reasonable basis' to commence an investigation,[11] must notify 'all States Parties and those States which . . . would normally exercise jurisdiction over the crimes concerned' of a pending investigation. If a State responds within one month that 'it is investigating or has investigated its nationals or others within its jurisdiction with respect to criminal acts which may constitute crimes referred to in Article 5 . . .' and requests deferral, the Prosecutor is required to defer to that State's investigation, unless the Pre-Trial Chamber otherwise authorizes (Article 18(2)).[12] Subsequent paragraphs allow the Prosecutor to review the deferral in case of 'a significant change of circumstances based on the State's unwillingness or inability genuinely to carry out the investigation' (Article 18(3)), permit appeals (including by States) against adverse rulings of the Pre-Trial Chamber (Article 18(4)) and enable the Prosecutor to seek exceptional authorization to take investigative steps during a deferral where evidence might otherwise be lost (Article 18(6)).[13]

This Article, introduced by the United States on the rationale that States should be given every—and the earliest—opportunity to investigate a case before the ICC intervenes, imposes significant limits on the ability of the Prosecutor to initiate cases. A presumption of deferral for six months at the earliest, 'reasonable basis' stage of an investigation, before the Prosecutor acquires the power to request cooperation of States Parties (and so, to begin to investigate in earnest) clearly presents dangers that evidence will later become unavailable.[14] While Article 18(6) takes account of this possibility in

[11] In the case of *proprio motu* proceedings, the 'reasonable basis' determination would trigger both the notice to States under Art. 18(1) and the application to the Pre-Trial Chamber for authorization to investigate: see Chapter IV, n. 41 above.

[12] Art. 18(2) itself does not list criteria to be considered by the Pre-Trial Chamber in deciding whether to authorize the Prosecutor to proceed notwithstanding a request for deferral, although the provisional Rule 55(2) adopted with the draft Rules of Procedure and Evidence on 30 June 2000 by the Preparatory Commission (Chapter IV, n. 26 above) would require the Court to consider the admissibility factors in Art. 17 (set out in text below).

[13] See Daniel D. Ntanda Nsereko, 'Commentary on Article 18', in Triffterer (1999), n. 9 above, 395; Holmes, n. 9 above, at 68–73.

[14] It is significant that after determining that there is a 'reasonable basis' to investigate (and subject to authorization of the Pre-Trial Chamber in the case of a *proprio motu* action: n. 11 above) the Prosecutor will apparently be able to investigate during the period between issuing the notice under Art. 18(1) and receiving a request for deferral under Art. 18(2). Such investigation, although generally requiring the cooperation of the State concerned (see pp. 155–9 below), could produce evidence of use in subsequent challenges to the sincerity of the State's intentions. In addition, the Prosecutor's ability under Art. 19(3) to invite the testimony of those who referred a situation, as well as of victims, will undoubtedly provide some compensation for the lack of formal investigative time.

contemplating exceptional investigative steps, there is a danger that the Prosecutor will not be able to satisfy the necessary burden of proof at such an early stage, where the investigation proper is yet to begin. Only the Court's eventual interpretation of this Article will determine the extent to which its abuse by States may endanger the subsequent viability of investigations. This potential danger will of course be multiplied where non-States Parties, which are under no subsequent duty to cooperate, avail themselves of this procedure.

Article 19 provides the main procedure for the Court's determinations of jurisdiction and admissibility, and is straightforward in its balancing of the interests of States and the requirements of effective investigation. It requires the Court to satisfy itself that it has jurisdiction in any case brought before it and allows it, on its own motion, to determine admissibility in accordance with Article 17 (Article 19(1)). Challenges to admissibility or jurisdiction may also be brought by a person under investigation, by a State with jurisdiction on the ground that it is investigating or has investigated the case, or by the territorial State of the crime or the national State of the accused (Article 19(2)). Significantly, the States bringing such motions need not be parties to the Statute. States are required to bring their challenges at the earliest opportunity (Article 19(5)), may only do so once, and must do so before the start of trial, although the Court has authority to allow otherwise in exceptional circumstances (Article 19(4)). These requirements are in part to prevent abuse of the process, given that the Prosecutor is called upon to suspend investigations, subject to limited exceptions, pending the outcome of the challenge (Article 19(7) and (8)). The Prosecutor has an independent power to seek rulings on admissibility or jurisdiction (Article 19(3)), and may request review of previous decisions on the basis of new facts (Article 19(10)).[15]

The substantive criteria of admissibility are presented in Articles 17 and 20, which are at the heart of the ICC regime.[16] Article 17(1) states:

the Court shall determine that a case is inadmissible where:
(a) The case is being investigated or prosecuted by a State which has jurisdiction over it, unless the State is unwilling or unable genuinely to carry out the investigation or prosecution;
(b) The case has been investigated by a State which has jurisdiction over it and the State has decided not to prosecute the person concerned, unless the decision resulted from the unwillingness or inability of the State genuinely to prosecute;
(c) The person concerned has already been tried for conduct which is the subject of the complaint, and a trial by the Court is not permitted under Article 20, paragraph 3;
(d) The case is not of sufficient gravity to justify further action by the Court.

---

[15] Christopher K. Hall, 'Commentary on Article 19', in Triffterer (1999), n. 9 above, 405; Holmes, n. 9 above, at 60–8.
[16] Holmes, at 43–60; Williams: both at n. 9 above. Also Immi Talgren, 'Commentary on Article 20', in Triffterer (1999), n. 9 above, 419.

This paragraph provides four situations in which cases will be *inadmissible* before the Court, the first three of which involve situations in which national proceedings are taking place or have taken place. The 'gravity' criterion of Article 17(1)(d) will apply to all situations, whether there have been national proceedings or not. Importantly, the phrasing of Article 17(1) allows cases that *do not* fall within the wording of Article 17(1)(a)–(c), assuming sufficient gravity, to be admissible before the Court (see below). For cases falling within Article 17(1)(a)–(c), admissibility depends on the Prosecutor satisfying the Court that the State in question is or was unable or unwilling genuinely to proceed (Article 17(1)(a) and (b)) or that the case falls within Article 20(3) (Article 17(1)(c)).

Where a national trial has already been completed, Article 17(1)(c) allows admissibility before the Court as an exception to the principle of *ne bis in idem* (double jeopardy) only where the terms set down in Article 20(3) are met. These criteria are essentially identical to those of Article 17(2), which define 'unwillingness' for the purposes of Article 17(1)(a) and (b). Article 20 (3) reads:

No person who has been tried by another court for conduct also proscribed under Articles 6, 7 or 8 shall be tried by the Court with respect to the same conduct unless the proceedings in the other court:
(a) Were for the purpose of shielding the person concerned from criminal responsibility for crimes within the jurisdiction of the Court; or
(b) Otherwise were not conducted independently or impartially in accordance with the norms of due process recognized by international law and were conducted in a manner which, in the circumstances, was inconsistent with an intent to bring the person concerned to justice.

In defining a State's 'unwillingness' genuinely to proceed, Article 17(2) states:

In order to determine unwillingness in a particular case, the Court shall consider, having regard to the principles of due process recognized by international law, whether one or more of the following exist, as applicable:
(a) The proceedings were or are being undertaken or the national decision was made for the purpose of shielding the person concerned from criminal responsibility for crimes within the jurisdiction of the Court referred to in article 5;
(b) There has been an unjustified delay in the proceedings which in the circumstances is inconsistent with an intent to bring the person concerned to justice;
(c) The proceedings were not or are not being conducted independently or impartially, and they were or are being conducted in a manner which, in the circumstances, is inconsistent with an intent to bring the person concerned to justice.

Articles 17(2) and 20(3) will encourage national authorities to comply with 'principles' (Article 17(2)) or 'norms' (Article 20(3)(b)) of due process recognized by international law, although these provisions do not require that national law conform to those standards as such. Rather, they make a case admissible where particular national proceedings fall short of such standards *and* show a 'purpose of shielding' or an 'inconsistency' of intent. It seems probable that the Court could find such a purpose or inconsistency where the lack of standards was egregious or where, for example, a sentence out of all proportion to the gravity of the offence is handed down. Generally, however, it is to be supposed that some additional bad faith or (at least in the case of 'inconsistency') a lack of good faith must be shown by the Prosecutor. States wishing to have the jurisdiction of their national authorities go unchallenged nevertheless have added reason to conduct proceedings in accordance with the applicable standards.[17] The risk of improper standards or of proceedings too flexible to ensure independence or impartiality will be particularly great where police, security forces, or the military are subject to their own courts or to special disciplinary procedures. Given a sufficiently rigorous admissibility jurisprudence, the Statute could therefore contribute to a upward levelling of standards between military and civilian jurisdictions, although the Statute takes no position on the use of military proceedings as such.

It must be assumed that the Court will require clear proof before it admits a case against the wishes of a State Party; the evidentiary burden on the Prosecutor can therefore be expected to be significant. Moreover, the success of the Court in conducting proceedings of its own depends on the willingness of the Assembly of States Parties (or the Security Council) to apply meaningful pressure on recalcitrant States (Chapter VIII). Whatever weakness the ICC regime may have with respect to enforceability, the possibility of a finding of 'unwillingness' and the public examination of factors such as independence and impartiality is certain to have some effect in prompting otherwise recalcitrant authorities to proceed, and to do so fairly or in a manner that appears to be fair. From this point of view, the ICC has at least some potential to encourage the separation of the judicial from executive process. The effect of the admissibility criteria on State practice awaits the jurisprudence of the Court, however.

'Unwillingness' (including Article 20(3)) and 'inability' are exceptions to the rule in Article 17(1) that cases are inadmissible before the Court where national proceedings are taking or have taken place.[18] Outside of these circumstances

---

[17] These will include the relevant provisions of international instruments defining human rights (the Universal Declaration of Human Rights, the International Covenant of Civil and Political Rights, and regional conventions) as well as humanitarian standards (especially the 1949 Geneva Conventions and their 1977 Additional Protocols), and may include non-treaty standards endorsed by international bodies (such as the UN Basic Principles on the Independence of the Judiciary, the UN Guidelines on the Role of Prosecutors; and the UN Basic Principles on the Role of Lawyers). For a survey of these standards, see Amnesty International, *Fair Trials Manual* (AI Index POL 30/02/98) (AI: London, 1998).

[18] 'Inability' for purposes of Art. 17(1)(a) and (c) presents fewer implications for national jurisdictions than does 'unwillingness'. It is defined in Art. 17(3): 'In order to determine inability in a particular case, the Court shall consider whether, due to a total or substantial collapse or unavailability of its national judicial system, the State is unable to obtain the accused or the necessary evidence and testimony or otherwise unable to carry out its proceedings.' The definition clearly contemplates a high threshold, and will arise before the Court with much less frequency than will cases of 'unwillingness'.

there exist situations in which, a case being of sufficient gravity to satisfy Article 17(1)(d), it will be potentially admissible because it falls outside the scope of Article 17(1)(a)–(c), i.e. because there have been no national proceedings at all. At least four such situations could present themselves. The first is where no State with jurisdiction has initiated domestic proceedings, and the second is where a State otherwise entitled to exercise jurisdiction voluntarily transfers the case to the Court. These are apparently straightforward (although the Prosecutor, or indeed the Court itself or the Assembly of States Parties, might encourage States to exercise their potential jurisdiction in order to spare ICC resources). The third is where a State does not commence proceedings or where proceedings are interrupted because of a bar under national law, such as a statute of limitations, immunity, or a grant of amnesty. Statutes of limitation present no difficulty, as the Statute expressly declares that the crimes within the jurisdiction of the Court are not to be subject to any such limitations (Article 29). Immunities, while of uncertain availability where the officials of other States are concerned, are similarly unavailable as between the State Party of the official's nationality and the Court (see pp. 136–46 below). A State Party the authorities of which refused to investigate and prosecute on the grounds of such a limitation or such immunity under national law would therefore be obliged to cooperate with the Court in its own exercise of jurisdiction. Amnesties present more complex considerations, and are discussed below (at pp. 93–102). The fourth situation in which cases would be admissible because no national proceedings are undertaken requires elaboration here.

This fourth situation is where a case becomes admissible before the Court when a State has exercised or is exercising its jurisdiction, but has done or is doing so on narrower grounds than contemplated by the Statute. This could occur where national laws bearing on criminal responsibility—be they definitions of crimes, general principles, or defences—define an area of responsibility markedly narrower than that provided for in the Statute, allowing *de facto* impunity for acts punishable by the Court.

Such admissibility gives States Parties wishing to preserve the right to exercise jurisdiction at the national level a powerful impetus to pass national laws in keeping with the substance of the Statute, in particular by ensuring that their criminal law makes available charges for the full range of crimes prohibited by the Statute. If any of the crimes defined in Articles 6–8 were not punishable under national law, the Court could in principle properly exercise jurisdiction. While many of these offences (murder, etc.) would form a part of the criminal law of all States, others may not. For example, criminal or especially military codes may not be sufficiently detailed to encompass the full range of sexual offences prohibited as crimes against humanity and war crimes,[19] may allow imprisonment or transfer of populations other than in

---

[19] 'Rape, sexual slavery, enforced prostitution, forced pregnancy, enforced sterilization, or any other form of sexual violence of comparable gravity' (Art. 7(1)(g)). Identical wording

accordance with international law,[20] or may not prohibit the use of child soldiers.[21]

Even with adequate definitions under national law, the application of narrower general principles than contemplated by the Statute could make a case admissible before the Court if national law thereby allowed impunity where the Court would punish. For example, were national law to provide a markedly narrower scope of responsibility than the Statute does in its articles on criminal[22] and command[23] responsibility the ICC could, in appropriate circumstances, admit the case. The same could apply where defences under national law are noticeably broader than those under the Statute.[24]

The foregoing discussion should make clear that significant implications for national law flow from the admissibility scheme of the Statute. The full extent of these implications will not be known until jurisprudence begins to flow from the ICC and until the willingness of the Assembly of States Parties (or of the Security Council) to enforce compliance with the Court is seen. Too much lenience in requiring conformity with international standards, or too high a level of proof needed to establish a 'purpose of shielding' or an 'inconsistency with an intent to bring the person concerned to justice', could be fatal to the Court's power to give States an effective incentive to do justice. The resulting weakness of the Court would also undermine any deterrent effect it might otherwise have through the increased activity of national authorities that it could stimulate. In addition to these uncertainties, the Court can be expected in its early complementarity jurisprudence to articulate a doctrine of the 'margin of appreciation' that it makes available to States, as some deference by the ICC to the apparently good faith efforts of national authorities will undoubtedly be granted, in light of the limited resources of the Court and

---

describes the corresponding war crime committed in international (Art. 8(2)(b)(xxii)) or non-international (Art. 8(2)(e)(vi)) armed conflict.

[20] Arts. 7(2)(d) (crimes against humanity), 8(2)(a)(vii), 8(2)(b)(viii) (international armed conflict), and 8(2)(e)(viii) (internal armed conflict).

[21] Arts. 8(2)(b)(xxvi) (international armed conflict) and 8(2)(e)(vii) (internal armed conflict).

[22] Art. 25(3) imposes criminal responsibility upon a range of actions (committing, ordering, aiding or abetting a crime, etc.), some of which (e.g. directly and publicly inciting others to commit genocide, Art. 25(3)(e)) reflect the particular nature of the crimes within the jurisdiction of the Court and may not otherwise be provided for under national law.

[23] Art. 28 is reasonably broad. Military commanders, or those effectively acting as such, are responsible for the crimes of subordinates where they knew or 'ought to have known' a crime was being or was about to be committed. Non-military superiors are responsible where they knew or 'consciously disregarded' the same (a narrower form of responsibility).

[24] Each ground for excluding responsibility under Art. 31 is carefully limited. For example, Art. 31(1)(c) excuses a person who 'acts reasonably to defend . . . in the case of war crimes . . . property which is essential for accomplishing a military mission, against an imminent and unlawful use of force in a manner proportionate to the degree of danger to the person or the other person or property protected'. A military code exonerating on wider grounds, by including e.g. more than 'essential' property or including responses to more than 'imminent and unlawful' uses of force, could lead to a case being ruled admissible.

the wide range of legal cultures and resource levels that States Parties will bring with them.[25]

Notwithstanding these potential curbs on the incentive structure of the Statute, States have begun taking steps to amend national law to reflect the jurisdictional scope of the Rome Statute.[26] Were this trend to extend widely, the resulting enhancement of the capacity of national law to prosecute international crimes, with any additional incentive provided by the jurisprudence of the ICC, could lay the foundations for a significant increase in the number and credibility of national proceedings against international crimes. If so, this would be one of the most significant effects of the Rome Statute.

3. AMNESTIES

(a) Introduction, relation to truth commissions

Amnesties, whether negotiated in political agreements, enshrined in treaties, or granted by national statutory or constitutional law, aim to prevent prosecution for acts otherwise criminal, typically in the name of promoting peaceful relations between those crafting the agreement. Frequently, even routinely, endorsed during transition from one regime to another, or as part of a peace settlement, amnesties ensure impunity against the ordinary process of the criminal law as a trade-off for the surrender of power or the cessation of hostilities. Being open to negotiation, they may apply to one or both sides of a conflict, to some or all officials (for example, by differentiating on the basis of rank), to certain crimes only, and may be limited by time, territory, or otherwise. As pre-conviction measures they are conceptually distinct from kindred post-conviction measures such as pardon, parole, and commutation of sentence. Where in force, the authorities are prevented from taking action within the scope of the amnesty, however unlawful the acts in question would otherwise be. The same, of course, is not true of authorities of jurisdictions not bound by the amnesty.

---

[25] Antonio Cassese, 'The Statute of the International Criminal Court: Some Preliminary Reflections' (1999) 10 E.J.I.L. 144, at 158–9.

[26] Canada passed the Crimes Against Humanity and War Crimes Act, Statutes of Canada 2000, c. 24, prohibiting genocide, crimes against humanity, and war crimes as defined in the Rome Statute, modifying relevant general principles, and providing procedures for cooperation with the ICC. New Zealand did the same with its International Crimes and International Criminal Court Act 2000 (1 October 2000), as did the United Kingdom with its International Criminal Court Act 2001, which received Royal Assent on 11 May 2001. South Africa has introduced an International Criminal Court Bill before the National Assembly (2001 Bill No. 42, online at http://www.parliament.gov.za/bills/2001/b42–01.pdf (site last visited on 21 July 2002)); Germany has adopted a *Code of Crimes Against International Law* (Chapter VI, n. 42 below); and Switzerland, and other countries are known to be working on similar legislative projects.

Amnesties for conduct amounting to serious violations of human rights or of humanitarian law are not a matter of merely historical importance.[27] A number of jurisdictions have introduced them in recent years, including Argentina, Cambodia, Chile, El Salvador, Guatemala, Haiti, South Africa, and Uruguay.[28] Nor were these met with uniform condemnation from the international community. In at least four instances, the UN 'pushed for, helped negotiate, and/or endorsed the granting of amnesty as a means of restoring peace and democratic government'.[29] Yet 'blanket' amnesties have come under increasing criticism on the grounds that they fail to affirm the rights of victims and are unable to secure lasting peace or meaningful recon-

---

[27] For the information in this section the author is indebted to Michael Scharf, 'The Letter of the Law: The scope of the international legal obligation to prosecute human rights crimes', in M.C. Bassiouni and Madeline H. Morris, eds., *Accountability for International Crimes and Serious Violations of Fundamental Human Rights* (1996) 59 L. and Contemp. Probs. 41, at 41–2; see also Michael Scharf, 'The Amnesty Exception to the Jurisdiction of the International Criminal Court' (1999) 32 Cornell Int'l L. J. For a thorough treatment, see Roht-Arriaza (1995), n. 7 above; and D. Orentlicher, 'Settling Accounts: The duty to prosecute human rights violations of a prior regime' (1991) 100 Yale L.J. 2537.

[28] See the sources at n. 8 above; also D. Cassel, 'Lessons from the Americas: Guidelines for international response to amnesties for atrocities' in Bassiouni and Morris (1996) n. 27 above, 197, at 200–4; and Scharf, 'The Letter of the Law', at 41–2, and 'The Amnesty Exception', at 507–12, both at n. 27 above. In El Salvador the parties to the civil conflict agreed, in negotiating the UN-brokered Salvadorean Peace Accords in 1992, to establish a supra-national process in the form of the United Nations Truth Commission for El Salvador, with 3 (non-Salvadorean) commissioners selected by the UN Secretary-General with the approval of the parties. In response to the Commission naming individual malefactors in its report, the Salvadorean legislature passing a blanket amnesty covering the persons named. For detailed history, see the Report of the United Nations Commission on the Truth for El Salvador, *From Madness to Hope: The 12-year war in El Salvador*, U.N. Doc. S/25500 (1993); and Thomas Buergenthal, 'The United Nations Truth Commission for El Salvador' (1994) 27 Vanderbilt J. Transnat'l L. 497; see also Douglass Cassel, 'Lesson from the United Nations Truth Commission for El Salvador', in Christopher C. Joyner, ed., *Reining in Impunity for International Crimes and Serious Violations of Fundamental Human Rights: Proceedings of the Siracusa Conference, 17–21 September 1998* (1998) 14 Nouvelles Etudes Pénales, 225 at 227. In Cambodia a 1994 law codified a practice that had existed since 1979, providing amnesty for Khmer Rouge members who surrendered to the government before the expiry of a six-month deadline: Craig Etcheson, 'The Persistence of Impunity in Cambodia' in Joyner (1998), n. 28 above, at 237–8. Despite halting pressure to establish a tribunal to try Khmer Rouge leaders, there is little sign that amnesties will be overturned or impunity substantially addressed overall: see n. 48 below. South Africa's Truth and Reconciliation Commission ('TRC'), the most sophisticated attempt to deal with a prior regime's systematic violations of fundamental norms, was empowered to recommend amnesties on an individualized basis in exchange for full and public disclosure of past abuses. The TRC brought to light an enormous amount of information, and through public disclosure by the perpetrators themselves, as well as compensation, provided at least a degree of closure to victims. Of course, only time will tell whether the high degree of impunity resulting from the TRC process will be outweighed by the measure of historical rectification, compensation, and reconciliation provided: see *Truth and Reconciliation Commission of South Africa Report* (5 vols.) (London: Macmillan, 1998); Jennifer J. Llewellyn and Robert Howse, 'Institutions for Restorative Justice: The South African Truth and Reconciliation Commission' (1999) 49 U. Toronto L.J. 355.

[29] Scharf, 'The Letter of the Law', n. 27 above, at 41 (citing Cambodia, Haiti, El Salvador, and South Africa).

ciliation.[30] Thus, for example, the United Nations distanced itself from an amnesty brokered in the negotiation of the Lomé Accords with respect to rebel forces credibly accused of war crimes and crimes against humanity in the civil war in Sierra Leone.[31] At the same time, amnesties accompanied by processes aimed at the rectification of the historical record through commissions of inquiry ('truth commissions'), compensating victims and reforming institutions have won broader (if uneven) acceptance.[32] The relationship of such reconciliation processes to criminal prosecution, and with it the question of amnesties, remains unsettled.

Amnesties typically remain a tribute paid, in negotiations, to the fact of present power, and their acceptability under any circumstances remains controversial, as any question setting pragmatism against normativity must. Yet increasing attention to the rights of victims and an emphasis on the criminal responsibility of individuals under international law has contributed to make the perceived legitimacy of amnesties limited and conditional, where it is acknowledged at all. An increasingly widespread view is that broader reconciliation processes are a desirable supplement to but no substitute for criminal prosecution.[33] This said, it remains true that criminal prosecution

[30] See Scharf, 'The Amnesty Exception', n. 27 above, at 512–14; Cassel, 'Lessons from the Americas', n. 28 above, esp. 228–9; M.C. Bassiouni, 'Searching for Peace and Achieving Justice: The need for accountability' in Bassiouni and Morris, n. 27 above, at 21; and Naomi Roht-Arriaza, 'Special Problems of a Duty to Prosecute: Derogation, amnesties, statutes of limitation, and superior orders', in Roht-Arriaza (1995), n. 7 above, at 57–60.

[31] See Preamble to Security Council Resolution 1315, para. 5 (U.N. Doc. S/Res/1315 [14 August 2000]) ('*Reaffirming* that the Special Representative of the Secretary-General appended to his signature of the Lomé Agreement a statement that the United Nations holds the understanding that the amnesty provisions of the Agreement shall not apply to international crimes of genocide, crimes against humanity, war crimes and other serious violations of international humanitarian law'); also *Report of the Secretary-General on the establishment of a Special Court for Sierra Leone*, U.N. Doc. S/2000/915 (4 October 2000), paras. 22–4 ('. . . the United Nations has consistently maintained the position that amnesty cannot be granted in respect of international crimes . . .'); Statute of the Special Court for Sierra Leone (Annex to the *Report of the Secretary-General*), Art. 10 ('An amnesty granted to any person falling within the jurisdiction of the Special Court in respect of the crimes referred to in Articles 2 to 4 ['Crimes against humanity', 'Violations of Article 3 common to the Geneva Conventions and of Additional Protocol II', and 'Other serious violations of international humanitarian law'] of the present Statute shall not be a bar to prosecution'). That the UN's view on the unacceptability of amnesties came late is widely known: 'Annan wrote that the United Nations "cannot stand between Sierra Leone's people and their only hope of ending such a long and brutal conflict." But the people of Sierra Leone had had no say in the matter, and the UN had actually been midwife to the agreement': William Shawcross, *Deliver Us from Evil: Peacekeepers, warlords and a world of endless conflict* (New York: Simon and Schuster, 2000) 389.

[32] For the tendency to see 'truth' and 'justice' as complementary and not mutually exclusive, see Juan E. Méndez, 'Accountability for past abuses' (1997) 19 H.R. Quarterly 255; Naomi Roht-Arriaza, 'Truth Commissions as Part of a Social Process: Possible guidelines' in Joyner (1998), n. 28 above, 279, and Peter A. Schey, Dinah L. Shelton, and Naomi Roht-Arriaza, 'Addressing Human Rights Abuses: Truth commissions and the value of amnesty' (1997) 19 Whittier L. Rev. 325, at 338–44.

[33] Cassel, 'Lessons from the Americas', n. 28 above, at 227–8. Rather than merely 'desirable', it has increasingly been argued that such inquiry processes are or are coming to be required as a

requires resources, institutions, and political will that may not exist in transitional societies. In such circumstances, amnesties (or simple *de facto* impunity) will only be prevented through concerted political action, nationally and internationally; and in the mobilization of international opinion, at least, arguments as to the lawfulness of amnesties are crucial.

(b) Amnesties and international law: General

The question of the lawfulness of amnesties under international law is of considerable importance to the project for a system of international criminal law based on the rule of law. If amnesties are not permissible with respect to a given offence, a State adopting one would thereby violate its obligations under international law, even if the measure were democratically adopted or endorsed.[34] Provided appropriate mechanisms are available, it would be possible to challenge such a measure in national or international fora.[35] Even barring formal procedures for ruling on lawfulness, the need for international legitimacy in the face of informal pressures has become a very real consideration for national governments faced with global media and NGO scrutiny. With this, determining the lawfulness of amnesties has become important.

As a general matter, amnesties are neither prohibited nor allowed under the express terms of international law, with one notable exception. This is Article 6(5) of Additional Protocol II to the 1949 Geneva Conventions, which provides: 'At the end of hostilities, the authorities in power shall endeavour to grant the broadest possible amnesty to persons who have participated in the armed conflict, or those deprived of their liberty for reasons related to the armed conflict, whether they are interned or detained'.

It has been credibly argued, however, that this provision does not authorize including within 'the broadest possible amnesty' conduct giving rise to individual responsibility under international law, or gross violations of human rights more generally, even if it has been cited in justification of amnesties for such acts.[36] Rather, the provision is intended primarily to discourage the prosecution under ordinary criminal law of those who have taken

consequence of a 'right to the truth': see Cassel, ibid., at 227; and Juan E. Méndez, 'The Right to Truth', in Joyner (1998), n. 28 above, 256.

[34] Cassel, 'Lessons from the Americas', n. 28 above, at 228–9, citing *Hugo Leonardo et al.,* Rep. No. 29/92, Cases no. 10.029 *et al.,* (1992–1993) Ann. Rep. Inter-Am. Comm'n H.R. 154, O.A.S. Doc. No. OEA/Ser.L/V/II.83, doc. 14, corr.1 (12 March 1993), in which the Commission found that an amnesty violated Uruguay's duty under the American Convention to protect human rights, despite the fact that it was approved by the populace in a referendum.

[35] As has been done: see Cassel, 'Lessons from the Americas', n. 28 above; and Roht-Arriaza, n. 30 above.

[36] For example, in the Decision of the Supreme Court of Justice of El Salvador on the Amnesty Law, Proceedings No. 10–93 (May 20, 1993), reprinted in Neil J. Kritz, ed., *Transitional Justice: How Emerging Democracies reckon with former regimes* (Washington D.C.: U.S. Institute of Peace, 1995) at 549, 555, and cited in Cassel, 'Letters from the Americas', n. 28 above, at 218.

up arms against the government in a civil conflict. In the view of the International Committee of the Red Cross:

Article 6(5) of Protocol II is the only and very limited equivalent in the law of non-international armed conflict of what is known in the law of international armed conflict as 'combatant immunity', i.e., the fact that a combatant may not be punished for acts of hostility, including killing enemy combatants, *as long as he respected international humanitarian law*, and that he has to be repatriated at the end of active hostilities. In non-international armed conflicts, no such principle exists, and those who fight may be punished, under national legislation, for the mere fact of having fought, even if they respected international humanitarian law. The 'travaux préparatoires' of [Article] 6(5) indicate that this provision aims at encouraging amnesty, i.e., a sort of release at the end of hostilities, for those detained or punished for the mere fact of having participated in hostilities. *It does not aim at an amnesty for those having violated international humanitarian law.*[37]

Article 6(5) therefore encourages reconciliation without infringing the principle of accountability under international law for crimes against humanity, genocide, and war crimes committed by either State or non-State agents during non-international armed conflict.

If international law does not directly address the subject of amnesties for conduct carrying individual responsibility, it becomes necessary to ask whether it forbids amnesties indirectly, by necessary inference. Here, the scope of any duty to prosecute will be determinative, as an absolute duty to prosecute cannot be compatible with measures aimed at preventing prosecution (at least, with blanket amnesties). On this reasoning, it has been asserted that States Parties to instruments prescribing such a duty would violate their international obligations were they to pass an amnesty with respect to the conduct defined by the instrument. This would apply to States Parties to the 1948 Genocide Convention,[38] to the 1949 Geneva Conventions (with respect to 'grave breaches' as well as to the relevant provisions of Additional Protocol I),[39] and to the Convention Against Torture,[40] all of which impose a duty to

---

[37] Letter from Dr Toni Pfanner, Head of the Legal Division, ICRC Headquarters, Geneva to Douglass Cassel, quoted in Cassel, ibid., in Bassiouni and Morris (1996), n. 27 above, at 218 [Cassel's emphasis]; see also Roht-Arriaza, n. 30 above, at 58–9 (pointing out the flexible, non-mandatory nature of the provision). Nonetheless, the ICRC Commentary on Art. 6(5) does not allude to any special consideration for crimes under international law: Yves Sandoz *et. al.*, eds., *Commentary on the Additional Protocols of 8 June 1977 to the Geneva Conventions of 12 August 1949* (Geneva: I.C.R.C./Martinus Nijhoff, 1987), at 1402.

[38] See Part II, n. 6 above, Art. 4.

[39] See Chapter VI, nn. 17 and 19 below.

[40] See Chapter VI, n. 21 below, Art. 7(1) ('The State Party in the territory under whose jurisdiction a person alleged to have committed any offense referred to in Article 4 is found shall . . . , if it does not extradite him, submit the case to its competent authorities for the purpose of prosecution'). The Committee Against Torture has held that, although it has no jurisdiction with respect to an amnesty law passed before the entry into force of the Convention for the jurisdiction enacting it, such a law is incompatible with the Convention's spirit and purpose: Decision on admissibility, dated November 23, 1989, Regarding Communications nos. 1/1988, 2/1988 and

prosecute. As the Geneva Conventions and Torture Convention also impose mandatory 'universal jurisdiction' (through a duty to extradite or prosecute) this prohibition on amnesties would extend beyond the State where the crime took place to encompass all States Parties.[41] Where applicable conventions are either non-existent or not widely ratified, it is necessary to construe other sources of law in search of a duty to prosecute. This is not difficult in the case of crimes against humanity, as it has been widely argued that there exists under customary law a duty to prosecute these and other international crimes (including, more recently, crimes committed in the course of non-international armed conflicts).[42] Such international criminalization is typically seen to bring with it both a duty to prosecute on the part of the territorial or national State, and a permissive universal jurisdiction on the part of all nations; both of which are difficult to reconcile with the (blanket) amnesties (see pp. 109–12 below).

Yet the existence of a duty to prosecute does not in itself resolve the difficulty presented by amnesties. While such a duty on the part of the territorial State might be clearly incompatible with a blanket amnesty, it is perhaps not equally clear that other forms of amnesty would be equally unacceptable. For example, where a State respects the right of victims to compensation and to 'truth', but prosecutes selectively (as in South Africa) is such a State in violation of its international obligation to prosecute? All States prosecute their ordinary criminal law selectively, of course, if they do not have unlimited resources, and as long as the selection is representative and is not made on discriminatory grounds it is difficult to object to this. Can the same apply to international crimes, and be used to justify limited amnesties? Here, it is relevant to note the decisions of human rights bodies which have arguably stopped short of holding that the obligation to protect human rights always gives rise to a duty to impose *criminal* procedure, or of holding that the obligation to prosecute is absolute.[43] It is true that these bodies were dealing with

---

3/1988 (*O.R., M.M., and M.S.* v. *Argentina*), *Report of the Committee Against Torture*, U.N. G.A.O.R., 45th Sess., Supp. No. 44, at Annex VI, U.N. Doc. A/45/44 (1990), cited in Scharf, 'The Letter of the Law' in Bassiouni and Morris, n. 27 above, at 47 n. 39.

[41] See generally the discussion in Scharf, ibid. at 43–8.

[42] Bassiouni (1999a) 221–4; Orentlicher (1991), n. 27 above, at 2585–95; Diane Orentlicher, 'Addressing Gross Human Rights Abuses: Punishment and victim compensation', in Louis Henkin and John L. Hargrove, eds., *Human Rights: An agenda for the next century* (Washington, DC: Am. Soc. Int'l L., 1994) 425; Theodor Meron, 'International Criminalization of Internal Atrocities', in Theodor Meron, *War Crimes Law Comes of Age* (Oxford: Clarendon, 1998).

[43] The ICCPR and the 3 regional human rights conventions do not expressly impose a duty to criminalize or to 'extradite or prosecute'. They do nevertheless require States to ensure the rights set out in them: International Covenant of Civil and Political Rights, Chapter II, n. 8 above, Art. 2(1) ('Each State Party . . . undertakes to respect and to ensure . . .'); *African Charter on Human and Peoples' Rights*, 27 June 1981, O.A.U. Doc. CAB/LEG/67/3 Rev.5, 21 I.L.M. 59, Art. 1 ('The Member States of the Organization of African Unity parties to the present Charter shall recognize the rights, duties and freedoms enshrined in this Charter and shall undertake to adopt legislative or other measures to give effect to them'); American Convention on Human Rights, 22

the wider category of gross and systematic violations of human rights, but the context of societies in conflict or in transition was the same. It is perhaps best to say that where one group is not in a position to impose a rigorous program of prosecution on another (as at Nuremberg), where two groups must continue to cohabit in society together, and where resources to devote to punishment and reconciliation are scarce, the best view is a more nuanced one. The obligation to undertake meaningful criminal prosecutions should not be undermined, but within this framework there may be room for principled flexibility so long as the need for reparation and the dignity of victims is also recognized.[44] It is possible that adequate acknowledgement, compensation and *bona fide* efforts at institutional reform might render acceptable a partial

November 1969, O.A.S.T.S. 36, O.A.S. Off. Rec. OEA/Ser.L/V/II.23, doc.21, rev.6, 9 I.L.M. 673, Art. 1 ('The States Parties . . . undertake to respect the rights and freedoms recognized herein and to ensure to all persons subject to their jurisdiction the free and full exercise of those rights and freedoms. . . .'); European Convention for the Protection of Human Rights and Fundamental Freedoms, 4 November 1950, 213 U.N.T.S. 221, E.T.S. 5, reprinted in Brownlie (1995) at 328, Art. 1 ('The High Contracting Parties shall secure . . . the rights and freedoms defined in . . . this Convention'). With respect to the ICCPR, commentators have cited the decisions and the interpretative comments of the Human Rights Committee in support of a duty to investigate and criminally prosecute serious violations of the rights set out in the instrument; this view has been contested, partly on the ground that the Covenant's drafters specifically rejected the inclusion of an express duty to prosecute: see Scharf, 'The Letter of the Law', n. 27 above, at 48–50, discussing the arguments of Orentlicher (1991), n. 27 above, at 2568 and Naomi Roht-Arriaza, 'Sources in International Treaties of an Obligation to Investigate, Prosecute and Provide Redress', in Roht-Arriaza (1995), n. 30 above, at 28–30 and 33 n. 64. The Inter-American Court of Human Rights has found that each party to the Convention has 'a legal duty . . . to use the means at its disposal to carry out a serious investigation of violations committed within its jurisdiction, to identify those responsible, impose the appropriate punishment and ensure the victim adequate compensation'. Despite this strong formulation, the Court did not specify that criminal as opposed to other disciplinary measures were necessary to fulfil the duty to 'punish', and the Court ordered the Honduran government to pay compensation to the victim's family without ordering it to instigate criminal proceedings: *Valasquez Rodriguez Case*, Judgment, 29 July 1988 (1988) Ann. Rep. Inter-Am. Court H.R., Appendix VI, at 35, OAS Doc. No. OAS/Ser.L/V/III.19, doc. 13 (31 August 1988), paras. 174, 194, cited in Scharf, 'The Letter of the Law', n. 27 above, at 50–1; see also Roht-Arriaza (1995), n. 30 above, at 30–2. Subsequent decisions from the Inter-American institutions, relating to amnesties in Argentina, Chile, El Salvador, and Uruguay, found amnesties to be inconsistent with the Convention, and found a duty to investigate, punish, and compensate, although Scharf, 'The Letter of the Law', at 50–2, emphasized the role played in these decisions by the denial of civil redress and punishment of any sort on the facts, arguing that like the Human Rights Committee, the Inter-American bodies appear inclined to take a contextualized, multi-faceted approach rather than one defined by an absolute duty to prosecute in all circumstances: see also Roht-Arriaza, n. 30 above, at 60–2.

[44] Scharf argues that although the Committee has stated that amnesties are 'generally incompatible' with State obligations relating to acts of torture, it is possible that these duty may be satisfied with measures short of criminal prosecution (dismissal from the military, payment of damages, etc.): 'The Letter of the Law', n. 27 above, at 50, discussing *General Comment No. 20(44) (Article 7)*, U.N. Doc. CCPR/C/21/Rev.1/Add.3 (7 April 1992), para. 15; see also Scharf, 'The Amnesty Exception', n. 27 above, at 514–21. Mendez, n. 33 above, at 261, formulates this as the rule that 'amnesty laws are incompatible with the international obligations of the state if their effect is to create a general environment of impunity for the most serious violations of the Covenant'.

and non-discriminatory failure to punish individuals through the criminal justice system.

Even where amnesties may, with some conditions, be unobjectionable alongside a duty to prosecute, they will often be limited and fragile. Where permissive universal jurisdiction arises at customary law (pp. 109–12 below) anyone benefiting from a national amnesty would risk prosecution by another State willing to exercise that jurisdiction (admittedly a rare occurrence); and where human rights conventions are relied upon, the lawfulness of amnesty, if it exists at all, is contingent on broader measures of truth-telling, compensation, and institutional reform that must be undertaken in good faith.

Although a flexible, contextualized approach to amnesties might be the most promising, the current situation reflects inconsistencies and an ongoing process of development. Whether (conditionally) lawful or not, the devolved nature of international legal enforcement in the international community means that the passage of amnesties will be determined not only or primarily by their lawfulness, but by their utility in light of domestic political pressures and the likely reaction they will bring from the international community. As will be seen, international consequences may change considerably as a result of the Rome Statute.

(c) Amnesties and international law: The Rome Statute

The Rome Statute represents a potentially significant development in the international regulation of amnesties. The Statute itself is silent on the subject. Moreover, the Statute does not follow the model of, for example, the Convention Against Torture, and imposes upon its States Parties no obligation to prosecute from which the unlawfulness of amnesties could be inferred (although the sixth paragraph of the Preamble does refer to such a duty, without specifying its scope). Nevertheless, the structure of the admissibility provisions raises the possibility that cases will be admissible before the Court when an amnesty bars prosecution at the national level.

As discussed above (pp. 86–93), cases are admissible before the Court unless made inadmissible by Article 17(1)(a)–(c). Amnesties appear not to fall within any of the listed situations (all of which involve national proceedings of some extent) and the necessary implication is that cases covered by an amnesty would be admissible if all other jurisdictional requirements were met (including, importantly, that the underlying conduct occurred after the entry into force of the Statute for the country in question).[45] The same cannot be

---

[45] The same opinion was held by the French Conseil Constitutionnel in its decision on the compatibility of the Rome Statute with the Constitution of France: '. . . *il résulte du statut que la Cour pénale internationale pourrait être valablement saisie du seul fait de l'application d'une loi d'amnistie ou des règles internes en matière de prescription . . .*' Decision 98–408 DC, *Traité portant statut de la Cour pénale internationale* (22 January 1999).

said for post-conviction measures such as pardon, parole, and commutation of sentence, which appear to fall outside the scope of the admissibility provisions. Such measures would presumably only accompany admissibility if they followed proceedings that were not themselves independent, fair, and otherwise in keeping with the criteria set out in Articles 17 and 20(3) (see discussion above).

If this view of the general admissibility of cases involving amnesties is confirmed in the eventual jurisprudence of the Court, it would reinforce the growing tendency to see amnesties as ineffective or counterproductive.[46] Such a view will nevertheless meet resistance from those asserting the ongoing utility or necessity in amnesties for purposes of restoring peace in some situations. A balance between these two views may be struck in a number of ways through the various organs of the Court. At one extreme, the Assembly of States Parties might respond to the non-cooperation of a State Party that respected a national amnesty in the same way it would in the face of any other non-cooperation, refusing to acknowledge the need for or legitimacy of such measures in any circumstances. Such a unified, strong view of matters is unlikely, even among the 'Like Minded' countries that will make up the bulk of the Assembly's initial members. If, as is more probable, the Assembly is divided in its view towards amnesties, it might respond in an *ad hoc* way, judging each situation in context and setting down no general guidelines. Such an approach would leave States Parties negotiating peace or transitions in an untenable position, however, as they would be unable to predict the Assembly's future response to measures they might adopt. Between these extremes, several points of compromise might be found.

First, it is not impossible that an individualized amnesty linked to a truth commission process (such as in South Africa) could be considered a *bona fide* decision not to proceed following an investigation, as contemplated by Article 17(1)(b), although this involves a broad view of the word 'investigation'. Such an interpretation (whether originating with the Prosecutor, the Court, or the Assembly of States Parties) could be limited to commissions inquiring into facts in a sufficiently rigorous and independent way, and offering amnesties (or 'deciding not to prosecute the person concerned' in the words of Article 17(1)(b)) on an individualized and principled basis.

Secondly, if a sufficient majority of the Assembly were convinced that amnesties might in exceptional circumstances form part of a satisfactory reconciliation process, the Assembly could set out rules on the basis of which it would forgo action on non-cooperation in certain cases admitted on the basis of an amnesty. The 'exceptional circumstances' could include that a genuine 'truth' process had been undertaken, that amnesties were linked to

---

[46] See generally Joyner (1998), n. 28 above; Bassiouni and Morris (1996), n. 27 above; and the sources cited in nn. 29 and 32 above.

full participation in that process, that prosecutions were otherwise available, and that fair compensation was available. In this way, the denial of justice would be minimized and the Assembly able to discourage blanket impunity. The difficulty with such an approach is that it would require States granting amnesties (even on an individualized basis linked to a commission of inquiry) to face a finding of non-cooperation before being 'exonerated' by the inaction of the Assembly, and the 'exoneration' itself would be highly contentious. This option is therefore undesirable.

A third option appears most likely to find expression in the practice of the Court. The resources of the Court will undoubtedly limit it to trying at most a few dozen cases a year.[47] Consequently the Prosecutor, operating under conditions of scarcity, will have to assign priority to prospective cases. She or he could potentially exclude situations involving rigorous truth commission/amnesty processes under the power not to initiate or to discontinue investigations where 'the interests of justice' would not be served (Article 53(1)(c) and (2)(c)); such decisions would be subject to review by the Pre-Trial Chamber (Article 53(3)). This practice could be clarified by an interpretative statement from the Prosecutor, and perhaps eventually by a provision in the Rules of Procedure and Evidence (particularly if the practice originated in the Assembly of States Parties). This approach would allow the ICC, in addition to discouraging impunity, to play a role in strengthening national practice with respect to the 'right to truth' and to compensation on the part of victims. Moreover, this third option does not involve the semantic contortions of the first or the procedural disadvantages of the second (above). It is therefore the most desirable, although the formulation of the factors determining when the Court would defer to national amnesties would be contentious, and perhaps fatally so.

In any event, it appears certain that the ICC will have the ability to review national processes resulting in amnesties, and to take jurisdiction in appropriate cases. This in itself is a major development. The consistent and principled approach which could—if only painfully—emerge might significantly impact on the practice of States Parties and potentially, in time, on the international community more widely.

4. CONCLUSION

As this Chapter has sought to demonstrate, the entry into operation of the International Criminal Court is likely to have a significant effect on the quantity and quality of national prosecutions relating to crimes under international law. This consequence of the Rome Statute should not be overstated.

---

[47] See Chapter VI, n. 37 below.

Domestic trials will remain fraught with all of the political, social, and resource difficulties that have always accompanied them, and the resulting imperfections will be slow to improve. Nonetheless, even this halting advance should be acknowledged and welcomed as one of the major consequences of recent developments in international criminal law, and as one of the factors that will most contribute to any movement towards the international rule of law.

A further consequence of the Rome Statute regime should be remarked. With the increased attention paid to efforts against impunity at the end of the twentieth century, a series of 'hybrid' efforts to promote accountability have joined those of the purely international *ad hoc* tribunals (see text at Chapter IV, n. 10 above). These are the processes in Sierra Leone, East Timor, and Cambodia where the United Nations has worked with domestic authorities and the international community to negotiate structures that aim to secure an adequate degree of accountability in an acceptably fair manner, while respecting the needs and sensibilities of the State concerned.[48] These initiatives, with

[48] The Special Court for Sierra Leone will be 'a treaty-based *sui generis* court' (unlike the *ad hoc* tribunals established by the Security Council) trying crimes under both international and Sierra Leone law, and 'incorporated in the national law of Sierra Leone in accordance with constitutional requirements': *Report of the Secretary-General*, n. 31 above, paras. 9, 19; see 'United Nations and Government of Sierra Leone sign agreement establishing Special Court', UNAMSIL Press Release (16 January 2002) (available online at http://www.un.org/Depts/dpko/unamsil/DB/160102a.htm (site last visited on 21 July 2002)). In East Timor, the United Nations Transitional Administration in East Timor (UNTAET), established by Security Council Resolution 1272 (25 October 1999), has promulgated regulations establishing a Public Prosecution Service in East Timor with a special Deputy General Prosecutor for Serious Crimes, as well as judicial panels (consisting of 2 international and 1 East Timorese judge) with exclusive jurisdiction to deal with 'serious criminal offences', which are defined to include genocide, crimes against humanity, war crimes, and torture: *Regulation No. 2000/16 on the organization of the Public Prosecution Service in East Timor*, U.N. Doc. UNTAET/REG/2000/16 (6 June 2000), s. 14 and *Regulation No. 2000/15 on the establishment of panels with exclusive jurisdiction over serious criminal offences*, U.N. Doc. UNTAET/REG/2000/15 (6 June 2000), ss. 1, 4–7, and 22. Under conditions of extreme resource constraint, the Special Panel for Serious Crimes of the Dili District Court had prosecuted over a dozen cases, and entered convictions for crimes against humanity in the trial of 4 individuals: *Report of the Secretary-General on the United Nations Transitional Administration in East Timor (for the period 16 October 2001 to 18 January 2002)*, U.N. Doc. S/2002/80 (17 January 2002), at paras. 39–43. In Cambodia, efforts to establish an international tribunal to prosecute the crimes of the Khmer Rouge were renewed in 1997: Etcheson, n. 28 above, at 238–9. The government of Cambodia came to an agreement on the form of a national tribunal with international participation in July 2000: United Nations, 'Press Briefing by the Under-Secretary-General for Legal Affairs and United Nations Counsel' (13 July 2000). However, the UN withdrew from negotiations early in 2002, citing lack of cooperation on the Cambodian side: 'Annan: Cambodia must change its position if it wants U.N. to help set up a tribunal' Associated Press (14 March 2002). Should the tribunal come to be established as envisioned, it would try both crimes under Cambodian law and international crimes; indictments would be brought by one international and one Cambodian Prosecutor, and cases decided by a majority of Cambodian and a minority of international judges at trial and two levels of appeal: *Law on the establishment of extraordinary chambers in the courts of Cambodia for the prosecution of crimes committed during the period of Democratic Campuchea* (available online at http://go.to/CambodiaToday (site last visited on 21 July 2002)).

all their shortcomings, are likely to be the forerunner of similar future efforts that will emerge as an ICC with limited resources, encountering crimes that the Statute aims to suppress, will give indirect encouragement to its States Parties (conceivably through the United Nations) to support initiatives that will provide accountability without taxing the abilities of the Court itself. The consequences of complementarity should therefore be understood not solely in terms of proceedings undertaken by national governments acting in isolation, but rather as 'joint ventures' placed at varying degrees between the national and the international planes.

VI

Universal Jurisdiction

This Chapter outlines the present state of universal jurisdiction over the 'core crimes' of international criminal law and situates it within the overall development of that law. It argues that, if regular enforcement is (as it should be) a goal of the emerging system of international justice, then universal jurisdiction will be an essential part of that system. At the same time, applying universal jurisdiction is laden with difficulties, not least because of its reliance on national authorities to enforce international norms, given the historical reluctance of those authorities to play this role. As reticence to apply (or indeed to implement) this doctrine rests in important part on fear of its uncontrolled exercise, it is argued below that the necessary controls be imposed through criteria—insufficiently clarified so far—that are applied in a transparent manner. Universal jurisdiction will not become a reliable pillar of the international rule of law until these difficulties are squarely faced, although the current trend supports a guarded optimism.

1. INTRODUCTION

Universal jurisdiction is at a turning point. After fifty years of relative neglect, and with renewed impetus lent by the *Pinochet* hearings in the United Kingdom[1] and by the adoption of the Rome Statute of the International Criminal Court,[2] this doctrine stands poised to become an integral, albeit supplemental component of the emerging international justice system. At the same time, serious obstacles stand in the way of its realization as a consistently available tool of fair and impartial enforcement. These obstacles are in some measure 'technical', bearing on the need for implementing legislation and appropriate international agreements. They are also to some extent inherent in the nature of universal jurisdiction. Because universal jurisdiction relies on national authorities to enforce international prohibitions, pivotal decisions can be expected to reflect, to a greater or lesser extent, domestic decision-makers' calculations as to the interests of justice, the national interest, and other criteria; and given that universal jurisdiction cases can be expensive, difficult to conduct, a magnet for both domestic and international controversy, and of little immediate connection to the exercising State, it is little wonder that local authorities are reluctant to 'normalize' this doctrine.

[1] See Chapter VII, n. 16, below.
[2] See above, pp. 70–6.

These factors ensure that a strong element of uncertainty is likely to prove durable, even where all the necessary agreements and legislation are in place. The practice of universal jurisdiction is therefore unlikely to become significantly more regular unless sustained aware-raising initiatives, programs of law reform, and a marked convergence of opinion affect domestic decision-makers over time.

In spite of such obstacles, it is clear that a number of governments, through the express provision for universal jurisdiction over core crimes during the process of ICC implementation (Chapter V, n. 26 above), are choosing a path that will speed rather than curb the entrenchment of this doctrine. The wave of legislative activity currently underway will in time give rise to cases, and these will oblige legal systems to find working solutions to problems which at present elude consensus. The extent to which universal jurisdiction becomes a reliable part of a system for promoting the international rule of law in practice depends in large measure on the unfolding of these developments over the coming years.

2. DEFINITION AND RATIONALE

Universal jurisdiction fills a gap left where other, more basic doctrines of jurisdiction provide no basis for national proceedings. Under universal jurisdiction, the fact that a crime did not occur within or have a discernible impact on the territory or security of a State (thus falling outside of territorial or protective principle jurisdiction) or that no national of the State perpetrated or was a victim of the act (active or passive personality jurisdiction) is no impediment to proceedings by that State's authorities.[3] Where international law recognizes this form of jurisdiction, States have in effect acknowledged that any other State may or must investigate and prosecute a given crime, even absent the usual jurisdictional links.

The words 'may or must' conceal an important nuance. In ordinary usage, 'universal jurisdiction' encompasses both *permissive* and *mandatory* forms, where a State *may* and where a State *must* exercise jurisdiction. This largely parallels the distinction between the doctrine's manifestations under customary and under conventional international law.

Treaties setting out a regime of 'universal jurisdiction' typically define a crime and then oblige all parties either to investigate and (if appropriate) prosecute it, or to extradite suspects to a party willing to do so.[4] This is the

---

[3] Kenneth C. Randall, 'Universal Jurisdiction under International Law' (1988) 66 Texas L. Rev. 785 at 786–8; Bassiouni (1999a), at 227; and Ian Brownlie, *Principles of Public International Law* (Oxford, Clarendon, 1988) at 303–14.

[4] Examples are found in relevant articles of the Geneva Conventions (including Additional Protocol I), Chapter II, n. 78 above and the UN Convention Against Torture, n. 21 and

obligation of *aut dedere, aut judicare* ('either extradite or prosecute').[5] Once a State ratifies or accedes to a treaty, it has no option in the matter.[6] Hence, this form of jurisdiction is not truly 'universal', but is a regime of jurisdictional rights and obligations arising among a closed set of States Parties.[7] Under customary law States are (at least in the prevailing view) merely *permitted* to exercise universal jurisdiction over e.g. piracy on the high seas or crimes against humanity. The phrase 'universal jurisdiction' is more accurately applied where it arises as a matter of custom than when used to describe the jurisdiction that arises only *inter partes* through a convention.

The rationales underlying international criminal law in general also support universal jurisdiction.[8] First, the serious crimes concerned are 'of universal concern',[9] deserving condemnation in themselves, and deemed to affect the moral and even peace and security interests of the entire international community.[10] Secondly, other bases of jurisdiction are insufficient to

accompanying text below. For treaties containing such provisions that do not deal with 'core crimes' of international criminal law, see n. 20 below.

[5] For an extensive discussion, see M. Cherif Bassiouni and Edward M. Wise, *Aut Dedere Aut Judicare: The duty to extradite or prosecute in international law* (Dordrecht: Martinus Nijhoff, 1995).

[6] A rare example of a treaty provision providing for permissive universal jurisdiction over a 'core crime' is found in Art. 5 of the 1973 Apartheid Convention: 'The persons charged with the crime of apartheid *may* be tried by a competent tribunal of any State Party to the Convention which may acquire jurisdiction over the person of the accused or by an international penal tribunal' [emphasis added]. With regard to the crime of piracy on the high seas, Art. 105 of the Convention on the Law of the Sea, 10 December 1982, 516 U.N.T.S. 205, reads:

On the high seas, or in any other place outside the jurisdiction of any State, every State *may* seize a pirate ship or aircraft, or a ship or aircraft taken by piracy and under the control of pirates, and arrest the persons and seize the property on board. The courts of the State which carried out the seizure *may* decide upon the penalties to be imposed, and *may* also determine the action to be taken with regard to the ships, aircraft or property, subject to the rights of third parties acting in good faith [emphasis added].

[7] The *Pinochet* decision clearly showed the potential significance of this in relation to the issue of immunity: see text accompanying Chapter VII, n. 27 below. See also Randall, n. 3 above, at 789 n. 19.

[8] For a fuller discussion, see pp. 44–51 above. The rationales outlined in the text following are those uniquely justifying the availability of universal jurisdiction (and the imposition of individual responsibility at international law). Of course, the rationales supporting the prosecution of all crimes at domestic law also apply—with all their uncertainties—to crimes giving rise to universal jurisdiction at international law. These include deterrence, obtaining justice, supporting the rule of law, facilitating social healing and reconciliation, revealing the truth, and providing protection from perpetrators: International Council on Human Rights Policy, *Thinking Ahead on Universal Jurisdiction: Report of a meeting hosted by the International Council on Human Rights Policy, 6–8 May 1999* (1999), at 14–21; International Law Association, Committee on International Human Rights Law and Practice, *The Exercise of Universal Jurisdiction in Respect of Gross Human Rights Offences: Final report* (London: Report of the Sixty-Ninth ILA Conference, 2000), at 3.

[9] *Restatement (Third) of the foreign relations law of the United States* (1986), para. 404.

[10] M.C. Bassiouni, *Crimes Against Humanity in International Criminal Law* (2d ed.) (The Hague: Kluwer, 1999), at 228–9; Christopher C. Joyner, 'Arresting Impunity: The case for universal jurisdiction in bringing war criminals to accountability' in M.C. Bassiouni and Madeline H. Morris, eds., *Accountability for International Crimes and Serious Violations of Fundamental Human Rights* (1996) 59 L. and Contemp. Probs. 153 at 166–7.

see perpetrators brought to account, as these acts are often committed by those who act from or flee to a foreign jurisdiction, or by those who act under the protection of the State. As a result of these normative and pragmatic rationales, universal jurisdiction does not arise with respect to any and all crimes (as does jurisdiction under e.g. the territorial principle) but only with respect to particular offences.[11] The pragmatic consideration is especially apparent with piracy on the high seas (the first crime to be subject to universal jurisdiction), slavery[12] and terrorism,[13] where the potential to evade justice through absconding and safe havens is great. The normative impulse is more apparent with crimes against humanity and war crimes, the prosecution of which reinforces the declared interest of all States in upholding fundamental principles of humanity. Nonetheless, both pragmatism and normativity play a role with respect to all these crimes. Pirates were labelled enemies of mankind (*hostis humani generis*),[14] emphasizing the moral aspect of the condemnation, while war crimes and crimes against humanity are often committed by those whose political power renders their State a *de facto* safe haven, a driving consideration in the post-War development of international criminal law generally.[15]

The imperative to defend the fundamental interests of the international community through criminal process has frequently been said to endow national courts exercising universal jurisdiction with the *de facto* status of

---

[11] If one accepts the doctrine set down in *The Steamship Lotus* (*France* v. *Turkey*), (1927) P.C.I.J. Ser. A, No. 10, that States are entitled by their sovereignty to exercise jurisdiction within their territory over acts committed abroad, without the requirement of any permissive rule of international law, provided only that to do so is not prohibited by a positive rule of international law, then universal jurisdiction could in principle arise with respect to any crime. This approach appears to be reflected in the law of some jurisdictions, which allow their courts to prosecute any crime over a certain threshold of seriousness: see e.g. Sweden's Penal Code, ch. 2, s. 3(7) (jurisdiction of Swedish courts over crimes committed abroad, where Swedish law punishes the crime by over 4 years' imprisonment), and Norway's General Civil Penal Code, Pt. 1, ch. 1, s. 12(4) (applicability of Norwegian criminal law to felonies committed abroad by a foreigner now resident in Norway, where the act is also punishable in the country where committed). Nonetheless, the general reluctance of States to exercise jurisdiction beyond the grounds traditionally sanctioned by international law without its specific authorization has resulted in the development of positive norms permitting or mandating universal jurisdiction for certain crimes: International Law Association, Committee on International Human Rights Law and Practice, *The Exercise of Universal Jurisdiction in Respect of Gross Human Rights Offences: Final Report* (London: Report of the 69th Int'l Law Assoc'n Conference, 2000), at 11.

[12] Rubin dissents on the availability of universal jurisdiction with respect to slavery: Alfred P. Rubin, *The Law of Piracy* (2d ed.) (Irvington-on-Hudson, NY: Transnational, 1997), at 11. For more on the crimes of piracy and slavery, see pp. 23–4 above.

[13] See n. 20 below.

[14] Sir Robert Jennings and Arthur Watts, eds., *Oppenheim's International Law* (9th ed.) (London: Longman, 1996), at 746; M. Cherif Bassiouni, 'The Sources and Content of International Criminal Law: A Theoretical Framework', in Bassiouni (1999b), at 224; for a comparison of the underlying rationales of piracy and the 'Nuremberg crimes', see Randall (1988), n. 2 above, at 803–4.

[15] See pp. 19–23 above.

agents of the international community, the declared values of which the proceedings vindicate.[16] To confer such a role on national authorities, however, raises complex practical difficulties that have only begun to be addressed (see pp. 118–27 below).

3. SCOPE OF UNIVERSAL JURISDICTION WITH RESPECT TO THE 'CORE CRIMES' OF ICL

Since the end of the Second World War, a considerable number of international conventions have established a duty to prosecute certain crimes. Such a duty does not always entail universal jurisdiction. For example, the 1948 Genocide Convention defines this crime, and states that '[p]ersons who commit genocide . . . shall be punished' (Article 4) and affirms that States Parties 'undertake to prevent and punish' it (Article 1). However, the Convention only refers to trial before the tribunals of the State within the territory of which the acts of genocide occur or before an international criminal court (Article 6), and does not provide for universal jurisdiction or the duty to extradite or prosecute (but see the discussion of customary law below).

Universal jurisdiction—in the form of the obligation to 'extradite or prosecute'—was recognized one year later in the four 1949 Geneva Conventions, which oblige all States Parties to prohibit 'grave breaches' of them.[17] Grave breaches are those violations of the Conventions that entail individual criminal responsibility.[18] States Parties are under a duty to search for persons alleged to have committed grave breaches, regardless of their nationality, and to bring them before their own courts, or alternatively to hand them over to another State Party for prosecution. The 'extradite or prosecute' obligation with respect to grave breaches under the Conventions was carried forward to the additional grave breaches of the first 1977 Additional Protocol.[19] The

---

[16] *Attorney-General of the Government of Israel* v. *Adolph Eichmann*, (12 Dec. 1961) 36 I.L.R. 18 (Isr. Dist. Ct., Jerusalem) *aff'd* (27 May 1962) 36 I.L.R. 277 (Isr. Sup. Ct.): 'international law is, in the absence of an International Court, in need of the judicial and legislative organs of every country to give effect to its criminal interdictions and to bring the criminals to trial. The jurisdiction to try crimes under international law is *universal*' (Dist. Ct., at 26); and referring to the State of Israel 'in the capacity of a guardian of international law and an agent for its enforcement' (Sup. Ct., at 304). As discussed with regard to the Rome Statute below, the need of international criminal law for the support of national courts exercising universal jurisdiction will not end with the establishment of the International Criminal Court.

[17] Geneva Convention I, Arts. 49, 50; Geneva Convention II, Arts. 50, 51; Geneva Convention III, Arts. 129, 130; and Geneva Convention IV, Arts. 146, 147.

[18] While States Parties to the Conventions are required to provide 'effective penal sanctions' with respect to grave breaches, they are only required to 'take measures necessary for the suppression' of violations other than grave breaches: Geneva Convention I, Art. 49; Convention II, Art. 50; Convention III, Art. 129; Convention IV, Art. 146.

[19] Additional Protocol I, Arts. 11, 85, 86, 88.

mechanism also became a characteristic feature of the terrorism-related conventions of the 1960s and 1970s, as well as others that followed.[20]

Finally, the Convention Against Torture[21] provides an explicit duty to make the crime of torture as defined in the Convention an offence under national law (Article 4). Each party is required to establish jurisdiction over the crime when committed on its territory, by one of its nationals, against one of its nationals (if the State feels it appropriate), or in any case in which the accused is present on its territory and it does not extradite him or her (Article 5). The State Party is then obliged, if it does not extradite the person, to submit the case to its authorities for prosecution (Articles 6, 7, and 12). Thus, at least in the Geneva Conventions and the Convention Against Torture, international law does provide a clear, mandatory form of 'universal' jurisdiction as between States Parties.[22] Where genocide, crimes against humanity, and other war crimes are concerned, one must turn to custom.

Customary law is less clear than law established by convention, but it has the advantage of applying to all States. For this same reason, its scope is often strongly contested. The clearly prevailing view is that genocide, crimes against humanity, and war crimes (including not only grave breaches of the Geneva Conventions but the 'Hague law' applicable in international armed conflict, as well as crimes arising in non-international armed conflicts) give rise to permissive universal jurisdiction at international law.[23] That customary law provided universal jurisdiction for the further grave breaches set out in Additional Protocol I, or for acts committed in non-international conflicts—indeed, whether the latter attracted individual responsibility under international law at all—has recently become less difficult to assert.[24] The

---

[20] 1970 Hague Convention, Art. 7; 1971 Montreal Convention, Art. 7; 1979 Hostages Convention, Art. 8; European Convention, Art. 7; all at Chapter II, n. 63 above.

[21] Convention Against Torture and Other Cruel, Inhuman or Degrading Treatment or Punishment, 10 December 1984, 1465 U.N.T.S. 85, 23 I.L.M. 1027.

[22] The limited effect of such jurisdiction is particularly noticeable where the convention involved is adopted by a regional organization, and is thus not even potentially universal: see the Inter-American Convention to Prevent and Punish Torture, 9 December 1985, P.A.U.S.T. 67, 25 I.L.M. 519, Art. 12.

[23] Randall (1988), n. 3 above, at 836; through the Draft Code of Crimes Against the Peace and Security of Mankind, the ILC would have required States to prohibit genocide, war crimes, and crimes against humanity, regardless of where and by whom committed (Art. 8) and either to prosecute or extradite individuals accused of these crimes (Art. 9): 1996 ILC Report, at 42–50.

[24] International responsibility under customary law for crimes committed in internal armed conflict was highly uncertain until recently, notwithstanding Common Article 3 of the 1949 Geneva Conventions and Art. 4 of 1977 Additional Protocol II to such conflicts. The jurisprudence of the ICTY and the Statute of the ICTR have supported international criminalization of acts committed in internal conflicts: see *Tadic* jurisdictional decision, at paras. 128–36; ICTR Statute, Art. 4; also 1996 Draft Code of Crimes, Art. 20(f) (affirming international individual responsibility for acts committed in non-international armed conflict), in 1996 ILC Report, Chapter II, n. 19 above, at 112, 118–19; Theodor Meron, 'International Criminalization of Internal Atrocities' in Theodor Meron, *War Crimes Law Comes of Age* (Oxford: Clarendon, 1998), at 248–53; see also International Law Association (2000), n. 8 above, at 6–7; also Chapter IV, n. 37 above.

Statutes and jurisprudence of the *ad hoc* tribunals for the Former Yugoslavia and for Rwanda, and the Rome Statute itself confirm the international criminality of at least some of these acts, and so strongly buttress claims that they give rise to customary universal jurisdiction.[25]

Some commentators go beyond the above view on permissive universal jurisdiction and argue with respect to some or all core crimes that such jurisdiction is mandatory at customary law, often adducing arguments of *jus cogens* and obligations *erga omnes* in support.[26] From this perspective, universal jurisdiction flows directly from the fact that the core crimes of international criminal law rest on norms of *jus cogens* that give rise to obligations *erga omnes*.[27] The evidence from practice and *opinio juris* nonetheless falls short of supporting such arguments unequivocally, at least at present.[28] As a

[25] Canada's implementing legislation for the Rome Statute declares that '. . . crimes described in Articles 6 [genocide] and 7 [crimes against humanity] and paragraph 2 of Article 8 [war crimes in international and internal armed conflict] of the Rome Statute are, as of July 17, 1998, crimes according to customary international law, and may be crimes according to customary international law before that date': Crimes against Humanity and War Crimes Act, Chapter V, n. 26 above, s. 6(4) (Offences outside Canada). The date chosen is that of the adoption of the Rome Statute.

[26] Bassiouni (1999a), at 220, focuses on crimes against humanity: 'Since "crimes against humanity" are international crimes for which there is universal jurisdiction . . . any and all states have the alternative duty to prosecute or extradite. Prosecution is premised not only on a state's willingness, but also on its ability to prosecute fairly and effectively. In the absence of these premises, the duty to extradite to a state willing and capable of prosecuting fairly and effectively arises.' See also M. Cherif Bassiouni, 'International Crimes: *Jus cogens* and *obligatio erga omnes*' in Bassiouni and Morris (1996), n. 10 above, 63; Amnesty International, *United Kingdom: Universal jurisdiction and absence of immunity for crimes against humanity* (AI Index EUR 45/001/1999) (London: AI, 1999), at 10–13, 23 ('Given that crimes against humanity are *erga omnes*, it follows that all states . . . are under an *obligation* to prosecute and punish crimes against humanity and to cooperate in the detection, arrest, extradition and punishment of persons implicated in these crimes').

[27] See Chapter II, nn. 68–9 above; M. Cherif Bassiouni, *Crimes Against Humanity under International Law* (Dordrecht: Martinus Nijhoff, 1992), at 510–527, and Amnesty International's thoroughly documented submission to the House of Lords in the *Pinochet* litigation: Amnesty International *The International Criminal Court: Fundamental principles concerning the elements of genocide* (AI Index: IOR 40/01/99) (London: AI, 1999).

[28] Even the most prominent advocate of the *jus cogens* approach, Cherif Bassiouni, admits:

Positive ICL does not contain . . . an explicit norm that characterizes a certain crime as part of *jus cogens* and the practice of states does not conform to the scholarly writings that espouse the views expressed above [by Professor Bassiouni]. States' practice evidences that, more often than not, impunity has been allowed for *jus cogens* crimes, the theory of universality has been far from universally recognized and applied, and the duty to prosecute or extradite is more inchoate than established, other than when it arises out of specific treaty obligations: M. Cherif Bassiouni, ed., *International Criminal Law* (2d ed.) (Ardsley, N.Y.: Transnational, 1999) (vol. I), at 39–40.

For the view that customary international law supports only permissive and not mandatory universal jurisdiction over core crimes at present, see Michael Scharf, 'The Letter of the Law', in M.C. Bassiouni and Madeline H. Morris, eds., *Accountability for International Crimes and Serious Violations of Fundamental Human Rights* (1996) 59 L. and Contemp. Probs. 41, at 52–9. Meron, n. 24 above, at 251–2 and 254–5, argues that universal jurisdiction is broadly available, but is not mandatory. A leading text that is non-committal about the existence of universal jurisdiction at all (apart from either a conventional manifestation, or piracy at customary law) and concedes only a 'gradual evolution' towards even permissive universal jurisdiction over crimes

result, the best that can be said with certainty is that customary law allows a permissive exercise of universal jurisdiction over genocide, crimes against humanity, and some war crimes, and may be evolving towards a mandatory one. This is less than ideal, as the *jus cogens* rationale would lend coherence to the ongoing evolution of international criminal law by pointing towards a vision of emerging international law that would incorporate the protection of fundamental rights as an integral part. The argument also makes practical sense, in that the ends of universal jurisdiction (to impose accountability for crimes of international concern and to eliminate safe havens) would be better served if the State where the perpetrator is found did not have any discretion—least of all a politically motivated discretion—as to whether to proceed. A permissive approach might be thought to tolerate the possibility of safe havens and thereby undermine accountability. The crystallization of a rule of customary law that would *oblige* States to extradite or prosecute those reasonably suspected of international crimes should therefore be encouraged.

Nonetheless, efforts to put into operation a workable system for the suppression of international crimes must be mindful of international life as it presently operates. While the coherence and effectiveness of the normative order should always be borne in mind, it is important not to put conceptual neatness ahead of the difficulties that arise in determining international law and in putting doctrine into practice. As discussed below (pp. 118–27), this requires that the hard legal problems be clarified in order to better realize the aims of this law.

4. CURRENT DEVELOPMENT OF UNIVERSAL JURISDICTION

To date, and notwithstanding a spate of activity in Belgium and other countries, the exercise of universal jurisdiction over core crimes of international criminal law has been sporadic at best, responding to selected situations at particular times. With the movement towards the entry into force of the Rome Statute, however, a process of national law reform has begun which has the potential to develop into a trend that would entrench universal jurisdiction as a relatively widely available means of accountability. Before it can do so, however, serious challenges remain to be faced.

Universal jurisdiction was explicitly recognized for the core crimes of international criminal law after the Second World War, although it seldom formed the exclusive basis of prosecutions that took place after the War.[29]

against humanity is Jennings and Watts (1994), n. 14 above, at 998. See also the *Restatement*, n. 9 above, para. 404.

[29] The Allies conducted over 1,000 trials in the tribunals of their national occupying forces following the end of WWII, and 'it is generally agreed that the establishment of these tribunals and their proceedings were based on universal jurisdiction': Randall (1988), n. 8 above, at 805,

Like other international justice initiatives, universal jurisdiction fell into neglect as post-War activity subsided into the stasis of the Cold War.[30] The *Eichmann* case brought the doctrine back to international attention in 1961.[31] The case did not lead to similar prosecutions in the short term, although it did inspire efforts to secure accountability for crimes committed against the Jewish people during the Second World War, and these efforts bore fruit in the legislative activity and related cases that arose in the 1980s and 1990s. During those years a number of countries passed legislation and undertook proceedings, generally without great success, against those alleged responsible for crimes during the Second World War.[32]

The establishment by the Security Council of *ad hoc* tribunals to try those responsible for crimes committed in the Former Yugoslavia and Rwanda led to a number of national prosecutions related to these situations.[33] The need

---

quoting *Demjanjuk* v. *Petrovsky*, 776 F.2d 571, 582 (6th Cir. 1985), *cert. denied*, 475 U.S. 1016 (1986); Amnesty International (1999), n. 27 above, at 17, quoting *In re List* (*Hostage* case), (1946–1949) 11 Trials of War Criminals 757 (U.S. Mil. Trib.—Nuremberg, 1948), at 1242: a State may 'surrender the alleged criminal to the state where the offence was committed, or . . . retain the alleged criminal for trial under its own legal processes'. Nonetheless, the jurisdictional basis of these proceedings was often not made explicit, and passive personality jurisdiction was evidently a factor in a number of them: Randall (1988), n. 3 above, at 805–10; International Law Association (2000), n. 8 above, at 22. For example, while in the *Hostage* case the tribunal did state that '[a]n international crime . . . cannot be left within the exclusive jurisdiction of the state that would have control over it under ordinary circumstances', it also restricted its remarks to 'the courts of the belligerent into whose hands the alleged criminal has fallen'—something decidedly less than universal jurisdiction: ibid., at 1241.

[30] See Chapter II, n. 17 and Part II, n. 8 and related text above.

[31] See n. 16 above.

[32] Australia passed the War Crimes Amendment Act in 1988, giving its courts jurisdiction for international crimes committed in Europe during the Second World War; of several cases commenced, only one resulted in trial (and acquittal for the defendant, Polyukhovich) before abandonment of the prosecutorial policy by the Australian government: Graham T. Blewitt, 'The Australian Experience', in Bassiouni, n. 28 above, (vol. III) 301; Gillian Triggs, 'Australia's War Crimes Trials: All pity choked', in T.L.H. McCormack and G.J. Simpson, eds., *The Law of War Crimes: National and International Approaches* (The Hague: Kluwer, 1997), 123. The United Kingdom passed the War Crimes Act in 1991, like Australia restricting its scope temporally and geographically (to acts committed during the Second World War in Germany or German-occupied territory), sentencing Anthony Sawoniuk to life imprisonment in 1999: Jane L. Garwood-Cutler, 'The British Experience', in Bassiouni, n. 28 above, (vol. III) 325; International Law Association (2000), n. 8 above, at 29. Canada passed a statute without the geographical or temporal time limits of the UK and Australian acts, but turned away from a policy of prosecutions when the *Finta* case resulted in an acquittal: Christopher A. Amerasinghe, 'The Canadian Experience', in Bassiouni, n. 28 above, (vol. III) 243; Sharon A. Williams, 'Laudable Principles Lacking Application: The prosecution of war criminals in Canada', in McCormack and Simpson (1997), above in this n., 151. During the same period the United States developed its own unique history of allowing civil suits with respect to crimes under international law: Jane L. Garwood-Cutler, 'Enforcing ICL Violations with Civil Remedies: The U.S. Alien Tort Claims Act', in Bassiouni, n. 28 above, (vol. III) 343.

[33] See Chapter IV, n. 10 above. Austria acquitted a Bosnian Serb (Cvjetkovic) in May 1995; in 1996 Belgian courts authorized proceedings against a Rwandan national (Ntezimana); Denmark convicted a Bosnian Muslim (Saric) in 1994; France initiated proceedings against a Rwandan (Munyeshyaka) in 1995; Germany convicted 4 Bosnian Serbs (Djajic, Jorgic, Sokolovic, Kusljic)

to pass national cooperation legislation and the presence of suspected criminals among refugee populations facilitated these proceedings, although the
Security Council imprimatur, declaring the crimes to threaten international
peace and security, may have contributed to the willingness of governments
to act.[34] Despite their limited temporal application and the limited success
(in terms of the number and completion of proceedings) to this point, these
activities did reflect an underlying endorsement of universal jurisdiction, and
opened the door for later developments in establishing a role to national
courts in enforcing fundamental norms of humanity.

Previous failings in the implementation and use of universal jurisdiction
have recently been compensated for, at least in part, by a combination of the
UK *Pinochet* proceedings and the adoption of the Rome Statute for the
International Criminal Court (with its related process of national implementation). These two events have made universal jurisdiction a subject of sustained debate in many of countries. Indeed, a number of countries have since
taken steps—often tentative and incomplete—to put universal jurisdiction
into practice.[35]

That the Rome Statute should stimulate the incorporation of universal
jurisdiction into national law was widely unforeseen, since the Statute
imposes no obligation on States Parties to prosecute the crimes it defines,
whether on a universal or any other basis. Rather, it provides a limited incentive to prosecute crimes committed by the nationals or on the territory of

in 1997 and 1999; the Netherlands initiated military court proceedings against a Bosnian Serb
(Knezevic) in 1997; a Swiss military court acquitted a Bosnian Serb (Grabez) in 1997, and convicted a Rwandan (Niyonteze) in 1999: Redress Trust, *Universal jurisdiction in Europe: Criminal
prosecutions in Europe since 1990 for war crimes, crimes against humanity, torture and genocide*
(London: Redress Trust, 1999), at 16–17, 19–20, 22, 26, 29, 35, 41–43; International Law
Association (2000), n. 8 above, at 24–7; Amnesty International (1999), n. 27 above, at 19–21. In
addition, in June 2001 a Belgian court convicted four Rwandans of crimes related to the 1994
genocide: Marlise Simons, 'Mother Superior Guilty in Rwanda Killings' *New York Times* (9 June
2001) A4; Paul Ames, 'Rwandan Nuns, Man Lose Appeals' Associated Press (9 January 2002).

[34] For examples and analysis of ICTY/ICTR cooperation legislation, see Amnesty
International, *International Criminal Tribunals: Handbook for government cooperation* (AI Index:
IOR 40/07/96) (London: AI, 1996).

[35] For example, former Chadian President Hissan Habré was arrested on charges of torture in
Senegal, but was released when Senegalese courts found that they did not have jurisdiction over
extraterritorial crimes in the absence of implementing legislation applicable to acts at the relevant
time: 'An African Pinochet' *New York Times* (11 February 2000) A30; International Law
Association (2000), n. 8 above, at 27; *Ministère Public et François Diouf contre Hissene Habré*,
(Arrêt no. 135 du 04–07–2000) (Cour d'Appel de Dakar). In the United States a retired Peruvian
army major and alleged torturer (Ricardo Anderson Kohatsu) was briefly detained by immigra-
tion officials before being released on the ground that he enjoyed diplomatic immunity (having
visited the U.S. to testify before the OAS): 'U.S. Frees Accused Torturer' *Washington Post* (11
March 2000) A1. In 1997 a Spanish investigating magistrate issued an international arrest warrant for former Argentine leader General Galtieri; Argentina did not cooperate: Redress Trust
(1999), n. 33 above, at 38. With respect to Senator Pinochet, the UK was requested to extradite
him not only to Spain, but also to Belgium, France, and Switzerland: Redress Trust (1999), n. 33
above, at 1, 20–21, 27, 43.

other States Parties (see pp. 86–93 above). Yet this incentive has been enough to prompt a wave of legislative activity as countries that have ratified or are contemplating ratification move to enable their domestic courts to meet the criteria of 'complementarity' set out in the Rome Statute. The question whether to provide for universal jurisdiction over these crimes has arisen at the same time.

The logic of providing for universal jurisdiction at the national level as part of the regime of international justice foreseen by the Rome Statute is compelling. The Rome Statute is premised on a desire to diminish impunity for the most egregious conceivable crimes (as evidenced in particular by the Preamble, and by the limited number of narrowly defined crimes in the Statute).[36] It anticipates, through its 'complementarity' mechanism, that national courts will bear the greater part of the burden in ensuring accountability, with the ICC playing a role only where national courts are unwilling or unable to act themselves. At the same time, it cannot be expected that the ICC will have the resources to try more than a very limited number of cases.[37] Thus, although the incentive provided by the complementarity mechanism is limited to crimes committed on the territory or by the nationals of State Parties, a role for universal jurisdiction presents itself clearly. If the ICC will be unable to try more than a fraction of alleged perpetrators at any one time, and if the most obvious States to exercise jurisdiction (the territorial State of the crime or the national State of the accused) will typically be unwilling or unable to act in a genuine manner, the sole choice remaining will often be the stark one between universal jurisdiction and impunity. The argument for national provision of universal jurisdiction is therefore a forceful one. Without the supplementary recourse that universal jurisdiction could provide via the courts of individual States, both the means of obtaining accountability and the credibility of the international community's claim that it desires accountability would be seriously reduced. States with the declared aim of ensuring that their courts are able to serve as complements to the ICC are therefore open to the argument that they must, to do so effectively, make

[36] The fourth preambular paragraph refers to the 'the most serious crimes of concern to the international community as a whole', as does Art. 5(1); see also discussions of the jurisdictional limits of the Court, pp. 76–8 above.

[37] One document has assumed a 'plausible' budget of U.S. $100m for an ICC with 60 States Parties and called upon to deal with 'one or two major situations': Cesare Romano and Thordis Ingadottir, *The Financing of the International Criminal Court: A discussion paper* (NY: Project on International Courts and Tribunals, New York University, 2000), at 11. As this amount is slightly less than the 1999 budget of the ICTY (ibid., at 29), the jurisdiction of which is limited to one (former) country, one gets some idea of how limited the capacity of even a well provisioned international court will be. At the final (July 2002) session of the ICC Preparatory COmmission, delegates adopted a draft budget for the first financial period of the Court totaling 30,893,500 euros, of which 24,040,800 euros was allocated for operational costs of the ICC: *Proposed Changes to the Text of Part Two of the Revised Draft Budget (PCNICC/2002/WGFYB/L.3)*, U.N. Doc. PCNICC/2002/WGFYB/L.6 (10 July 2002).

universal jurisdiction available for genocide, crimes against humanity, and war crimes. Without such a decision by a critical mass of States, the ICC's aim of eroding impunity for the worst of crimes is likely to be seriously impaired.

A skeptic might reply that, while this argument has some force as part of a doctrinal effort to achieve a coherent vision of individual accountability at international law, it would not necessarily be compelling to States engaged in questioning how best to legislate in their national interest. From this perspective there could be a gap between the international interest in the rule of law and the immediate interests of an individual State or government. It is, at the time of writing, too early to describe definitively the direction of the emerging trend, but at the early stage of the process of ICC implementation a number of States have shown a willingness to follow the above reasoning.

Canada was the first country to pass legislation implementing the Rome Statute. Its Crimes Against Humanity and War Crimes Act of 2000 established the jurisdiction of its national courts over genocide, crimes against humanity, and war crimes as defined by customary or conventional international law, declaring the definitions of the Rome Statute to constitute custom as of at least 17 July 1998.[38] With regard to acts committed outside of Canada, the legislation applies to conduct prior to its entry into force, to the extent that international law allows (section 6(1)). The jurisdiction is limited by the requirements of section 8:

A person who is alleged to have committed an offence under section 6 or 7 [offences outside Canada] may be prosecuted for that offence if
(a) at the time the offence is alleged to have been committed,
    (i) the person was a Canadian citizen or was employed by Canada in a civilian or military capacity,
    (ii) the person was a citizen of a state that was engaged in an armed conflict against Canada, or was employed in a civilian or military capacity by such a state,
    (iii) the victim of the alleged offence was a Canadian citizen, or
    (iv) the victim of the alleged offence was a citizen of a state that was allied with Canada in an armed conflict; or
(b) after the time the offence is alleged to have been committed, the person is present in Canada.

This last criterion constitutes the 'universal jurisdiction' provision.[39] New Zealand has legislated more broadly in some respects giving its courts,

---

[38] See n. 25 above, ss. 4–8.
[39] Crimes Against Humanity and War Crimes Act, n. 25 above. It appears that the presence requirement will prevent Canada from opening an investigation against an alleged perpetrator who is known not to be present in Canada, thus foreclosing the possibility of extradition requests (unless another ground of jurisdiction applies, e.g. the victim was Canadian). The shortcoming of this limitation is discussed further at pp. 126–7 below.

through section 8(1)(c) of its legislation,[40] jurisdiction to try Rome Statute crimes:

regardless of
   (i) the nationality or citizenship of the person accused; or
   (ii) whether or not any act forming part of the offence occurred in New Zealand; or
   (iii) whether or not the person accused was in New Zealand at the time that the act constituting the offence occurred or at the time a decision was made to charge the person with an offence.

Belgium, which amended its legislation even before ratification of the Rome Statute, provided for similar jurisdiction, and with no presence requirement.[41] Germany has adopted legislation, while South Africa and others have expressed intention to follow suit, albeit with a requirement that the accused be present.[42] On the other hand, the United Kingdom, a third

---

[40] International Crimes and International Criminal Court Act 2000, Chapter V, n. 26 above, ss. 8–11. The legislation appears to open the door for extradition requests. It should be noted that investigations into cases against Senator Pinochet were initiated in Spain, France, Switzerland, and elsewhere without the presence of the accused in the investigating country (although France could only do this where the case is based upon passive personality and not universal jurisdiction): Redress Trust (1999), n. 33 above, at 11.

[41] *Loi relative à la répression des violations graves de droit international humanitaire* (10 February 1999), published in the *Moniteur belge* (23 March 1999), s. 7. This law amends an existing statute (the 1993 *Loi relative à la répression des violations graves du droit international humanitaire*) to add genocide and crimes against humanity (as defined in the Rome Statute) to serious violations of the 1949 Geneva Conventions and their Additional Protocols, for all of which Belgian law now provides universal jurisdiction. However, in June 2002 a Belgian appeal court interpreted this law as requiring the presence of the accused before the commencement of proceedings, thus threatening to end a number of cases alleged perpetrators residing abroad: Constant Brand, 'War Complaints vs. Sharon Dropped' Associated Press (26 June 2002). Two subsequent legislative proposals would correct this ruling's effect of imposing a presence requirement: Sénat de Belgique, Session de 2001–2002, *Proposition de loi interprétative de l'article 7, alinéa 1er, de la loi du 16 juin 1993 relative à la répression des violations graves du droit international humanitaire*, document legislatif 2–1255/1 (18 July 2002) [for cases based on existing law]; *Proposition de loi modifiant la loi du 16 juin 1993 relative à la répression des violations graves du droit international humanitaire*, document legislatif 2–1256/1 (18 July 2002) [for cases based on this proposed amendment to the existing law]. For the ruling of the International Court of Justice on the legality of an arrest warrant made possible by the immunities provision of the same law, see pp. 146–8 below.

[42] Germany has included the principle of universality in its *Code of Crimes Against International Law*, which entered into force on 30 June 2002, and was passed in order to enable German courts to meet (and surpass) the requirements of the 'complementarity test' of the Rome Statute. Multiple translations of the Code, with introductory materials are available online at http://www.iuscrim.mpg.de/forsch/online_pub.html. For background, see Franck Jarasch and Claus Kress, 'The Rome Statute and the German Legal Order', in Claus Kress and Flavia Lattanzi, eds., *The Rome Statute and Domestic Legal Orders: General aspects and constitutional issues*, vol. 1 (Baden-Baden: Nomos, 2000). At a conference on the International Criminal Court held at Pretoria on 5–9 July 1999, officials from 13 Member States of the Southern African Development Community (SADC) adopted the Pretoria Statement of Common Understanding on the International Criminal Court, which recommended a (non-binding) Model Enabling Act developed at the conference (on file). This act would provide for universal jurisdiction over all Rome Statute crimes: s. 5(ii). With respect to South Africa's draft legislation, see Chapter V, n. 26 above.

example among members of the Commonwealth, declined to include such jurisdiction in its own legislation.[43]

The provision of universal jurisdiction even by a significant minority of ratifying States will be an enormous advance for the doctrine. More importantly, the jurisprudence that could be expected to follow from this legislative process will offer an opportunity to wrestle with the thorny legal and political problems that attend universal jurisdiction.

5. PRACTICAL AND POLITICAL PROBLEMS TO BE ADDRESSED

The political and practical problems that arise in attempting to put universal jurisdiction into practice are neither few nor lightly to be dismissed. The political will of States to go forward with the legislative changes necessary to make universal jurisdiction effective is conditioned in part by their understanding of how these problems are to be dealt with. Although cases pursued under the legislation passed during the process of ICC implementation will undoubtedly uncover new difficulties, the main contours of the obstacles to come appear to be well known, and have recently been the object of increasing scrutiny and discussion.

(a) Basic legislative shortcomings

The first level of difficulties relates to the legislative basis for the exercise of universal jurisdiction by national authorities. Even assuming the will and resources were present, prosecutors or investigating judges in many countries simply would not have the necessary legal means to investigate or prosecute on the basis of universal jurisdiction. For example, in the United States torture alone is subject to universal (in fact, merely extra-territorial) jurisdiction.[44] Genocide,[45] other crimes against humanity, and war crimes[46] are not. Many countries are in a similar position.[47] For universal jurisdiction to fulfil its potential as part of an international system for the suppression of

---

[43] Crimes Against Humanity and War Crimes Bill, presented to the House of Commons on 24 July 2000.

[44] 18 USC §2340A (1999) (applying only to acts committed outside the United States).

[45] Genocide is prohibited under U.S. law (18 USCA §1091 (1999)), but only when committed within the U.S. or when the alleged offender is a U.S. national.

[46] The 1996 War Crimes Act made punishable certain war crimes only when committed by or against members of the U.S. armed forces: 18 USCA §2441 (1996).

[47] 'Until recently, only a few dozen states had provided their courts with the specific competence to try certain gross human rights offences under the principle of universal jurisdiction. Even in those states legislation tended to be quite a patchwork': International Law Association (2000), n. 8 above, at 12.

impunity, such legislation should also be of adequate scope and not subject to temporal, spatial, or other restrictions.[48] In principle, such legislation could even be retroactive to the extent that the conduct gave rise to individual responsibility at international law at the time it was committed; politically, this will often be difficult.[49] While adoption of the Rome Statute, with its reasonably comprehensive definitions, is likely to lessen dispute at least about the scope of universal jurisdiction at customary law (see pp. 109–12 above), broader doubts about the application of the doctrine will still have to be overcome.

The incorporation of definitions and provision of jurisdiction at national law are not the end of the task. Even after jurisdictional and definitional difficulties are overcome, the full implementation of universal jurisdiction into national law requires the adaptation of adjacent areas of law affecting the exercise of such jurisdiction. These areas include laws relating to immunity (see pp. 131–50 below), to mutual legal assistance (to facilitate the exchange of evidence, witnesses, etc.), and to extradition. Without a comprehensive system of laws at the national level, and without such laws being adopted by a sufficient number of States, universal jurisdiction cannot be expected to function in practice as a working pillar of the international justice system. This is an area of legal reform that has only begun to receive sustained attention in the wake of the UK *Pinochet* proceedings.

(b) Evidence/Mutual legal assistance[50]

The exercise of universal jurisdiction raises special evidentiary challenges, in particular because the major part of the evidence necessary to make out a case

---

[48] 'The inadequacies of national legislation vary, but common problems are a failure to provide specifically for jurisdiction over crimes committed abroad, failure to sufficiently define crimes, and failure to provide penalties. The problems seem to be just as serious in "monist" countries where international law is part of, and even often superior to, national law, as in "dualist" systems such as the UK. The implications of these problems are that states may not be able to initiate and complete criminal proceedings against alleged violators': Redress Trust (1999), n. 33 above, at 7. One example is the legislation of France, which enables French courts to punish genocide and crimes against humanity taking place abroad, but only where the acts are committed by or against French nationals; another is the UK's 1991 War Crimes Act, n. 32 above: ibid., at 24, 44.

[49] The *Habré* case failed in Senegal because of the lack of implementing legislation under Senegalese law at the relevant time, notwithstanding that (at least in principle) the civil code-based legal system of Senegal incorporates international law directly: see n. 35 above. Canada has taken action to prevent such an occurrence in its jurisdiction, enabling Canadian courts, under the Crimes Against Humanity and War Crimes Act, Chapter V, n. 26 above, to prosecute genocide, crimes against humanity, and war crimes, when committed outside Canada, either before or after the entry into force of the Act, to the extent that the relevant acts constituted crimes according to customary international law or conventional international law at the time and place of commission (s. 6(3)).

[50] See the discussion in International Council on Human Rights Policy (1999), n. 8 above, at 48–50.

may lie in the control of another jurisdiction: and indeed, of the jurisdiction where the alleged crime occurred and where the accused may be a standing official. State officials may make difficult or impossible visits to sites or access to witnesses and documents indispensable to proving the alleged crime. Even where documents can be obtained, courts other than those of the States most directly involved may sometimes find it difficult to assess their authenticity.

Such problems are the traditional domain of mutual legal (or judicial) assistance. Mutual legal assistance is a complex area of law governed by many bilateral and multilateral treaties or agreements, with corresponding national implementing legislation. Typically, these agreements and this legislation allow the requested State a wide latitude of discretion, and may allow the State to refuse to provide assistance on a number of grounds, including because the offence is not recognized under its own law, because the proceedings in the requested State would be unfair (in the requested State's judgement), or because the national interest of the requested State dictates that assistance be refused. Given the legal problems attendant on the exercise of universal jurisdiction and the politically sensitive matters that typically arise in cases involving crimes under international law, these factors pose obvious problems.

Mutual legal assistance agreements do not at present deal specifically with the issue of crimes under international law and universal jurisdiction. This is in spite of the fact that international instruments have called on a number of occasions for a high degree of cooperation in this area.[51] Partly as a result of the evidentiary problems arising in the absence of an effective system of international cooperation, most cases based on universal jurisdiction have relied essentially on eyewitness testimony that was available in the prosecuting State.[52] States legislating for universal jurisdiction should therefore review their mutual assistance arrangements, taking into account the exercise of this doctrine with respect to international crimes, and should revise laws or agreements as necessary to address relevant issues, including:

---

[51] 1977 Additional Protocol I, Art. 88 ('1. The High Contracting Parties shall afford one another the greatest measure of assistance in connexion with criminal proceedings brought in respect of grave breaches of the Conventions or of this Protocol. . . . 3. The law of the High Contracting Party requested shall apply in all cases. The provisions of the preceding paragraphs shall not, however, affect the obligations arising from the provisions of any other treaty of a bilateral or multilateral nature which governs or will govern the whole or part of the subject of mutual assistance in criminal matters.'); 1984 Convention Against Torture, Art. 9 ('1. States Parties shall afford one another the greatest measure of assistance in connection with criminal proceedings brought in respect of any of the offences referred to in Article 4, including the supply of all evidence at their disposal necessary for the proceedings. 2. States Parties shall carry out their obligations under paragraph 1 of this Article in conformity with any treaties on mutual judicial assistance that may exist between them.'). See also, *Principles of International Cooperation in the Detection, Arrest, Extradition and Punishment of Persons Guilty of War Crimes and Crimes Against Humanity*, G.A. Res. 3074 (XXVIII) (3 December 1973), para. 6.

[52] International Law Association (2000), n. 8 above, at 17.

a) <u>On site investigations</u> It may be desirable for investigators, counsel for the defense or prosecution, judges or juries to visit or examine sites related to the alleged crime. Such visits require the permission of the requested State, as well as adequate facilities for their proper conduct (such as protection for the investigators, where necessary).[53]

b) <u>Obtaining evidence</u> This would include 'conducting searches and seizures, interviewing witnesses, excavating graves, producing documents, and supplying material evidence'.[54] Agreements could provide for making evidence available across borders either in writing or by audio or video link, but would have to take into account problems of verification, of cross-examination, and of the sanctioning of false testimony.

c) <u>Protection of victims and witnesses</u> The prosecuting State is not in a good position to provide protection for witnesses abroad either during trial or in the long term. A practical precondition to obtaining the cooperation of witnesses may therefore be obtaining verifiable assurances that they will be protected by authorities in their home State, or even allowing the witness to relocate to the prosecuting State. Without such assurances, witnesses may understandably be reluctant to testify, particularly where the accused and his or her supporters retain significant power in the State of the crime.

d) <u>Reasons for refusal to provide assistance</u> In the case of serious crimes under international law, such refusal should be subject to restrictions, including restrictions on the national security and political offence grounds for refusal.

Systematic amendments to mutual assistance arrangements will no doubt entail a comprehensive review and reform of commitments in this complex and often overlapping area of law. Nonetheless, such changes to the mutual legal assistance regime are potentially indispensable to the eventual effective exercise of universal jurisdiction.

---

[53] In the *Niyonteze* case, arising from the 1994 genocide in Rwanda, the Swiss court (a military tribunal) visited Rwanda to collect statements from witnesses who would be unable to attend trial in Switzerland: International Law Association (2000), n. 8 above, at 28 (citing *Jugement en la cause Fulgence Niyonteze*, Tribunal militaire de division 2, Lausanne, 30 April 1999). A Belgian magistrate traveled to Chad in March 2002 to interview witnesses in an investigation against Hissène Habré, the former president of that country: 'Un juge belge part enquêter au Tchad sur l'ex-président Hissène Habré' Agence France Presse (26 February 2002).

[54] Christopher Keith Hall, *Outline of Some Legal and Practical Obstacles to Prosecution Based on Universal Jurisdiction and Some Possible Solutions*, paper prepared for the International Council on Human Rights Policy meeting on Universal Jurisdiction, 6–8 May 1999, and quoted in International Council on Human Rights Policy (1999), n. 8 above, at 50. See also Amnesty International, *Universal Jurisdiction: The duty of states to enact and implement legislation* (AI Index No. IOR 53/002/2001) (London: AI, 2001) ch. 14.

(c) Extradition[55]

The primary shortcoming relating to extradition with respect to crimes under international law is the lack of comprehensive and express treaty obligations. As international law treats extradition generally as a matter of comity, subject to the discretion of the requested State in the absence of a treaty obligation,[56] specific obligations to extradite must emerge either through treaty or through a rule of customary law. The emergence of an obligation to extradite or prosecute at customary international law would represent an important development.[57] Without such a duty, international law provides only the existing conventional obligations to prosecute or extradite for grave breaches and torture.[58] With or without such a customary duty, changes to national extradition laws will be needed.

Even once the basic possibility of extradition for crimes under international law is established, a host of difficulties remain. *Pinochet* made clear the extent to which national laws relating to extradition can impose problems and delay in the exercise of universal jurisdiction. The intricacies that mark extradition law often make proceedings exceedingly slow. Issues include those raised in the UK proceedings (primarily, whether the offence was punishable under the law of the requested State at the relevant time)[59] and go farther to encompass a range of other matters. These may involve such restrictions as the bar in many constitutions of extradition of nationals,[60] political offense exceptions,[61] national interest or national security factors, statutes of limita-

---

[55] See the discussion in International Council on Human Rights Policy (1999), n. 8 above, at 45–6.

[56] I.A. Shearer, *Extradition in International Law* (Manchester: Manchester U.P., 1971) at 23–7.

[57] See n. 26 and related text above.

[58] 1949 Geneva Conventions, Art. 49 (Convention I), Art. 50 (Convention II), Art. 129 (Convention III), Art. 146 (Convention IV) (that a High Contracting Party is obliged to bring those responsible for grave breaches, whatever their nationality, before its own courts or, if it prefers, to hand them over to another Party that has made out a *prima facie* case); 1977 Additional Protocol I, Art. 8 (that subject to the obligations under the Geneva Conventions, 'and when circumstances permit, the High Contracting Parties shall cooperate in the matter of extradition. They shall give due consideration to the request of the State in whose territory the alleged offence has occurred'); 1984 Convention Against Torture, Art. 7(1) ('The State Party in the territory under whose jurisdiction a person alleged to have committed any offence referred to in Article 4 is found shall in the cases contemplated in Article 5, if it does not extradite him, submit the case to its competent authorities for the purpose of prosecution'). See also *Principles of International Cooperation,* n. 51 above, para. 5; the 1948 Genocide Convention, Art. 7, provides that States Parties pledge themselves to grant extradition 'in accordance with their laws and treaties in force', although the Convention requires prosecution only by the State on the territory of which the crime was committed (Art. 6).

[59] See Chapter VII, n. 19 below.

[60] Michael Plachta, '(Non-)Extradition of Nationals: A never-ending story?' (1999) 13 Emory Int'l L. Rev. 77.

[61] 1948 Genocide Convention, Art. 7 (that genocide shall not be considered a political crime for purposes of extradition).

tion,[62] the perceived possibility of unfairness in the proceedings, humanitarian grounds, *non bis in idem*, and more.[63] Importantly, such factors are often left to the discretion of political rather than judicial authorities, without adequate transparency and possibility of review.

While some of these factors would (at least in certain circumstances) remain legitimate in cases involving international crimes (fair trial guarantees, *non bis in idem*), others would not (political offense exception, statutes of limitation). As with mutual legal assistance, each State that wishes to have an effective international system for the exercise of universal jurisdiction will have to undertake a thorough review of its extradition laws to ensure that they treat crimes under international law appropriately.[64]

(d) The decision to proceed

Even where the legal basis is adequate, the questions of who makes the decision to proceed, based on which factors, are likely to become pivotal as universal jurisdiction shifts from an aspiration to a working legal reality. Because these questions will determine how often universal jurisdiction will be exercised, and on what conditions, they call for more sustained examination than they have so far received. The ability of proceedings to withstand criticisms that they are politically motivated or represent 'jurisdictional imperialism',[65] and the consequent support of governments for the exercise of universal jurisdiction, will clearly be affected by the manner in which discretion is exercised in the prosecuting State.

The discretion of the relevant officials, whether political or legal, should be structured so as to take into account legitimate factors for limiting the exercise of universal jurisdiction. These (cumulative) factors include the following:

(a) <u>The presence of the defendant</u> If the defendant is not present, authorities in the prosecuting State will have to assess the likelihood of cooperation from the relevant State or States in his or her extradition (if extradition requests are possible under national law).[66]

---

[62] Convention on the non-applicability of statutory limitations to war crimes and crimes against humanity, 26 November 1968, 754 U.N.T.S. 73, 8 I.L.M. 68, reprinted in Bassiouni (1992), n. 27 above, 703.

[63] See M. Cherif Bassiouni, 'Law and practice of the U.S.', in Bassiouni (1999b), n. 28 above, (vol. II) 191, at 229–51; Amnesty International, *The International Criminal Court: Making the right choices, Part III* (AI Index IOR 40/013/97) (London: AI, 1997), at 40–50.

[64] Canada, in implementing the Rome Statute into domestic law, modified its extradition act to eliminate ordinary reasons for refusal in proceedings related to surrender to the ICC: *Crimes Against Humanity and War Crimes Act*, n. 25 above, s. 52. This streamlining was not extended (in relevant part) to extradition proceedings to States seeking to exercise universal jurisdiction over Rome Statute crimes.

[65] International Council on Human Rights Policy (1999), n. 8 above, at 26.

[66] See discussion above, nn. 39–40 and related text. The German Code of Crimes Against International Law, Art. 3(5) (see n. 42 above) takes the likelihood of future presence into account.

(b) <u>The availability of sufficient evidence</u> An inability to acquire adequate evidence (particularly where the State of the accused is not disposed to assist) can effectively block proceedings. Absent sufficient evidence, the possibility of cooperation will again have to be weighed. In this context, the need to provide adequate protection for victims and witnesses must also be considered.

(c) <u>Severity</u> Prosecuting authorities could also take into account the seriousness of the acts with which the accused is charged, the rank and role of the accused in the crimes alleged, the impact of the relevant situation on the international community, and the presence in the prosecuting State of a victim community or of some other connection to the country or conflict in question.

(d) <u>Situation in the territorial State</u> If the territorial State or national State of the accused is demonstrably willing and able to prosecute the accused in a fair manner, or if there is another, clearly more appropriate forum, the State considering universal jurisdiction should ordinarily defer to its courts. If the territorial or national State is not in a position to proceed effectively, authorities in the investigating State will have to consider the attitude towards prosecution of civil society (victims, non-governmental organizations, society at large) in the territorial State,[67] as well as the possibilities that proceedings will either prevent or deter further abuses (particularly where the conflict to which they relate is ongoing), or will stimulate more robust action in the territorial State or national itself.[68] The stability of the other country, the attitude of the government there towards impunity, including the occurrence and context of a 'truth commission' or of an amnesty, will all be relevant to this important, notoriously difficult calculation.[69] A prosecutor could legitimately choose not to proceed in light of all the circumstances, even for example where a decision to limit (but not exclude) prosecutions has been made in the context of a credible 'truth commission' process in which full disclosure of the accused's acts was

---

[67] International Council on Human Rights Policy (1999), at 34.

[68] David Bosco, 'Dictators in the dock' *American Prospect* (14 August 2000) 26 ('the international involvement "expanded the space for Chilean society and institutions to confront their dark past themselves"', quoting American academic Diane Orentlicher).

[69] For preliminary proposals on the evaluation of national amnesties and truth commissions respectively, see Priscilla B. Hayner, 'International guidelines for the creation and operation of truth commissions: A preliminary proposal' and D. Cassel, 'Lessons from the Americas', in Bassiouni and Morris, eds., *Accountability for International Crimes and Serious Violations of Fundamental Human Rights* (1996) 59 L. and Contemp. Probs. The provision in the German Code of Crimes Against International Law, Art. 3(5), n. 42 above, for halting proceedings when the offence is being prosecuted by a territorial State of the crime, the national State of the accused, or the national State of the victim seems imperfect (at least on its face) in that it does not take into account the rigour or fairness of the other proceedings.

made and the right of victims to reparations was fully respected (see discussion of amnesties, pp. 93–102 above).

(e) <u>Resources available to the prosecutor</u> Apart from other constraints, prosecutors may be loath to expend resources on crimes having no or only slight direct connection to their own jurisdiction. Having budgetary limits to consider, authorities will want to examine the cost implications of universal jurisdiction proceedings. Even where evidence is available the cost of such proceedings can be exorbitant, with correspondingly high opportunity costs in terms of resources available to pursue local matters potentially important in themselves. National authorities, particularly in over-stressed systems, will eventually have to struggle with the question of when the service to the international community of a universal jurisdiction prosecution is counterbalanced by the need for prosecution of local crime. While the cost of exercising jurisdiction will often not be unmanageably high, and would not in any event excuse inaction (as extradition to a State willing to take proceedings would still be possible), the reality of the resource factor points, at the least, to the need to make sensitive the responsible officials to the crucial role of national courts in enforcing international law.

(f) <u>Relation to the other country</u> Universal jurisdiction contains what is probably an irreducible element of political friction. Jurisdiction may be unlikely to be exercised where the government is able to influence the decisions of national prosecutors and where national interests might, in the view of the government, be harmed by prosecution. At present, the law of many States accords a pivotal role to political officials.[70] Yet political officials are typically required to take the full national interest into account in their decisions, and this typically involves weighing a multiplicity of trade, strategic, and other factors. To eliminate this 'interference' one must either structure the discretion of the political officer or eliminate it. The rule of law would presumably be better served if all relevant decisions were taken in a transparent and accountable manner by prosecutors and judges. If States remain reluctant to eliminate the discretion of political officials, the second-best alternative would be to subject the exercise of ministerial discretion to controls that ensured to the extent possible the legitimacy of the decisions made. This might include provision for public guidelines outlining the factors to be considered, followed by provision for judicial review in which the exercise of discretion could be challenged.

---

[70] Examples (requiring the consent of the Attorney-General to initiate proceedings) include Canada (Crimes Against Humanity and War Crimes Act, s. 9(3)); New Zealand (International Crimes and International Criminal Court Act 2000, s. 13); and the United Kingdom (International Criminal Court Act 2001, s. 53(3): see n. 26 above.

At present, officials have little experience and little authoritative guidance on the appropriate exercise of discretion in the specific context of universal jurisdiction over the (often politically charged) core crimes of international criminal law. Those who promote universal jurisdiction should recognize that States have a legitimate desire to ensure that the case-load likely to lay claim to the resources of their authorities is manageable. Similarly, even governments that are committed proponents of accountability will want to have a reasonable degree of clarity as to the potential political fallout of universal jurisdiction proceedings. Concerns about the potentially real consequences of universal jurisdiction proceedings on inter-State relations are not trivial. It would be one thing for France to prosecute a former Head of State of Haiti before its domestic courts, and quite another for the Marshall Islands to prosecute a former President of the United States. If regular enforcement—the rule of law—is to become even a clearly *emergent* reality, then supporters of universal jurisdiction will have to propose credible means of addressing the complex decisions and (sometimes 'political') value-judgements faced by those operating in real-world situations.

6. CONCLUSION

The requirement, in the legislation of Canada and other States,[71] that an accused be present in the investigating country places an imperfect limit on the exercise of universal jurisdiction. It is not difficult to imagine circumstances in which the international community, and the particular States involved, would favour extradition and trial in another country. Yet a full 'presence requirement' will prevent this, by conditioning investigation on the prior presence of the accused, making an arrest warrant and extradition request impossible until the person is within the territory of the investigating State. Such a requirement would do so, moreover, without providing answers as to when universal jurisdiction is best exercised by the forum contemplating it; even when a potential defendant is present in the territory of a given State, difficult questions will remain as to whether prosecution is desirable. It would, in principle, be preferable to enable authorities to open an investigation of a suspect absent from the investigating State's territory, with the aim of requesting extradition, in the context of clear policy grounds underlying the decision to proceed. Yet these 'policy grounds' would have to be sufficiently clear to ensure that universal jurisdiction proceedings would neither become a financial drain nor an unmanageable political or diplomatic burden before a greater number of States could be expected to take this step. Thus, practical concerns about the feasibility of universal jurisdiction will have to be addressed thoroughly and convincingly, in terms relevant to those

---

[71] See n. 39 above.

confronting them most directly (that is, prosecutors and policy-makers). This has not so far been done, and States are cautious accordingly. Even once the international community develops a sufficient degree of experience and consensus about how best to make the decisions required, the weightiness of the decisions to be made, affecting as they may the internal situation of the country in question, as well as the prosecuting State's interests in its relations with that country, is all but certain to make many governments hesitate before reforming their law to allow for the full and effective exercise of universal jurisdiction.[72]

Despite these difficulties, there is reason to believe that universal jurisdiction is deeply consonant with the underlying aim of international justice. As part of a comprehensive regime for ensuring accountability for the core crimes of international criminal law, such jurisdiction will be indispensable as a complement to and a surrogate for the ICC. At the same time, such jurisdiction will by its nature always be a supplementary jurisdiction, of last resort, and it will often not be feasible to exercise it. Even with wide availability among States of an adequate legal basis and with full and transparent prosecutorial (not political) control, universal jurisdiction would always be subject to 'political' and resource judgements that themselves create tensions, involving as they do consideration of a wide range of justice and reconciliation factors. Such judgements will require the development of special expertise and administrative arrangements for the establishment of such jurisdiction as a working norm. Even so, judgements about the wisdom of proceeding will vary among good faith actors from State to State, resulting in an irreducible element of controversy. This tension is inherent in delegating to national authorities the enforcement of international law.

These problems have scarcely begun to be addressed in the way that a working legal system requires. Until now, the exercise of universal jurisdiction has depended on the largely fortuitous convergence of the presence of a defendant, of members of the public interested in a case, of availability of evidence (in particular from victims or other eye-witnesses), of the necessary legal regime, of political and prosecutorial will and the necessary resources. An element of the fortuitous is probably inherent in the exercise of this form of jurisdiction, given the many contingencies involved. Nonetheless, its entrenchment in the international system as a means of fair and regular enforcement will require wide-ranging law reforms and education, the difficulties of which should not be underestimated.

---

[72] The Belgian case against the (now former) Foreign Minister of the Congo (pp. 146–8 below) resulted from a Belgian extradition request pursuant to a law not requiring a presence requirement (n. 41 above). As an apparent result of this law being applied without a clear overarching policy regarding the commencement of proceedings, the Belgian government is currently considering amendments to its law to impose limits on the exercise of universal jurisdiction: see *Proposition de loi modifiant la loi du 16 juin 1993 relative à la répression des violations graves du droit international humanitaire*, n. 44 above.

VII

Immunity

1. INTRODUCTION

With increasing potential for the application of international criminal law to individuals acting—or purporting to act—in an official capacity, the question arises whether such individuals should ever, and if so under what circumstances, be shielded from arrest and prosecution by doctrines of immunity. For reasons flowing from the Nuremberg principles,[1] immunity should be irrelevant for the same reason that superior orders or prior legality under national law are irrelevant. To acknowledge claims of immunity would in effect allow States to choose whether or not their agents would be responsible under international law, making regular enforcement (the rule of law) all but impossible. Such 'checker-boarding' would undermine the enforcement of international criminal law and weaken its role in promoting peace and security. Nonetheless, a lack of practice and the strength of the underlying rationale of immunities at international law have hindered the emergence of any straightforward consensus. The discussion below shows that further practice and analysis are needed before such consensus is likely to emerge; it also shows that international law is likely, if it attends to the issues on both sides of the balance sheet as it develops, to set clear limits on the applicable doctrines of immunity while leaving a space within which these continue to operate.

2. OFFICIAL IMMUNITIES: A SKETCH

The international law of immunities is sometimes clearly codified, but is often uncodified and unclear. Diplomatic immunities are set out in the widely supported Vienna Convention on Diplomatic Relations,[2] and supplemented by custom. Head of State immunity[3] and State immunity[4] *per se*—which

---

[1] Pages 19–23 above; see also M. Cherif Bassiouni *Crimes Against Humanity in International Criminal Law* (2d ed.) (The Hague: Kluwer, 1999), at 505–8.

[2] 18 April 1961, 500 U.N.T.S. 95 ['VCDR']. See generally Eileen Denza, *Diplomatic Law: A commentary on the Vienna Convention on Diplomatic Relations* (2d ed.) (Oxford: Clarendon, 1998).

[3] See generally Sir Arthur Watts, 'The Legal Position in International Law of Heads of States, Heads of Governments and Foreign Ministers' (1994) III *Recueil des Cours* 9, at 35–81. Watts, at 52, describes the body of rules governing the status of Heads of States at customary law as one 'which is in many respects still unsettled, and on which limited State practice casts an uneven light'. Another writer states that '[w]hile a survey of the international community's approach to head of state immunity reveals wide agreement that heads of state are entitled to some immunity,

protects the State as such from the jurisdiction of foreign courts—are largely matters of (sometimes rather thin) custom. The position of officials other than diplomatic agents and Heads of State—including heads of government, where different from Head of State—is even less certain.[5]

Immunity for State representatives derives from deeply rooted doctrines of international law aimed at facilitating relations between States, in part by preventing the authorities of one jurisdiction from interfering with the sovereignty of another. As the ICJ stated: 'The Vienna Conventions [of 1961, and its 1963 companion on Consular Relations], which codify the law of diplomatic and consular relations, state principles and rules essential for the maintenance of peaceful relations between States and accepted throughout the world by nations of all creeds, cultures and political complections'.[6]

As the VCDR recognizes in relation to diplomatic immunities, 'the purpose of . . . privileges and immunities is not to benefit individuals but to ensure the efficient performance of the functions of diplomatic missions as representing States' (Preamble, para. 4). The same impersonal, functional aim applies equally, *mutatis mutandis*, to Heads of State and other officials.

Basic concepts of this area of law, which will be relevant in seeking to harmonize it with international criminal law, are inviolability and immunity. Denza writes:

Inviolability in modern international law is a status accorded to the premises, persons or property physically present in the territory of a sovereign State but not subject to its jurisdiction in the ordinary way. The sovereign State—under the Vienna Convention the receiving State—is under a duty to abstain from exercising any sovereign rights, in particular law enforcement rights, in respect of inviolable premises, persons or property.

The Vienna Convention confers inviolability on a range of premises, persons, and property. Some kinds of property are, however, given specified immunities which fall short of inviolability—for example the means of transport of the mission and the diplomatic bag [at 112].

---

there is no consensus on the extent of that immunity': Jerrold L. Mallory, 'Resolving the Confusion over Head of State Immunity: The defined right of kings' (1986) 86 Columbia L. Rev. 169 at 177.

[4] Immunities attaching to diplomats, heads of State, and other officials are distinct from the State immunity that attaches to the State as such: see generally Jürgen Bröhmer, *State Immunity and the Violation of Human Rights* (The Hague: Martinus Nijhoff, 1997).

[5] Heads of State, heads of government, foreign ministers, and other officials are protected by the immunities set down in the Convention on Special Missions, 8 December 1969, 1400 U.N.T.S. 231, 9 I.L.M. 127, when visiting other countries on the missions covered by the Convention. While important as an indication that immunities like those in the VCDR may apply by analogy to other officials, this instrument has not been widely ratified. It has nonetheless been taken as a basis for analysis by Watts (1994), n. 3 above, at 38ff.

[6] *United States Diplomatic and Consular Staff in Tehran (United States of America v. Iran), Judgment of 24 May 1980*, (1980) I.C.J. Rep. 3, at 25 ['*Hostages* case'].

Inviolability is therefore, strictly speaking, the highest and most impervious form of immunity.[7] The VCDR makes diplomatic agents personally inviolable (Article 29), confirming 'the oldest established rule of diplomatic law'.[8] It also makes inviolable their residence and property (Article 30) and makes them immune from the criminal jurisdiction of the receiving State (Article 31).[9] This immunity lasts until the agent leaves the country at the end of their posting, and continues thereafter with respect to acts performed in the exercise of that person's official functions (Article 39). The official correspondence of the mission (Article 27) and its archives and documents (Article 24) are also inviolable. Diplomatic immunity is a privilege of the sending State, not a right of the person, and may be waived by that State (but only expressly) (Article 32). In the negotiation of the Vienna Convention, the decision was made to make inviolability absolute, without allowance even for 'exceptional circumstances' or cases of 'extreme urgency'.[10] Exceptions to inviolability have not been supported because States have relied upon the remedies that the framework of the VCDR contemplates against abuse of immunity and inviolability, i.e. to declare an individual *persona non grata* (Article 9) and to sever diplomatic relations with the sending State.[11]

The absolute immunity that attaches to the person of a diplomat in their capacity as a representative of their sending State is known as immunity *ratione personae*, and applies to all acts performed during tenure of the posting, regardless of whether performed within the scope or purported scope of the person's official functions.[12] The immunity enjoyed by a Head of State at customary international law during their tenure in office is generally recog-

---

[7] The distinction between immunity and inviolability is discussed at length in J. Craig Barker, *The Abuse of diplomatic privileges and immunities: A Necessary evil?* (Aldershot: Dartmouth, 1996), at 70–79 and 230–234.

[8] Denza (1998), n. 2 above, at 210. Denza describes the incident at the US Embassy in Teheran as 'probably the only significant breach by a Contracting Party of Article 29 of the Vienna Convention. . . .' (at 217). In ordering provisional measures in response to that breach, the ICJ stated: 'There is no more fundamental prerequisite for the conduct of relations between States than the inviolability of diplomatic envoys and embassies. . . .' ((1979) I.C.J. Reports at 19). See *Hostages* case, n. 6 above, at 42.

[9] Although subject to early assertions that it should not apply in cases of treason, 'the rule of immunity from criminal jurisdiction continued virtually unchallenged until its incorporation into the Vienna Convention' (Denza, n. 2 above, at 230). The ICJ stated in the *Hostages* case, n. 6 above: 'if the intention [declared by the Iranian authorities] to submit the hostages to any form of criminal trial or investigation were to be put into effect, that would constitute a grave breach by Iran of its obligations under Article 31, paragraph 1, of the 1961 Vienna Convention' (at 37).

[10] Denza (1998), n. 2 above, at 121. Denza remarks: 'An incident where during a fire in the United States Embassy in Moscow the local "fire-fighters" proved to be KGB agents illustrates why this is so' (ibid.) Nonetheless, 'a very limited exception to the prohibition on arrest or detention may be implied on the basis of self-defence or of an overriding duty to protect human life' (ibid., at 219–20).

[11] Denza (1998), n. 2 above, at 123–6; see also *Hostages* case, n. 6 above, at 38–40.

[12] VCDR Art. 31(1) provides three express exemptions to this immunity *ratione personae*, but these do not reduce the immunity from criminal jurisdiction.

nized to be of the same sort.[13] The immunity enjoyed by a diplomat after completion of his or her posting, however, is an immunity attaching only to acts performed in an official capacity (i.e. immunity *ratione materiae*). The same limited immunity is increasingly said to apply to a former head of State at customary law; thus, jurisdiction has been exercised over former heads of State for acts done in a personal capacity (as e.g. for personal enrichment).[14] This same lesser form of immunity applies to lesser officials both during after their time in office.[15]

Absent waiver, immunity imposes a formidable barrier to the application of criminal process by one State against the personnel of another, whether under universal or any other theory of jurisdiction. The pressing questions, for international criminal law, are whether (and to what extent) immunities *ratione personae* and *ratione materiae* are subject to exceptions where criminal responsibility arises directly under international law, and whether the answer varies between national and international tribunals. Since March 1999 the first place one must turn to address these questions has been the House of Lords' decision in the *Pinochet* case.

3. PINOCHET

The *Pinochet* decision of 24 March 1999 has become a landmark for its direct treatment of these questions. It was, as Lord Browne-Wilkinson described it, 'the first time . . . when a local domestic court has refused to afford immunity to a head of state or former head of state on the grounds that there can be no immunity against prosecution for certain international crimes.'[16] The decision's international importance is therefore considerable—not as a binding

---

[13] This conflation of diplomatic and Head of State immunity has been criticized on the ground that the duties of a Head of State and a diplomatic agent are incomparable: Hazel Fox, 'The Pinochet Case No. 3' (1999) 48 I.C.L.Q. 687, at 693–4. Sir Arthur Watts describes the consideration due a Head to State to be an *a fortiori* case of that owed an Ambassador: Watts (1994), n. 3 above, at 40.

[14] See Sir Robert Jennings and Sir Arthur Watts, *Oppenheim's International Law* (9th ed.) (London: Longman, 1996), at 1037–44.

[15] Watts (1994), n. 3 above, at 102–4, states that the immunities owing to heads of government are not the equivalent of those owing to heads of States because heads of government do not personify the State in the same way as heads of States do. Espousing a functional approach, Watts asserts that heads of government should enjoy immunity from criminal and civil suit during foreign visits, citing the 1969 Special Missions Convention, Art. 31. See also Jürgen Bröhmer, *State Immunity and the Violation of Human Rights* (The Hague: Martinus Nijhoff, 1997), at 26–32. With regard to others, the VCDR applies immunity from criminal jurisdiction to the family of a diplomatic agent and to the members of the mission's technical and administrative staff. Members of the mission's service staff enjoy immunity only for acts performed in the course of their duties (Art. 37).

[16] *R.* v. *Bow Street Metropolitan Stipendiary Magistrate and Others*, ex parte *Pinochet Ugarte (Amnesty International and Others intervening)* (No. 3) [1999] 2 All E.R. 97 (H.L.), at 111.

precedent, but for what it reveals about the current state of international law, and of legal attitudes in at least one influential State. For those concerned with the ability of the ICC to perform its functions, it underscores the need for effective implementing legislation, without which international norms often lack the foundation for practice (see pp. 63–6 and 84–93 above).

Senator (formerly General) Pinochet, head of State of Chile during a period of severe and systematic human rights abuses between 1973 and 1990, came to the United Kingdom to seek medical treatment in 1998. Judicial authorities in Spain transmitted two international arrest warrants to the United Kingdom, seeking the Senator's arrest and extradition for crimes alleged during his time as head of State. Universal jurisdiction formed the basis of most of the charges. He was arrested on provisional warrants issued in response to the Spanish requests. On 28 October 1998 (eleven days after the arrest) the Divisional Court quashed both warrants. The decision relating to the second warrant (quashed on the basis that the Senator was entitled to immunity as a former head of State) was appealed to the House of Lords. Pending appeal, Spain issued a formal request for extradition that greatly expanded the charges in the second warrant. On 25 November, a five-judge panel of the House of Lords overturned the Divisional Court decision by a majority of three to two, holding that a former head of State was not entitled to immunity for crimes under international law, as these could not form part of the official functions defining that immunity.[17] This ruling proved unstable, however. The failure of one of the judges in the majority, Lord Hoffmann, to declare his involvement with a fundraising charity linked to one of the intervenors (Amnesty International) resulted in an unprecedented subsequent ruling to set this decision aside.[18] An expanded seven-judge panel reheard the case in early 1999 and issued its reasons on 24 March.

At the rehearing the House of Lords considered two issues of law: were the crimes alleged against Senator Pinochet extradition crimes under UK law; if so, did he enjoy immunity from arrest and prosecution for them? The first issue turns upon UK law more than does the second, but it was only with respect to confirmed extradition crimes that the issue of immunity could arise.

On the first issue the judges agreed that, for an extradition crime to exist, the alleged conduct had to be criminal and subject to extra-territorial jurisdiction under UK law at the time it took place, not just at the time the extradition was requested.[19] Torture and conspiracy to torture were therefore held to become extradition crimes only upon the entry into force of the legis-

---

[17] *R.* v. *Bow Street Metropolitan Stipendiary Magistrate and Others,* ex parte *Pinochet Ugarte* [1998] 4 All E.R. 897, [1998] 3 W.L.R. 1456 (H.L.).

[18] *R.* v. *Bow Street Metropolitan Stipendiary Magistrate and Others,* ex parte *Pinochet Ugarte (Amnesty International and Others intervening)* (No. 2) [1999] 1 All E.R. 577, [1999] 2 W.L.R. 272 (H.L.).

[19] Lord Browne-Wilkinson sets out the reasoning (at 104–7). All other judges concurred: *Pinochet (No. 3),* n. 16 above.

lation giving UK courts universal jurisdiction over them. That date was 29 September 1988, precluding extradition on the vast part of the crimes for which Pinochet's extradition was sought.[20] Torture and conspiracy to torture after 1988 remained extraditable.[21]

On the second issue of immunity, none of the judges doubted that immunity *ratione personae* is absolute and applies to acts done in both a private and a public capacity, such that Pinochet would have been protected from any legal process (absent a waiver) had he still been Head of State at the time the warrant was issued.[22] The only exception to such immunity is where an instrument establishing an international tribunal expressly provides for the responsibility of heads of State.[23]

In the crucial ruling, six of the seven judges[24] agreed that there are crimes under international law to which immunity *ratione materiae* is not applicable, that torture is one of these crimes, and that, on the facts of the case, claims of immunity were unavailable with respect to it after 1988. The reasons of the majority for arriving at these conclusions vary somewhat, but the entry into force of the Torture Convention is essential to all of them in affirming that claims to immunity are unavailable as between parties to it.[25]

While the prohibition of torture was agreed to be a peremptory norm of international law, a number of the Law Lords were of the view that something more express is called for before it can be assumed that the courts of one State can try the officials of another for acts performed in the course of their official functions.[26] In support of this view, Lord Hope quoted with approval the judgment of the House of Lords' previous hearing of the case:

[20] Lord Millett alone argued that English statutory jurisdiction over criminal law is supplemented by the common law and that, since customary law forms part of the common law, English courts have always had extra-territorial jurisdiction over crimes giving rise to universal jurisdiction at customary law (ibid., at 177). If accepted, this reasoning would have made all allegations of torture and conspiracy to torture extradition crimes, even prior to the 1988 passage of the UK legislation.

[21] All the judges expressly supported Lord Hope's reasoning (ibid., at 137–45) with respect to which crimes were extraditable, including Lord Millett (despite preferring his own broader view, n. 20 above). Allegations not based on universal jurisdiction, i.e. of conspiracies *in Spain* to commit murder or torture *in Spain*, also remained extraditable before 29 September 1988, but were held to give rise to immunity.

[22] The rationale for this distinction is not apparent, and it has been said that if immunity *ratione materiae* is inconsistent with Art. 1 of the Torture Convention, equally is immunity *ratione personae*: Fox (1999), n. 13 above, at 700; Eileen Denza, '*Ex Parte Pinochet*: Lacuna or leap?' (1999) 48 I.C.L.Q. 949 at 954.

[23] *Pinochet (No. 3)*, n. 16 above, Lords Browne-Wilkinson (at 114), Goff (at 120–1), Hope (at 147) and Phillips (at 189).

[24] Lord Goff dissented, supporting complete immunity, which he saw as being compatible with the terms of the Torture Convention (ibid., at 126–30).

[25] Spain, Chile, and the United Kingdom. The UK was the last to ratify the Torture Convention; it did so on 8 December 1988.

[26] The decision in *Pinochet (No. 3)*, n. 16 above, reflects a broad interpretation of official functions: Lords Goff (at 125–6), Hope (at 147), Saville (at 169), Millett (at 172), and Phillips (at 189–90). This stands in contrast to the majority in the previous decision, n. 17 above, which relied

So it is necessary to consider what is needed, in the absence of a general international convention defining or cutting down head of state immunity, to define or limit the former head of state immunity in particular cases. In my opinion it is necessary to find provision in an international convention to which the state asserting, and the state being asked to refuse, the immunity of a former head of state for an official act is a party; the convention must clearly define a crime against international law and require or empower a state to prevent or prosecute the crime, whether or not committed in its jurisdiction and whether or not committed by one of its nationals; it must make it clear that a national court has jurisdiction to try a crime alleged against a former head of state, or that having been a head of state is not defence and that expressly or impliedly the immunity is not to apply so as to bar proceedings against him. The convention must be given the force of law in the national courts of the state; in a dualist country like the United Kingdom that means by legislation, so that with the necessary procedures and machinery the crime may be prosecuted there in accordance with the procedures to be found in the convention.[27]

Three other judges either supported this reasoning or expressed doubt as to any limit to immunity before the entry into force of the Torture Convention.[28] The result was the same: to turn to the terms of the Convention to justify any absence of immunity.

Lord Browne-Wilkinson reasons that any official immunity *ratione materiae* is incompatible with the terms of the Torture Convention, which expressly aims to facilitate the prosecution of public officials. Chile could not claim immunity since it had, by ratifying the Convention, agreed to outlaw official torture and had recognized the duty of other States Parties to extradite or prosecute officials of other States Parties (at 114–15). Lords Hope, Hutton, Saville, Millett, and Phillips apply similar reasoning.[29]

more upon the argument that conduct criminal under international law could not form part of official functions. This reasoning was reflected in the third hearing in the decisions of Lord Hutton (at 165–6) and, more narrowly, of Lords Browne-Wilkinson (at 113–14) and Phillips (at 192). Scholarly opinion has generally supported the potential inclusion of acts of torture within the compass of 'official acts': J. Craig Barker, 'The Future of Former Head of State Immunity after *Ex parte Pinochet*' (1999) 48 I.C.L.Q. 937, at 943; Denza (1999), n. 22 above, at 952–6; John Hopkins, 'Case and Comment: Former head of foreign state: extradition; immunity' (1999) Camb. L.J. 461, at 464; Ruth Wedgwood, 'International Criminal Law and Augusto Pinochet' (2000) 40 Virg. J. Int'l L. 829, at 840.

[27] Lord Hope (at 147–8) quoting Lord Slynn from the earlier judgment, n. 17 above, at 1475.
[28] Lords Browne-Wilkinson (at 114), Goff (at 117), and Saville (at 168).
[29] At 152, 165, 169, 179, and 190 respectively. Three (Lords Browne-Wilkinson, Hope, and Saville) held the relevant date to be that on which the Torture Convention became binding as between Spain, Chile, and the UK: this was the date that the last of these countries ratified it (the UK, on 8 December 1988). Lord Hutton thought the relevant date to be that of the entry into force of the law giving UK courts extraterritorial jurisdiction over torture (29 September 1988). Lords Millett and Phillips agree that the terms and entry into force of the Convention clarify the lack of immunity, but also find that immunity has never existed with respect to crimes of *jus cogens* giving rise to universal jurisdiction, and that the Torture Convention merely recognizes this. Lord Goff (at 125) was of the view that ratification of the Convention Against Torture could not amount to waiver; some scholars have supported this: Hopkins (1999), n. 26 above, at 464; Denza (1999), n. 22 above, at 955.

Three possible readings of the *Pinochet* decision—relevant to consideration of the Rome Statute (pp. 136–46 below)—suggest themselves. First, it may be that immunity is limited not as a matter of customary law, but by the terms of the Convention.[30] Secondly, it may be that the Convention did not change customary law and did not expressly limit immunity but gave rise to a kind of estoppel as between States Parties, preventing them from bringing claims of immunity for proceedings related to torture before the courts of another State Party.[31] In either of these two cases the implications of the *Pinochet* decision are limited to situations in which the country of the person sought, the requesting State, and the requested State are all parties to the Convention. Thirdly, it may be that the Torture Convention caused an emerging rule of customary law to crystallize, such that immunity is now limited with respect to all States for allegations of torture against their officials before the courts of all other nations, whether parties to the Convention or not.[32]

Although the decisions of the Law Lords resist easy harmonization, the first of these three readings is the most plausible reading of the case. Three judges expressly articulated the view, Lord Hope's view is compatible with it, and the two judges who would have found no immunity even before 1988 supported the reasoning as proper, if too narrow. Although the third possibility is arguable, only two of the seven judges express belief in a change at customary law in general, and the reasoning of the others is carefully worded to either discount or avoid the possibility.[33] This leaves a restricted, context-specific, and fact-driven view of the extent to which *Pinochet* limits immunity.[34]

[30] Lord Browne-Wilkinson: '. . . Chile had agreed with the other parties to the Torture Convention that all signatory states should have jurisdiction to try official torture (as defined in the Convention) even if such torture were committed in Chile' (at 115). Lord Saville: 'I do not reach this conclusion by implying terms into the Torture Convention, but simply by applying its express terms. . . . To my mind these terms demonstrate that the states who have become parties have clearly and unambiguously agreed that official torture should now be dealt with in a way which would otherwise amount to an interference in their sovereignty' (at 169–170). Lord Hutton: 'Therefore having regard to the provisions of the Torture Convention, I do not consider that Senator Pinochet or Chile can claim that the commission of acts of torture . . . were functions of the head of state' (and therefore within the scope of immunity) (at 165).

[31] Lord Hope: 'I would not regard this as a case of waiver. Nor would I accept that it was an implied term of the Torture Convention that former heads of state were to be deprived of their immunity . . . It is just that the obligations which were recognised by customary international law in the case of such serious international crimes by the date when Chile ratified the Convention are so strong as to override any objection by it on the ground of immunity *ratione materiae* to the exercise of the jurisdiction over crimes committed after that date which the United Kingdom had made available. . . . Chile, having ratified the Convention . . . which Spain had already ratified, was deprived of the right to object to the extra-territorial jurisdiction which the United Kingdom was able to assert over these offences' (at 152).

[32] See n. 29 above for the views of Lords Millett and Phillips, who go farther than this.

[33] See nn. 27 and 28 above.

[34] Without prejudice to the need to appreciate the full complexity of the judgment, references to 'the *Pinochet* judgment' or 'the reasoning of the Law Lords' in the remainder of this Chapter refers to this understanding of the central rationale of the majority. Even such a narrow reading

The decision is a cautious one, taking a somewhat traditional view of State consent in the light of the role that diplomatic and Heads of State immunities play in the smooth interaction of States. This rationale should not be ignored or undervalued. Criminal proceedings by one State against the officials of another have a clear ability to disrupt friendly relations and the effect of this disruption must, without exaggeration or diminution, be weighed against the advantages of lifting immunities for international crimes. On one hand, absence of immunity is as necessary a part of the Nuremberg doctrines as is the absence of a defence of prior legality or of superior orders. A State's ability to manipulate the law to protect its agents from responsibility is removed in each case. Critics could therefore argue that the Law Lords in effect recognized a State's right to decide whether or not its officials would be held to account for international crimes, by requiring what amounts to an express agreement to limit immunity. On the other hand it is possible, as the Law Lords appear to have viewed it, that norms intended to promote stability—by holding agents of State to account for crimes that often cause or aggravate breaches of international peace and security—when enforced by an international tribunal, may actually damage it when enforced by national courts. This perspective deserves some weight, given the lack of common standards and equivalent capacity across criminal justice systems, the lack of independence among judges and prosecutors in a great many jurisdictions, and the need to preserve the effective functioning of the system of diplomacy. This is probably the strongest argument available in support of the decision's high threshold for recognizing any change in the law of immunity.

4. IMMUNITY UNDER THE ROME STATUTE

The relative weight given to the sanctity of diplomacy in the face of the exigencies of international accountability is certain to influence interpretation of the Rome Statute. The balance struck between these in the jurisprudence of the Court is certain to have a great impact on the ICC's effectiveness. The *Pinochet* decision's emphasis on convention and legislation as against customary and common law highlights the need for clear provisions in both international conventions and national legislation. Clear legislation will guarantee better than appeals to custom that national courts perform their role in enforcing international criminal law. Like universal jurisdiction, any limits to the availability of immunities would be most reliable if expressly provided for

has, of course, been criticized as being overly broad. Lord Goff reasoned in dissent that waiver of immunity must be express and that no such express waiver could be found in the terms of the Convention Against Torture. Fox (1999) n. 13 above, at 697–8, and Denza (1999), n. 22 above, at 955, agree.

through national legislation. The Rome Statute does provide a limited incentive for States to pass such legislation.

The role of immunities in the Rome Statute regime can be examined in relation to (a) proceedings before the ICC itself; (b) surrender of suspects by their State of nationality, pursuant to a request from the Court; and (c) to surrender of a suspect, pursuant to an ICC request, by a State other than the State of that person's nationality.

(a) Proceedings before the ICC itself

The situation regarding the assertion of immunities before the ICC itself—that is, once the accused is in Court custody—is straightforward. As the Law Lords in *Pinochet* confirmed[35] and the practice of international tribunals has made clear, no immunity may be claimed before an international tribunal providing in its constituent instrument for loss of immunity or the equal responsibility of officials. Thus, the Charter of the Nuremberg Tribunal declared official capacity irrelevant; Karl Dönitz, who became acting head of State after Hitler's suicide at the conclusion of World War II, was convicted; and the Tribunal expressly affirmed the rule set down in the Charter.[36] The Proclamation establishing the Tokyo Tribunal did the same, although it did not specifically refer to head of State, since a decision had already been taken not to try the Japanese emperor.[37] Similar formulations followed in other instruments.[38] The Yugoslav and Rwanda tribunals each affirmed the broader formulation of the Nuremberg tribunal, and the practice of each lends support to the doctrine.[39]

---

[35] See n. 23 above.

[36] Art. 7 of the Nuremberg Charter, Chapter I, n. 33 above, reads: 'The official position of the defendants, whether as Heads of State or responsible officials in Government Departments, shall not be considered as freeing them from responsibility or mitigating punishment'. Dönitz was charged, convicted, and sentenced to 10 years' imprisonment: IMT Judgment, Chapter I, n. 33 above, at 310–15. The Tribunal declared that '[t]he principle of international law, which under certain circumstances, protects the representative of a state, cannot be applied to acts which are condemned as criminal by international law': IMT Judgment, Chapter I, n. 33 above, at 223.

[37] Part II, n. 1 above, Art. 6 ('Neither the official position, at any time, of an accused, nor the fact that an accused acted pursuant to order of his government or of a superior shall, of itself, be sufficient to free such accused from responsibility for any crime with which he is charged, but such circumstances may be considered in mitigation of punishment if the Tribunal determines that justice so requires'); Gary Jonathan Bass, *Stay the Hand of Vengeance: The Politics of War Crimes Tribunals* (Princeton: Princeton U.P., 2000), at 151.

[38] 1948 Genocide Convention, Art. 4 ('Persons commiting genocide or any of the other acts enumerated in Art. III shall be punished, whether they are constitutionally responsible rulers, public officials or private individuals'); see also Allied Control Council Law No. 10, Art. 4(a) (essentially identical to Art. 7 of the Nuremberg Charter); 1996 Draft Code of Crimes, Chapter II, n. 19 above, at 39, Art. 7 (essentially the same as the Nuremberg Charter); see Amnesty International, *The International Criminal Court: Fundamental Principles concerning the Elements of Genocide* (A.I. Index: IOR 40/01/99) (London: AI, 1999), at 27–42.

[39] The Statute of the International Criminal Tribunal for the Former Yugoslavia, Art. 7(2), reads: 'The official position of any accused person, whether as Head of State or Government or

Article 27 of the Rome Statute makes clear the extent to which the International Criminal Court will disregard the immunities of those brought before it:

1. This Statute shall apply equally to all persons without any distinction based on official capacity. In particular, official capacity as a Head of State or Government, a member of a Government or parliament, an elected representative or a government official shall in no case exempt a person from criminal responsibility under this Statute, nor shall it, in and of itself, constitute a ground for reduction of sentence.
2. Immunities or special procedural rules which may attach to the official capacity of a person, whether under national or international law, shall not bar the Court from exercising its jurisdiction over such a person.

In keeping with previous international tribunals, Article 27(1) ensures that norms of responsibility apply without any distinction based on official capacity.[40] Express provision for the criminal responsibility of officials was enough, in the context of the Torture Convention, for the judges in the *Pinochet* decision to hold that immunity *ratione materiae* could no longer be asserted (as between States Parties),[41] although the Law Lords held that immunities *ratione personae* would continue to apply except before an international tribunal.[42] By adding to official responsibility a clear reference to immunities under national or international law, Article 27(2) ensures that the consequences of the responsibility recognized by Article 27(1) are not frustrated by claims of immunity or other procedures.[43] Once it has custody, the ICC will therefore be able to proceed with respect to both standing and former offi-

as a responsible Government official, shall not relieve such person of criminal responsibility nor mitigate punishment'. The Statute of the Rwanda Tribunal, Art. 6(2), is identical. The ICTY indicted Slobodan Milosevic while in office as President of the Federal Republic of Yugoslavia: *Prosecutor* v. *Milosevic* et al., *Indictment* (ICTY Case No. IT–99–37) (24 May 1999); see further *Prosecutor* v. *Milosevic, Decision on preliminary motions* ICTY Case No. IT–99–37) (8 November 2001), paras. 26–34. The ICTR convicted Jean Kambanda, Interim Prime Minister of Rwanda during the 1994 conflict, for crimes performed during his time in office, citing the abuse of his official position as an aggravating factor in sentencing: *Prosecutor* v. *Jean Kambanda, Judgment and Sentence* (ICTR Case No. 97–23-S) (4 September 1998), para. 61(B)(vii). No immunities were asserted before the ICTR on Kambanda's behalf, of course, as it was the current government of Rwanda that had overthrown Kambanda's government.

[40] The ICTY has declared Art. 7(2) of the ICTY Statute and Art. 6(2) of the ICTR Statute to be 'indisputably declaratory of customary international law': *Prosecutor* v. *Furundzija, Judgment* (ICTY Case No. IT–95–17/1) (10 December 1998), para. 140.

[41] See n. 29 above and accompanying text.

[42] See n. 23 above.

[43] These immunities established by international law for the officials of other States are compounded by the immunities frequently available under national legislation or constitutional law to a nation's own head of State, high officials, members of parliament, or officials generally. See Otto Triffterer, 'Commentary on Article 27', in Triffterer, ed., *The Rome Statute of the International Criminal Court: Observers' notes, article by article* (Baden-Baden: Nomas, 1999) at 501; Helen Duffy and Jonathan Huston, 'Implementation of the ICC Statute: International obligations and constitutional considerations', in Claus Kress and Flavia Lattanzi, eds., *The Rome Statute and Domestic Legal Orders: General aspects and constitutional issues* (vol. 1) (Baden-Baden: Nomas, 2000), 29.

cials, including heads of State. Among other effects, this enhances the potential of the Court to take action with respect to a continuing situation.[44] It also promotes equal application of the law, exposing the few officials entitled to immunity *ratione personae* to the same criminal proceedings as lower officials entitled only to immunity *ratione materiae*.

(b) Surrender to the ICC

(i) Surrender by the State of nationality

Because of its complementarity to national jurisdictions (pp. 86–93 above), the Rome Statute gives States a real incentive to exercise jurisdiction over their own officials if they wish to avoid the Court doing so. As a result, the Statute is prompting significant changes of national law for a number of (prospective) States Parties. Once the Court does exercise jurisdiction, States Parties are required to cooperate with it (Article 86) and to adjust their laws accordingly (Article 88) (see pp. 155–9 below). National laws and constitutions, which frequently provide conditional or unconditional exemption from criminal proceedings for those who hold certain offices, may sometimes stand in the way either of domestic proceedings pursuant to the complementarity principle or of surrender to the ICC, and as such will call for attention in a number of States. Yet amending frequently long-honoured immunities of national constitutions—and for the purpose of accommodating an international institution that opponents will argue undermines sovereignty—may give rise to intractable political obstacles in some States. Governments have therefore sought ways around such problems either by making amendments only to allow surrender to the ICC, without removing the immunities that will prevent their authorities from investigating themselves, or by interpreting national immunities in a manner that allows both domestic proceedings and surrender to the ICC.[45]

France provides an example of the former approach.[46] As a preliminary step to ratification, the government of France referred the Rome Statute to its constitutional court on 24 December 1998. The Conseil Constitutionnel recognized that Article 27 was potentially incompatible with the provisions of the French Constitution that establish immunities and special procedures for France's head of State and for members of government and parliament.[47] In

---

[44] The Statute specifically contemplates the issuance of an arrest warrant 'to prevent the person from continuing with commission of that crime [for which reasonable grounds exist to believe the person is responsible] or a related crime . . .' (Art. 58).

[45] See the discussion in Duffy and Huston, n. 43 above, at 36–42.

[46] See the discussion in Antoine Buchet, 'L'Intégration en France de la Convention Portant Statut de la Cour Pénale Internationale: Histoire breve et inachevée d'une mutation attendue', in Kress and Lattanzi (2000), n. 43 above, at 74–82.

[47] See Chapter V, n. 45 above.

response, the French government amended its constitution to indicate that the Republic of France 'may recognize the jurisdiction of the ICC in the conditions set out in the treaty signed 18 July 1998'.[48] This would appear to allow France to surrender individuals to the ICC, thus opening a path towards fulfilment of its obligation to cooperate with the Court under Article 86. Yet because France has not amended its constitutional immunities *per se*, the new provision does nothing to increase the power of French authorities to meet the full requirements of the complementarity test with respect to proceedings before their own courts. The ICC is therefore the only venue for trying a limited set of high French officials (barring the exercise of universal jurisdiction). Such an approach allows governments to avoid many of the political difficulties involved in changing their laws or constitution or in initiating proceedings, and may prove attractive for others.[49]

An example of the latter approach is found in Germany.[50] The German constitution provides in Article 46(2) that a member of parliament may only be arrested and punished with the prior authorization of that body; Article 60 applies the same procedure to the President. The potential for conflict with Germany's obligations under the Rome Statute is obviated by the possibility of prior authorization, thus making it possible that statutory obligations could be fulfilled.[51] For many countries with constitutional immunities subject to waiver, this approach will allow governments to avoid the political difficulties involved in constitutional amendment.

Both France, with its use of 'may' instead of 'shall' in its constitutional amendment, and Germany, with its reliance on future parliaments to authorize cooperation with the ICC, have allowed their national authorities a certain margin of discretion in deciding whether or not they will fulfil their country's obligations under the Statute. Others can be expected to follow suit, or to go even farther, as they work through the process of implementation, weighing domestic political factors, the desire to preserve 'sovereignty' (i.e.

---

[48] 'La République Peut Reconnaître la Juridiction de la Cour Pénale Internationale dans les Conditions Prévues par la Traité Signé le 18 juillet 1998': Loi constitutionelle nr. 99–568 du 8 juillet 1999 (9 July 1999) *Journal Officiel de la République Française (lois et décrets)*, p.10175, Art. 53–2.

[49] It is understood that a number of Francophone African States may follow the French example.

[50] See the discussion in Frank Jarasch and Claus Kress, 'The Rome Statute and the German Legal Order' in Kress and Lattanzi (2000), n. 43 above, 91, at 105–7.

[51] Jarasch and Kress, ibid., at 105–6, argue that no conflict arises, on the ground that the German Constitution (in Art. 24(1)) allows the rules of international organizations to take priority over national laws where the two conflict and where the national law does not form part of core constitutional principles. Were the Rome Statute not deemed to have priority, however, prior authorization would be essential to Germany's ability to fulfil its Rome Statute obligations. Granting priority to the Rome Statute is key in the case of the German Constitution's indemnity (in Art. 46(1)) for words spoken in parliament, however, as no waiver of this indemnity is provided. While words spoken in parliament might theoretically include incitement to genocide, the chance of such an eventuality arising must be extremely remote: ibid., n. 43 at 106.

discretion at the national level), and the likelihood that the ICC will ever exercise jurisdiction over their own officials. Article 27(2) therefore allows for a potentially complex relationship between the Court and States, and leaves a range of legislative options open to governments.

(ii) Surrender by another State

The *Pinochet* judgment confines its limiting of immunity to States Parties of the Torture Convention. In the case of the Rome Statute, which creates no obligations to extradite or prosecute between States Parties, the main concern lies in the place of immunities between States Parties and the Court. Article 27(2) clearly limits immunity with respect to *the Court's* exercise of jurisdiction. The State Party of which, for example, an accused is Head of State may therefore not claim immunity before the ICC or allow any immunities to intrude between its own authorities and the ICC-related requests that they are obliged to fulfil. Whether the same is true for claims of immunity that such a State might bring before the courts of other States Parties is a far more challenging question.

Whether the Rome Statute contemplates an absence of immunity before the courts of a requested State for the officials of *other* States requires a discussion of Article 98(1):[52] 'The Court may not proceed with a request for surrender or assistance which would require the requested State to act inconsistently with its obligations under international law with respect to the State or diplomatic immunity of a person or property of a third State, unless the Court can first obtain the cooperation of that third State for the waiver of the immunity.'

Before exploring the paths along which the jurisprudence of the ICC might be guided by the different possible interpretations of this paragraph, it is important to note that Articles 98(1) and 27(2) are not necessarily contradictory.[53] Rather, Article 27(2) makes clear that immunities under national or international law 'shall not bar *the Court* from exercising *its* jurisdiction . . .' (emphasis added). Article 98(1) instead pertains to the obligations under international law *of the requested State*, as well as to the exercise of jurisdiction by such States, rather than by the Court. The Court may be free to act where States remained constrained by doctrines of immunity, as discussed below. It should also be noted that the paragraph refers to obligations under

[52] Article 98(2), n. 66 below, is also relevant to the execution of such requests but this paragraph, which aims primarily at Status of Forces Agreements (SOFAs) and not immunities *per se*, is dealt with below, see pp. 148–9.

[53] The chair of the Working Group responsible for Art. 27 at the Rome Diplomatic Conference suggests that there may be a contradiction between that article and Art. 98(1), owing to the fact that each was negotiated by a different Working Group at the Conference: Per Saland, 'International Criminal Law Principles', in Roy S. Lee *The International Criminal Court: Issues, negotiations, results* (The Hague: Kluwer, 1999) 189, n. 25 at 202.

international law, meaning that national law pertaining to immunities will not be able to block cooperation with the Court except to the extent that it reflects the international law accounted for in this paragraph.[54] Furthermore, and importantly, the paragraph implies—although it avoids firmly declaring— that it is the Court, and not the requested State, which decides the scope of any available immunity.[55]

Turning to the potential effect of Article 98(1) in the practice of the Court, the pressing question becomes, what exactly are a State's 'obligations under international law with respect to the . . . immunity of a person . . . of a third State'?[56] Is immunity a potential bar to the execution by a State Party of a request from the Court to arrest and surrender an official from another State, or have immunities under international law ceased to exist with respect to Rome Statute crimes? Will the outcome differ if the official in question is the national of a non-State Party? Does the result depend upon the nature of the available immunities (*ratione materiae* or *ratione personae*)? Broadly speaking, the Court could decide (1) that immunities continue as prior to the Statute's entry into force, without distinction between States Parties and non-States Parties, (2) that relevant immunities have been lifted as between States Parties, but continue with respect to non-States Parties, and (3) that immunities have ceased to exist altogether in relation to Rome Statute crimes, making the distinction between parties and non-parties irrelevant.

The ICC might hypothetically rely on *Pinochet* to support the proposition that States Parties could not arrest and surrender officials from another State (whether party to the Statute or not) without a waiver of immunities, since the Statute does not follow the Convention Against Torture in expressly

---

[54] The obligation on States Parties to ensure that procedures are available under national law for required cooperation with the Court (Art. 88), when read together with Art. 98(1), might be argued to entail an obligation to narrow statutory immunities to those available under international law, in order to allow the fullest cooperation with the ICC. Section 48 of Canada's ICC implementing legislation, Chapter VI, n. 25 above, can be understood in this light. The section amends Canada's *Extradition Act* to include the following:

6.1 Despite any other Act or law, no person who is the subject of a request for surrender by the International Criminal Court or by any international criminal tribunal that is established by resolution of the Security Council of the United Nations and whose name appears in the schedule, may claim immunity under common law or by statute from arrest or extradition under this Act.

The absence of any reference to immunities under international law is presumably significant.

[55] This interpretation is supported by a rule adopted by the Preparatory Commission for the ICC in the Finalized Draft Rules of Procedure and Evidence adopted 30 June 2000, Chapter IV, n. 26 above. Rule 195(1) grants States the rights to provide information to the Court relevant to any determination under Art. 98. Even here, however, the text carefully avoids stating that it is the Court that decides: 'When a requested State notifies the Court that a request for surrender or assistance raises a problem of execution in respect of Article 98, the requested State shall provide any information relevant to assist the Court in the application of Article 98. Any concerned third State or sending State may provide additional information to assist the Court.'

[56] Head of State immunity is sometimes assimilated to either State or diplomatic immunity, sometimes declared *sui generis*: see Bröhmer (1997), n. 4 above, at 29–31. There is no reason to assume it does not fall within the words of Art. 98(1).

contemplating the arrest and prosecution of the officials of States Parties by the authorities of other States Parties. It is true that the crimes within ICC jurisdiction are considered as much a part of *jus cogens* as torture is, and that permissive universal jurisdiction is ordinarily assumed to exist for these crimes.[57] Yet this in itself would not satisfy the *Pinochet* requirements for making immunities unavailable. Without any requirement *aut dedere, aut judicare*, immunities would arise to the extent permitted by international law outside the Statute. Applying similar reasoning to that of the Law Lords, immunity *ratione personae* would be absolute whereas that *ratione materiae* would be unavailable where clear obligations exist to exercise jurisdiction over the officials of other States and the relevant other State had recognized these. This would occur where the requested State and the third State are both parties to the Geneva Conventions or the Convention Against Torture, but presumably seldom otherwise; if the Court took an (over-)broad reading of the International Court of Justice's reasoning in the *Congo* v. *Belgium* case, such exceptions might not be found at all (pp. 146–8 below).

The shortcomings inherent in applying the narrow reasoning of the Law Lords to the regime of the Rome Statute are immediately apparent. Officials enjoying immunities *ratione personae* would go untouched while those with lesser protection *ratione materiae* would be liable to arrest and surrender: but only where properly incorporated instruments such as the Geneva Conventions or the Convention Against Torture established the foundation. The result would be an arbitrary patchwork presenting narrow windows of vulnerability not corresponding to the gravity of the offence or otherwise relating to the individual's responsibility.

Moreover, the recognition of immunities before the courts of requested States would leave only the official's State (where a State Party) under an unconditional obligation to surrender him or her to the Court. Yet this could place the conduct of ICC proceedings in great peril. At the outset of an investigation the Prosecutor will have notified all States Parties and other States that would normally exercise jurisdiction, and will have deferred to any giving notice that it was taking proceedings itself, except under limited circumstances (Article 18). If no notice was given and the Prosecutor continued to investigate, States would still be able to challenge admissibility on the grounds that they were investigating or prosecuting themselves (Article 19). Given the ample opportunity for a State to act through the Court to prevent action being taken with respect to its officials, it is most likely that the State of which the accused is or was an official will resort to a claim of immunity before the court of another State Party only in situations where no action has

---

[57] The Statute's sixth preambular paragraph reads: 'Recalling that it is the duty of every State to exercise its criminal jurisdiction over those responsible for international crimes'. Whether this implies 'international crimes *wherever committed*' or 'international crimes *committed within the ordinary jurisdiction of their courts*' appears deliberately to have been left open to interpretation.

been taken domestically (perhaps because of an amnesty) or where proceedings have been taken with respect to which the Court has found a 'purpose of shielding the person' or an 'inconsistency with the intent to bring the person concerned to justice' (Article 17) (see pp. 86–93 above). In such circumstance, if a claim of immunity were recognized and the accused returned to his or her home State, that State would almost certainly refuse to hand the person over to the Court. To allow immunities in such situations might well obstruct justice completely in many instances.

Counsel for the States involved will no doubt argue that, although immunities are on one level incompatible with the Nuremberg principles (as giving States a way to shield officials from the law), the drafters of the Rome Statute deliberately established a regime in which obligations would bind a given State to the requests of the Court with respect to that State's own officials. It will be argued that this would prevent the disruptions to inter-State relations that would necessarily follow from States taking on an enforcement role with respect to each others' officials, in particular where different standards of judicial and prosecutorial independence might exist. Yet the potential consequences of such an approach on the effectiveness of the ICC seem too drastic to have been intended.

This leads to the second approach, whereby States Parties would be deemed to have waived immunities as between themselves.[58] Support for this position rests on one or all of the arguments that, first, the Rome Statute has transformed customary law, secondly, the object and purpose of the Statute is best fulfilled by this approach, and thirdly, States Parties in agreeing to limit immunity in relation to the Court could be taken to have done so as between themselves. Where the Court has ruled a case admissible, the State Party of which the accused is an official would therefore be unable to claim immunity before the courts of another State Party that was acting pursuant to a request from the ICC. One might be tempted to formulate this as a duty upon States Parties to grant the waiver of any existing immunities; such a duty would not

---

[58] The following text, produced by Canada and the United Kingdom, was circulated informally during the negotiation of the Rules of Procedure and Evidence at the July–August 1999 session of the Preparatory Commission. Although not taken up in the Rules, it may provide a basis for future interpretative arguments:

The question has been raised of the interrelationship between diplomatic and State immunity on the one hand and the obligations of States Parties to the Statute to surrender an accused person to the Court on the other.

Article 98(1) of the Statute requires the Court to obtain a waiver of immunity before proceeding with a request for surrender 'which would require the requested State to act inconsistently with its obligations under international law' with respect to the immunity of a third State. Does this provision require the Court to request a waiver even where the State enjoying the immunity is a State Party? The question would arise where, say, the person whose surrender is requested by the Court is a diplomatic agent of a State Party, accredited to another State Party.

The interpretation which should be given to Article 98 is as follows. Having regard to the terms of the Statute, the Court shall not be required to obtain a waiver of immunity with respect to the surrender by one State Party of a head of State or government, or diplomat, of another State Party.

The above does not affect the question of inviolability of premises or documents.

of course be shared by non-States Parties.[59] A better approach would simply be to assume that, with their ratification of the Rome Statute, immunities no longer existed as between States Parties with respect to cooperation requests from the ICC.[60]

Part of the rationale for this lifting of immunities as between States Parties lies in the delegation to the Court of decisions which, in the hands of national authorities, might easily lead to real acrimony between States. Article 98(1) in effect allows States to delegate responsibility for difficult decisions to the Court: provided, that is, that the paragraph is interpreted to give the Court the final say in such decisions. Because States Parties are obliged only to give effect to the decisions of the Court, and do not themselves take direct responsibility for the decisions, one could argue that diplomatic relations cannot be tarnished (or tarnished as much) thereby. The requested State Party is exercising no discretion to remove the immunity—and so cannot credibly be said to be manipulating legal process for political advantage—but is merely acting in response to the finding of an institution to which both requested and requesting States Parties have agreed to surrender a degree of their own discretion in such matters.

Because a purposive reading of the Statute drives this reasoning, it cannot apply with equal force to the officials of non-States Parties. If the person sought were accused of crimes on the territory of a State Party but was an official of a non-State Party, the immunities available under applicable international law would then apply. If the Court were to follow the *Pinochet* reasoning, it would then recognize complete immunity *ratione personae* for heads of State and diplomatic agents and immunity *ratione materiae* for lesser and former officials. It would presumably limit the latter where a treaty binding on the requested and the 'third' State expressly contemplated foreign prosecution of officials (as does the Convention Against Torture and the Geneva Conventions). If the Court were instead to follow an expansive reading of the ICJ's *Congo* v. *Belgium* decision (below) it might not find even the latter limits. Assuming that the 'third State' was unwilling or unable to proceed against its own official, either approach would impose a real limit on the effectiveness of the ICC in favour of affirming the 'good relations' rationale underlying the law of immunities. Such a limit would, however, be subject to erosion over time if the trend to limit immunities were to continue.

---

[59] Bert Swart and Gören Sluiter, 'The International Criminal Court and International Criminal Cooperation', in Herman A.M. von Hebel, Johan G. Lammers, and Julien Schukking, eds., *Reflections on the International Criminal Court: Essays in honour of Adriaan Bos* (The Hague: T.M.C. Asser Press, 1999) 91 at 120–1.

[60] One authority on immunities points out that a 'duty to waive immunity' is impracticable, both because it would be impossible to enforce and because States could only be relied upon to fulfil the duty where they would have been willing to waive immunity in any event: Barker (1996), n. 7 above, at 203–4.

This leads to the third and boldest approach. The Court could decide (like Lord Phillips in *Pinochet (No. 3)* at 189–190) that immunity is incompatible with international criminal responsibility as such, and that the status of the accused as the national of a State Party or of a non-State Party is irrelevant. Belgium did so in amending its law, in preparation for its own ratification of the Rome Statute, to make immunities relating to a person's official capacity irrelevant to the exercise of universal jurisdiction for international crimes.[61] Such a position offers equality of treatment for suspects, without distinction based on whether the State of which they are or were an official is party to the Statute. It therefore conforms closely to the Nuremberg principles, removing from States the means of controlling whether or not their officials bear responsibility for the gravest crimes. At the same time, the approach would put the ICC well ahead of the general development of international law (see below) and would be certain to draw strong criticism from non-Party States, which would accuse the ICC of ignoring fundamental norms of international law. In any event, the ICJ's decision on the immunities affected by one investigation under Belgium's law, as well as the process of reconsideration that this decision prompted in Belgium, have made it even more unlikely than it would otherwise have been that the ICC will follow the 'Belgian model' (below).[62]

5. IMMUNITY OUTSIDE OF THE ROME STATUTE

(a) Trial by national courts after Congo v. Belgium

Once outside the Rome Statute regime, and given the lack of explicit reference to international crimes in the VCDR and other instruments, the immunity of officials from prosecution (other than before their own courts) is a matter of some uncertainty, and is likely to develop unevenly as States take a range of legislative and judicial action. What appears certain on the basis of experience to date is that the immunities *ratione personae* enjoyed by current high officials and diplomatic agents will be slow to erode, and will—outside the context of international tribunals—enjoy ongoing support from States as a necessary component of inter-State relations. The House of Lords' decision in *Pinochet*, the judgment of the French Cour de Cassation in the proceedings

---

[61] *Loi relative à la répression des violations graves de droit international humanitaire* (1999), Chapter VI n. 41 above. Art. 5(3) reads: '*L'immunité attachée à la qualité officielle d'une personne n'empêche pas l'application de la présente loi.*'

[62] Under a proposal put forward by Belgian legislators on 18 July 2002, Art. 5(3) of the Belgian law would be amended to read '*L'immunité internationale attachée à la qualité officielle d'une personne n'empêche l'application de la présente loi que dans les limites établies par le droit international*': see *Proposition de loi modifiant la loi du 16 juin 1993 relative à la répression des violations graves du droit international humanitaire*, Chapter VI, n. 41 above, Art. 4.

against *Ghaddafi*, the New York Southern District Court's decision in the civil suit of President Mugabe, and the recent ICJ judgment in *Congo* v. *Belgium* all unequivocally support this assertion.[63]

The development of exceptions to the immunities *ratione materiae* enjoyed by lesser and former officials is likely to be both more noticeable and more uneven. More liberal States will tend to join Belgium in finding exceptions to internationally-recognized immunities for international crimes, albeit without going as far as Belgium.[64] More conservative States will either find full immunities with respect to crimes under international law, perhaps on the basis of a (mis-)reading of the ICJ's decision in *Congo* v. *Belgium*;[65] or they will follow the majority in *Pinochet* in respecting functional immunities except where a ratified treaty between the relevant States as well as applicable

---

[63] For *Pinochet*, see n. 23 and related text above. On 13 March 2001 the French Cour de Cassation ruled that Mouammar Ghadaffi, as head of State of Libya, was entitled to immunity from the jurisdiction of French courts for alleged involvement in the terrorist bombing of a civilian aircraft: see Salvatore Zappalà, 'Do Heads of State in Office Enjoy Immunity from Jurisdiction for International Crimes? The Ghaddafi case before the French Cour de Cassation' (2001) 12 E.J.I.L. 595. On 30 October 2001 a United States court of first instance dismissed a suit, alleging torture and other crimes, against the current President and Foreign Minister of Zimbabwe, accepting a Suggestion of Immunity from the U.S. Department of State: *Tachiona et al.* v. *Mugabe et al.*, Decision and Order, 31 October 2001 (00 Civ. 6666 [VM], unreported) (U.S. Dist. Ct., S.D.N.Y.). The Democratic Republic of the Congo, in its application to the International Court of Justice, challenged the Belgian law that had facilitated the issuance of an arrest warrant against its Foreign Minister while in office, arguing that Art. 5 of the law (n. 61 above) and the related arrest warrant constituted a violation of 'the diplomatic immunity of the Minister for Foreign Affairs of a sovereign State, as recognized by the jurisprudence of the Court and following from Article 41, paragraph 2, of the Vienna Convention of 18 April 1961 on Diplomatic Relations': *Arrest Warrant of 11 April 2000 (Democratic Republic of the Congo* v. *Belgium), Judgment*, 14 February 2002, para. 1. In its judgment, the ICJ decided that the issuance and international circulation of the Belgian arrest warrant 'failed to respect the immunity from criminal jurisdiction and the inviolability which the incumbent Minister for Foreign Affairs of the Democratic Republic of the Congo enjoyed under international law': ibid., para. 78(2); see also paras. 58–61. A Belgian legislative proposal would limit its law to take the effect of the ICJ into consideration: see n. 62, above.

[64] Zappalà (2001), n. 62 above, argues that immunities *ratione materiae* do not apply at all to crimes under customary law (chiefly genocide, war crimes, and crimes against humanity).

[65] The ICJ judgment could be construed as authority for the proposition that foreign ministers (and by extension heads of State and heads of government) continue to enjoy immunities even with respect to crimes under international law on the ground that these fall within the 'official functions' for which the ICJ found continuing immunity after the immunity-holder leaves office. Such an interpretation would be overbroad, however, and would imply that the Court considered the *Pinochet* decision to be wrongly decided: a result too drastic to deduce from the ICJ's extremely terse judgment. It is true that the ICJ did not address the possibility of an exception to the functional immunities of former foreign ministers with respect to crimes under international law: *Congo* v. *Belgium, Judgment*, n. 62 above, paras. 58–61. It did, however, limit its holding to the situation of the case at the time the case was initiated, at which time the accused remained an incumbent foreign minister entitled to full personal immunities: ibid., paras. 26–8. Moreover, a separate opinion of 3 judges concurring in the overall judgment referred to the growing trend to recognize such an exception, and urged that the judgment be read in light of such a trend: see *Congo* v. *Belgium, Joint separate opinion of Judges Higgins, Kooijmans and Buergenthal*, paras. 74–85, 89. Given the developments outlined in this Chapter, it is the view of this author that the latter path is the better one.

implementing legislation exists. Between these extremes will be shades of gray, where national authorities take into account existing treaty obligations and developments at customary law in deciding whether to recognize immunities. Notwithstanding the ICJ decision in *Congo* v. *Belgium*, the general trend appears certain to continue in the direction of the reduction of immunities *ratione materiae* over crimes under customary international law. This can only be accelerated by the entry into operation of the International Criminal Court, with the international culture of accountability that it will promote.

(b) Status of Forces Agreements (SOFAs)

One further area should be mentioned briefly. Under Article 98(2) of the Rome Statute, an exception to the obligation of States Parties to cooperate with the Court is allowed where the consent of a 'sending State' is required to surrender an individual.[66] This is intended to encompass Status of Forces Agreements ('SOFAs'), the most typical of which are those entered into between the United Nations and States hosting a peace-keeping operation, and those between the North Atlantic Treaty Organization ('NATO') and its Member States.[67] In both cases, the State on the territory of which foreign military personnel find themselves cedes its jurisdiction over serious crimes to the State contributing the forces: an allocation of jurisdiction creating immunity from local courts' jurisdiction.[68] While this opens the door to potential impunity for criminal behaviour, UN practice has not yet shown any sign of

[66] 'The Court may not proceed with a request for surrender which would require the requested State to act inconsistently with its obligations under international agreements pursuant to which the consent of a sending State is required to surrender a person of that State to the Court, unless the Court can first obtain the cooperation of the sending State for the giving of consent for the surrender.'

[67] United Nations agreements typically consist of a Status of Forces Agreement with the State on the territory of which the operation is active, and Contribution Agreements with the nations providing the personnel: *Model Status-of-Forces Agreement for Peace-Keeping Operations*, U.N. Doc. A/45/594 (9 October 1990); *Model Agreement Between the United Nations and the Member States Contributing Personnel and Equipment to United Nations Peace-Keeping Operations*, U.N. Doc. A/46/185 (23 May 1991). See also *Agreement Between the Parties to the North Atlantic Treaty Regarding the Status of their Forces* (19 June 1951), (1953) Canada T.S. No. 13. UN agreements are sometimes referred to as 'Status of Mission Agreements' or SOMAs. The United States, which has far more foreign-based troops than any other nation, has numerous bilateral SOFAs as well; on US efforts to extend these to provide 'protection' from the ICC see below, Ch. IX, pp. 178–81.

[68] The UN Model SOFA assigns to the contributing State exclusive jurisdiction over the criminal acts of its military personnel within the territory of the operation (Art. 47(b)). The NATO SOFA assigns to the contributing State 'the primary right to exercise jurisdiction' over its military personnel with respect to 'offences arising out of any act or omission done in the performance of official duty', although the contributing State shall give 'sympathetic consideration' to a request to exercise jurisdiction by the host state where the contributing State chooses not to exercise its own primary right (Art. 7(3)).

changing. This is no doubt largely from a desire to avoid giving States any cause to limit contributions to UN operations. Nonetheless, an allusion to the complementarity principle, while imperfect, has recently been seen in the case of the Sierra Leone Special Court.[69] Whether this will become a trend towards ensuring accountability in future remains to be seen. The successful effort of the United States, in July 2002, to obtain passage of a Security Council resolution temporarily deferring any possible ICC investigation of peacekeeping personnel from States not party to the Rome Statute makes enhanced accountability of peacekeepers seem unlikely outside the ICC regime: see below, Ch. IX, p. 180.

6. CONCLUSION

What approach to immunities the ICC ultimately adopts will depend on many factors, not least of which is the culture among its judges when they take up the issue. The judges of the ICC will be charged, not with upholding the constitutional order of a given State, but with impartially applying the Rome Statute by its terms and in accordance with its object and purpose. As such, and having been elected by States willing to ratify the Rome Statute, these judges, in weighing the needs of diplomacy against those of justice, are likely to give greater weight to the latter than were the the Law Lords who decided *Pinochet*. It is therefore likely that these judges will decline to recognize immunities at least as between States Parties, with respect to requests for arrest and surrender from the ICC. It is possible that such a finding would, in turn, contribute to a gradual erosion of doctrines of immunity with respect to crimes under international law.

Here a crucial proviso must be expressed. The above discussion has related to the potential role of immunity of officials from criminal process and, by implication, with inviolability for purposes of arrest. Even if the ICC should decide that such immunities do not apply as between States Parties or otherwise, it should be understood that the erosion of broader immunities and

---

[69] The Statute of the Special Court for Sierra Leone, Art. 1(2), provides that the sending State shall have primary jurisdiction over 'transgressions' by its personnel within the territory of Sierra Leone, while Art. 1(3) provides that '[i]n the event that the sending State is unwilling or unable genuinely to carry out an investigation or prosecution, the Court may, if authorized by the Security Council on the proposal of any State, exercise jurisdiction over such persons'. That it is left to the Security Council, a political body, to determine which personnel are prosecuted may do more to harm than to promote the appearance of fair justice. Nonetheless, the underlying principle that the allocation of jurisdiction typical to SOFAs should be subordinate to the need for accountability is a positive one. The Statute of the Special Court forms an Annex to the Agreement between the United Nations and the Government of Sierra Leone on the establishment of a Special Court for Sierra Leone, 16 January 2002, and is available on-line at http://www.sierra-leone.org/specialcourtstatute.html (site last visited on 21 July 2002).

inviolability would not necessarily follow.[70] Given the evolution of the law of individual accountability in recent years, it would probably be no unacceptable leap in international law to allow the authorities of one State Party to arrest and surrender the officials of another, provided they act pursuant to the request of the ICC. Yet to allow national officials to breach the inviolability of a diplomatic mission to conduct a search (for example) would be a step of a higher magnitude altogether. Given the fundamental importance attached to such inviolability, and the potential for abuse by the officials of the enforcing State,[71] it is almost unthinkable that the ICC would take such a step.

Immunities have been and are likely to remain subject to controversy from time to time.[72] These criticisms have led to the many inroads that perforate the doctrine today. Yet efforts to advance areas of international law that might run into conflict with the purposes served by doctrines of immunity would best take into account the important international interest served by immunities and seek out ways to safeguard these interests while advancing the progressive developments of international law.

[70] The Canada/UK text from July–August 1999 makes this distinction in its last line: see n. 58 above.

[71] See n. 10 and related text above.

[72] Michael B. McDonough, 'Privileged Outlaws: Diplomats, crime and immunity' (1997) 20 Suffolk Transnat'l L. Rev. 475, examines proposals to reform immunities (at 491–6) and suggests that more immunities and inviolability be restricted to allow national authorities better to combat 'terrorism' (at 496–9); he does so without looking with care at potential negative consequences of such restrictions. Peter Evans Bass, 'Ex-Head of State Immunity: A proposed statutory tool of foreign policy' (1987) 97 Yale L.J. 299, argues at 316–19 that US statutory immunities should not extend to violations of international human rights norms.

VIII

ICC enforcement: Cooperation of States, Including the Security Council

1. INTRODUCTION

Should States be unwilling or unable to exercise their jurisdiction (whether territorial, national, or universal) to bring to account those accused of international crimes, the International Criminal Court will presumably be the only forum remaining in which to do so. The Security Council is more likely to avail itself of its power to refer cases to the ICC (pp. 78–9 above) than to agree to incur the costs of establishing further *ad hoc* tribunals, given that two permanent members of the Security Council (France and the United Kingdom) will be among the parties to the Rome Statute. Notwithstanding that political factors and financial realities could, along with the incentive for domestic prosecutions provided by the Rome Statute, lead to an increase in the use of 'hybrid' tribunals,[1] the ICC itself must be the cornerstone of any emerging system of international justice. It is equally true that the Court will ultimately depend on the good will and active support of States for its effectiveness. Yet, as will be seen in this Chapter, both the experience of the *ad hoc* tribunals and the design of the Rome Statute give ample cause for caution with regard to State cooperation. Far from subordinating sovereignty to a supra-national criminal justice institution, the ICC places some of its most critical functions at the disposal of its States Parties' processes and decisions, albeit within a framework that ensures a dialogue that is ultimately likely to favour the Court's aims.

2. THE AD HOC TRIBUNALS: FORESHADOWING THE ICC

Without attempting here to present a history of the *ad hoc* tribunals for the Former Yugoslavia and for Rwanda, it is important to emphasize the way in which their experience shows how political context will determine the degree and kind of cooperation that governments will be willing and able to give to an international tribunal. This is true both of the countries most immediately affected by the crimes themselves, and of the decision-making countries in the Security Council or in the multilateral missions on the ground. Political considerations play an overriding role, notwithstanding the 'innovative and

---

[1] See Chapter V, n. 48 above.

sweeping' obligation to cooperate with a tribunal established under the Security Council's Chapter VII mandate.[2] As a 'giant without arms or legs', dependent on States for the cooperation that makes it operative, the ICTY undoubtedly foreshadows in important respects the experience that awaits the ICC.[3] Cooperation can be viewed from three perspectives: that of the 'target' (territorial, national, or victim) State, that of the States controlling the decisions of the Security Council and/or multilateral missions, and that of third States (i.e. of the international community at large).

In Rwanda, one might have expected a high degree of cooperation, given that most of the crimes within the ICTR's jurisdiction were committed by a prior regime of which the present government of Rwanda was the successor and erstwhile enemy. The post-conflict Tutsi-led government was nonetheless equivocal at the start,[4] and its subsequent relationship with the Tribunal has been troubled.[5] In the Former Yugoslavia, willingness to cooperate has

---

[2] *Prosecutor* v. *Tihomir Blaskic, Judgment on the Request of the Republic of Croatia for Review of the Decision of Trial Chamber II of 18 July 1997* (ICTY Case No. IT–95–14) (29 October 1997) (Appeals Chamber), para. 64. Art. 29(1) ('Cooperation and judicial assistance ') of the ICTY Statute provides: 'States shall cooperate with the International Tribunal . . . .' Art. 29(2) provides a non-exhaustive list of required forms of compliance with 'any request for assistance or an order issued by a Trial Chamber'. In para. 4 of Res. 827, establishing the Tribunal, the Security Council, acting under Chapter VII of the UN Charter:

Decide[d] that all States shall cooperate fully with the International Tribunal and its organs in accordance with the present resolution and the Statute of the International Tribunal and that consequently all States shall take any measures necessary under their domestic law to implement the provisions of the present resolution and the Statute, including the obligation of States to comply with requests for assistance or orders issued by a Trial Chamber under Art. 29 of the Statute.

This obligation binds States to accept and carry out the Security Council's decision through Art. 25 of the UN Charter. Art. 28 of the ICTR Statute, and para. 2 of Res. 955, is identical (*mutatis mutandis*): see Chapter IV, n. 10 above. The Rules of Procedure and Evidence of each tribunal contain a rule authorizing the President of the Tribunal to make a finding of non-compliance for transmission to the Security Council: *Rules of Procedure and Evidence* (Doc. No. IT/32/Rev.18) (14 July 2000) (ICTY) and (3 November 2000) (ICTR), 7*bis*.

[3] Antonio Cassese, 'On the Current Trends towards Criminal Prosecution and Punishment of Breaches of International Humanitarian Law' (1998) 9 E.J.I.L. 2, at 13.

[4] See Virginia Morris and Michael P. Scharf, *The International Criminal Tribunal for Rwanda* (2 vols.) (Irvington-on-Hudson, N.Y.: Transnational, 1998) (vol. I), at 59–72. In September 1994 the newly-formed Rwandan government invited the Security Council to establish the Tribunal (ibid., at 69) but then, while promising to cooperate with the Tribunal, voted against the Resolution adopting its Statute (Chapter IV, n. 10 above) citing concerns over its temporal jurisdiction and failure to apply the death penalty (ibid., at 72, n. 366). The concern with temporal jurisdiction was based on the fact that post-genocide revenge killings by Tutsis would be within the Tribunal's powers.

[5] Scharf (1998) n. 4 above, (vol. I), at 637–60, esp. 652–3. A major incident occurred in 1999, when the ICTR Appeals Chamber ordered the release of a suspect whose rights were found to have been violated by unreasonable delay awaiting trial. In protest, the Rwandan government pledged to suspend its cooperation with the Tribunal, and the Prosecutor applied for review of the decision. The Chamber reversed itself: *Barayagwiza* v. *Prosecutor, Decision (Prosecutor's Request for Review or Reconsideration)* (ICTR Case No. 97–19–AR72) (31 March 2000) (Appeals Chamber); see 'Rwanda Normalizes Relations with UN Tribunal' *Internews* (10 February 2000) (quoting the Rwandan Prosecutor General saying, while the Appeals Chamber contemplated its decision, 'I think the Tribunal will have a better idea of its future after the decision'); also 'The

varied with the position of the government in question and the political context of the day. The Bosnian Muslim authorities of Bosnia-Herzegovina have proven the most supportive: unsurprisingly, given that it is primarily their opponents who are facing prosecution.[6] The government of Croatia, although subject to persuasion when circumstances converged appropriately, was generally unresponsive to requests for extradition of its nationals and for provision of evidence.[7] The Bosnian Serb authorities and authorities in the Federal Republic. of Yugoslavia have proven the most refractory, causing serious problems for the Tribunal, notwithstanding transitions that were predicted to increase the likelihood of cooperation.[8] Changes of government have improved the prospects of cooperation, although improvements are likely to be uneven and improvement slow.

As for the Security Council/troop-contributing countries in the Former Yugoslavia, support for the ICTY has been intermittent at best, with NATO forces giving highest priority to self-protection and with political or public pressure being sporadic and generally weak.[9] Troops stationed in the Former Yugoslavia have nonetheless been essential to the success of the ICTY, and in favourable circumstances have made significant arrests and given important assistance.[10] In general it has been where risks are reduced, public pressure

Politics of Justice at the International Criminal Tribunal for Rwanda' *Internews* (29 February 2000) (quoting the Prosecutor, in argument before the Chamber, saying '[w]hether we like it or not, we must come to terms with the fact that we depend on the government of Rwanda'). A subsequent motion of the defendant for review was dismissed: *Prosecutor* v. *Barayagwiza, Decision on Review and/or Reconsideration* (ICTR Case No. 97–19-AR72) (14 September 2000) (Appeals Chamber).

[6] Gary Jonathan Bass, *Stay the Hand of Vengeance: The Politics of War Crimes Tribunals* (Princeton: Princeton U.P., 2000), at 257.

[7] *Report of the International Tribunal for the Prosecution of Persons Responsible for Serious Violations of International Humanitarian Law Committed in the Territory of the Former Yugoslavia since 1991*, U.N. Doc. A/54/187 (25 August 1999) ['*1999 ICTY Report*'], at paras. 100–5 (describing 'Croatia's persistent failure to comply with Prosecution requests for assistance'). Croatia handed over indictees Tihomir Blaskic and Zlatko Aleksovski after the United States threatened to block international loans: Bass (2000), n. 6 above, at 255–6, 264, 270–1.

[8] 1999 ICTY Report, at para. 91–9 (describing 'a pattern of non-compliance [on the part of the FRY], including the failure to defer to the competence of the Tribunal, failure to execute warrants, failure to provide evidence and information and the refusal to permit the Prosecutor and her investigators into Kosovo'), and para. 106 ('[o]f the thirty-six publicly indicted persons at liberty at the end of [July 1999], the Office of the Prosecutor believes that approximately twenty-five are in the Republika Srpska').

[9] See Theodor Meron, 'Answering for War Crimes: Lessons from the Balkans', in Meron, *War Crimes Law Comes of Age: Essays* (Oxford: Clarendon, 1998) at 279–80; see also chapter 6 in Bass (2000), n. 6 above, 206. In its early years Tribunal officials felt strongly that the Security Council did not take its complaints of non-cooperation seriously: Bass, ibid., at 223–4 (quoting President Cassese characterizing the Council's response: 'We deplore their attitude, we condemn their attitude. Either deplore or condemn. . . . Maybe next time they'll find a third word.'). Despite an improvement in NATO support (see following note) these concerns persist: see *Letter from President McDonald to the President of the Security Council concerning outstanding issues of State non-compliance* (ICTY Press Release JL/P.I.S./444-E, 2 November 1999).

[10] The practice of issuing sealed indictments has, by lessening the danger to troops, led to a significant increase in the willingness to use SFOR personnel to arrest indictees: Bass (2000), n. 6

and political will high, and other factors favourable that States have shown a willingness to undertake meaningful action on enforcement.

Developments within the wider circle of States have not been unencouraging, providing a significant precedent for the ICC. A number of States have passed or amended legislation to allow cooperation with the Tribunals.[11] This legislation has provided a basis for the transfer of suspects, the supply of witnesses, the acceptance of convicted prisoners, and other forms of cooperation.[12] With or without legislation, States have provided practical assistance to the Tribunals,[13] and a number of States have prosecuted individuals on the basis of universal jurisdiction.[14]

The experience of the *ad hoc* tribunals has only underscored the interplay between law and politics in the enforcement of international criminal law. This has sparked claims that only a real willingness to use force and a marked decline in respect for sovereignty can make such tribunals effective.[15] The Rome Statute, which will be unable to rely even on the uneven benefits of

above, at 265–7; 1999 ICTY Report, paras. 125, 131, 134. Fear of Serb reprisals has nonetheless ensured that even this expedient is cautiously enforced; also, the ongoing troop-protection policy ensures that major figures, like former Bosnian Serb leader Radovan Karadjic, the most prominent indictee in Bosnian Serb territory, remain at large. Leading NATO States appear to have decided that the indictment of President Milosevic was in, or at least not against, their interests, and supplied the Prosecutor with the intelligence feeds that made the indictment possible. Such selective provision of cooperation nonetheless risks politicizing the Tribunal: Bass (2000), n. 6 above, at 272–4; William Shawcross, *Deliver Us from All Evil: Peacekeepers, warlords and a world of endless conflict* (New York: Simon and Schuster, 2000), at 382.

[11] Amnesty International, *International Criminal Tribunals: Handbook for government cooperation* (AI Index: IOR 40/07/96) (London: AI, 1996) Supplements 1–3 (containing the legislation of 20 States). As of 1999, 23 States had passed legislation, 4 had indicated that no such legislation was required to enable cooperation, and others had indicated the intent to pass legislation in the near future: 1999 ICTY Report, at para. 187. In addition, 5 States had entered agreements to allow persons convicted by the ICTY to serve sentences in their jurisdictions: ibid., at para. 188.

[12] Such legislation has nonetheless been criticized, for example by the former President of the ICTY, owing to 'the tendency to subsume cooperation with the ICTY under the traditional model of *inter-state* judicial cooperation': Cassese (1998), n. 3 above, at 13–14; see Amnesty International (1996), n. 11 above, at 45–61, esp. 58–61; and n. 22 below.

[13] Over the course of 1996 and 1997, Zambia arrested and detained 2 individuals indicted by the ICTR, Kenya handed over several more, and Cameroon cooperated in delivering 4 others; arrests were also made with the assistance of France, the United Kingdom, Belgium, Denmark, and Tanzania: Scharf (1998), n. 4 above, (vol. I), at 655–8; *Fifth Annual Report of the International Criminal Tribunal for the Prosecution of Persons Responsible for Genocide and Other Serious Violations of International Humanitarian Law Committed in the Territory of Rwanda and Rwandan Citizens Responsible for Genocide and Other Such Violations Committed in the Territory of Neighbouring States between 1 January and 31 December 1994, for the period 1 July 1999 to 30 June 2000*, U.N. Doc. A/55/435 (2 October 2000), para. 135. See also Amnesty International (1996), n. 11 above, at 12–14, 22–4.

[14] See Chapter VI, n. 33 and related text above.

[15] Cassese (1998), n. 3 above, at 11–17, esp. 17 ('So long as states retain some essential aspects of their sovereignty and fail to set up an effective mechanism to enforce arrest warrants and to execute judgments, international criminal tribunals may have little more than normative impact').

Security Council support in most instances, was not negotiated in a way that would allay such critiques.

3. COOPERATION WITH STATES UNDER THE ROME STATUTE

For the obvious reason that it will have no police powers of its own and will have limited resources for investigation and prosecution, the ICC would be entirely unable to function without the cooperation of States. The cooperation provisions of the Statute are set out primarily in Part 9, Articles 86 to 102.[16] These provide a basic framework within which necessary forms of cooperation can be requested and non-cooperation determined by the Court, although the ultimate power to enforce cooperation lies with States acting through the Assembly of States Parties or the Security Council, and not with the ICC itself. As with other key portions of the Statute (pp. 76–82 above), the cooperation provisions reflect a balance between the needs of an effective Court and the prerogatives of the sovereign States whose support for the Statute will underlie its success.

All States Parties are under a basic obligation to cooperate with the requests of the Court (Article 86): a significant and hard-won strength of the Statute, given that the Court will not automatically enjoy the peremptory powers of the Security Council (n. 2 above). Parties are also obliged to provide any necessary procedures under national law for the cooperation called for under Part 9 (Article 88). This latter requirement alone will have significant effects, as Part 9 calls for cooperation in the arrest and surrender of accused persons and in a number of other forms of cooperation (taking testimony, ensuring attendance of witnesses, locating evidence, etc.). The Statute contemplates that States will apply the procedures of their national law in cooperating with Court requests, but requires that the cooperation called for under the Statute be possible. In other words, national law may govern procedures, but will lead to violations of the Statute if it inhibits the cooperation required. The extent to which new or amended legislation is needed depends, of course, on the existing legal and constitutional order of a given State. States Parties or prospective States Parties have begun to prepare and pass the necessary laws.[17]

---

[16] For the negotiating history, see Phakiso Mochochoko, 'International Cooperation and Judicial Assistance', in Roy S. Lee, ed., *The International Criminal Court: Issues, negotiations, results* (The Hague: Kluwer, 1999), at 305, as well as the relevant Comments in Otto Triffterer, ed., *The Rome Statute of the ICC: Observers' notes, article by article* (Baden-Baden: Nomos, 1999) and in particular Claus Kress, Kimberly Post, Angelika Schlunck, and Peter Wilkitzki, 'Preliminary Remarks', ibid., 1045.

[17] See generally, Otto Triffterer, 'Legal and Political Implications of Domestic Ratification and Implementation Processes', and Helen Duffy and Jonathan Huston, in Claus Kress and Flavia Lattanzi, eds., *The Rome Statute and Domestic Legal Orders* (vol. 1) (Baden-Baden,

Where a State Party (or another State agreeing to cooperate for purposes of a particular case) fails to cooperate, the Court may refer the matter to the Assembly of States Parties (or the Security Council, if the Council referred the case) (Article 87(5) and (7)).[18] The Assembly, in turn, is obliged to '[c]onsider . . . any question relating to non-cooperation' (Article 112(2)(f)). The consequences that will flow from this consideration and their ability to compel cooperation are essential to the ICC's effectiveness, but will remain unknown until the Assembly of States Parties develops its practice in this area. Many States were reluctant to grant to the Court the authority to make findings of non-cooperation, and it is an important assurance of the Court's credibility. At the same time, the omission of the consequences of non-cooperation from the Statute is a sign of the sensitivity of the issue, and of the wish of the Statute's drafters not to delay or endanger the adoption of the Statute by examining it too closely. What is clear is that the Assembly will be limited in the range of responses available to it by the international law to which its members are subject. Thus, while the Security Council might be able to authorize the use of force in support of the Court where it has itself referred a situation using its Chapter VII powers, the Assembly cannot do so, and would be limited to a range of peaceful measures.[19] A number of options will

Nomos, 2000). Canada, New Zealand, and the United Kingdom have all passed ICC cooperation legislation (Chapter V, n. 26 above), as have Finland, Norway, and Sweden: Act on the implementation of the provisions of a legislative nature of the Rome Statute of the International Criminal Court and on the application of the Statute, No. 1284/2000 (28 December 2000) (Finland); Act No. 65 of 15 June 2001 relating to the implementation of the Statute of the International Criminal Court of 17 July 1998 (the Rome Statute) in Norwegian law (Norway); both of these laws are available on-line at http://www.legal.coe.int/criminal/icc/Default. asp?fd=docs&fn=Docs.htm (site last visited on 21 July 2002). Argentina, Australia, Austria, Germany, Liechtenstein, South Africa, Switzerland, and others have all made progress towards implementing similar legislation: Irene Gartner, 'Implementation of the ICC Statute in Austria' in Kress and Lattanzi (2000), n. 17 above, at 55; Franck Jarasch and Claus Kress, 'The Rome Statute and the German Legal Order', ibid. 91, at 93; Jonathan Huston, 'Ratification of the Rome Statute in the Principality of Liechtenstein: General considerations and constitutional questions', ibid. 139, at 142; Sivuyile S. Maqungo, 'Implementing the ICC Statute in South Africa', ibid. 183, at 183–4; and Michael Cottier, 'The Case of Switzerland', ibid. 219, at 219–20. Portugal enacted a judicial cooperation law in 1999 that allows cooperation with international tribunals established through a treaty ratified by Portugal, although some details of cooperation will require further amendments: Paula Escarameia, 'Notes on the Implementation of the Rome Statute in Portugal', ibid. 151, at 165.

[18] In the case of States Parties, the Court makes a 'finding' of non-cooperation (Art. 87(7)), while in the case of a non-State Party the Court merely 'informs' the Assembly or Council (Art. 87(5)). Whether the Assembly could then take any action on behalf of the Court against an uncooperative non-State Party would depend on the terms of that State's initial agreement to cooperate with the Court: Claus Kress and Kimberly Prost, 'Commentary on Art. 87', in Triffterer (1999) n. 16 above, 1055, at 1063–4. For detailed analysis of the cooperation legislation in various countries, written largely by those involved in the drafting, see Bruce Broomhall, Claus Kress, and Flavia Lattanzi, eds., *Constitutional Issues, Cooperation and Enforcement*, vol. 2 of *The ICC and Domestic Legal Orders* (Nomos, forthcoming 2003).

[19] '. . . [T]he Assembly of States Parties is entitled to ask for immediate compliance with the Court's request and may condemn the State Party's failure. It may go beyond this and consider

remain open to the Assembly in responding to non-cooperation findings, but the need to maintain overall support for the Court, to avoid polarization along regional or cultural lines, to avoid punishing the citizenry of a State for the intransigence of its leaders, and other political considerations will at times undoubtedly work against effective, regular and impartial enforcement.

The surrender to the Court of persons sought by it will obviously be indispensable to ICC proceedings.[20] After setting out preconditions for the issue of a warrant (Article 58), the Statute provides an unequivocal obligation to arrest and surrender a person sought by the Court (Articles 59 and 89–92).[21] The obligation to surrender is not at the discretion of a State Party in the way that an obligation for extradition from another State may be. The Statute anticipates that national requirements for surrender will 'not be more burdensome, and will wherever possible be less burdensome' than those applicable to extradition from one State to another (Article 91(2)(c)).[22] The rule of speciality is made available (Article 101) but the Statute makes no allowance for factors often considered (and sometimes constitutionally mandated) in inter-State extradition, such as the political offence exception or

the appropriateness of collective countermeasures, such as economic sanctions, against the non-cooperating State. By contrast, the termination of the treaty *vis-à-vis* the non-cooperating State is not an option given its integral nature and its overall humanitarian goal.' In the absence of a sufficient majority of the Assembly in support of countermeasures, individual countermeasures may be possible: Kress and Prost, n. 18 above, at 1068.

[20] The requirement that the accused be present at trial (in all but limited circumstances) is set out in Art. 63.

[21] A summons to appear might be enough in some cases. These are available under Art. 58 where the Prosecutor satisfies the Court that there are reasonable grounds to suspect the person of a crime within the jurisdiction of the Court, but where the necessity of arresting the person (to secure their appearance, among other things) is not established.

[22] This simplicity of procedure is embodied in the distinction between 'extradition' to another State and 'surrender' to the Court (Art. 102). It reflects the assumptions (1) that Court procedures conform to the highest international standards and therefore do not raise the fairness issues that might arise in extradition; (2) that the Court is not a foreign jurisdiction, but is a supplementary mechanism exercising in limited circumstances the (delegated or pooled) jurisdiction available to the requested State; and (3) that the crimes in question are of unequalled gravity and concern the international community as a whole. A similar streamlining was called for by the President of the ICTY in guidelines sent to UN Member States, calling for surrender to the Tribunal 'without resort to extradition proceedings' (although the jurisdictional basis of the ICTY, created by Security Council resolution, is different from that of the ICC): see *Tentative guidelines for national implementing legislation of United Nations Security Council Resolution 827 of 25 May 1993*, sent by the President of the Yugoslav Tribunal to Members of the United Nations on 15 February 1995, reprinted in Supplement 1 of Amnesty International (1996), n. 11 above; see also ibid., at 58–61; Cassese (1998), at 13 (arguing that '[e]xtradition to a state and surrender to an international jurisdiction are two totally different and separate mechanisms'); and Duffy and Huston, n. 17 above, at 45 (arguing that surrender to the ICC does not involve the same 'abandonment' of an individual that extradition to another State does, since the surrendering State Party participates in the management of the ICC through the Assembly of States Parties). In their ICC legislation, Canada (s. 52) and New Zealand (s. 55) provide that the reasons for refusal available in extradition proceedings do not apply to proceedings of surrender to an international tribunal: Chapter V, n. 26 above.

non-extradition of nationals.[23] Not even objections on national security grounds are provided for with respect to surrender of an accused.[24] Also, a State Party could not object to arrest and surrender on account of immunities attaching to the official capacity of one of its officials, and at least in some circumstances is probably obliged to fulfil such requests with respect to the officials of other States.[25]

Apart from arrest and surrender, Part 9 includes under Article 93 an obligation to cooperate in a wide range of situations related to the provision of evidence and testimony and the facilitation of investigation and trial generally.[26] The cooperation listed is subject to certain limits, notably where the requested State Party objects on national security grounds (a provision certain to give rise to fundamental disputes: Article 93(4), and n. 24 above), or where execution of the request is prohibited by 'an existing fundamental legal principle of general application' (Article 93(3)). In either case, a duty to consult with the Court to seek an alternative means of providing the assistance arises, thus limiting the potential for bad faith non-cooperation while opening a window for delay. As with requests for arrest and surrender, the forms of cooperation contemplated under Article 93(1) may be regulated by national law but not to the detriment of the cooperation called for under the Statute.[27]

[23] The Statute does deal expressly with *ne bis in idem* (double jeopardy) challenges (Art. 89(2)), national proceedings against an accused with respect to other crimes (Art. 89(4)), or conflicting international obligations of the requested State (Arts. 90, 98): see Claus Kress and Kimberly Prost, 'Comment on Art. 89', in Triffterer (1999), n. 16 above, at 1071. The question whether the obligation to *surrender* nationals to the ICC conflicts with constitutional prohibitions on the *extradition* to other States of such nationals is a major one for a number of potential ratifying States: see Duffy and Huston, n. 17 above, at 43–6 (citing, at 43 n. 68, 25 constitutions prohibiting extradition of nationals, and 8 more subjecting such prohibition to international treaties). Some States, including Austria and Switzerland, have already adopted the view that surrender to the ICC does not fall within the purview of prohibitions on extradition to another State: Gartner, n. 17 above, at 60–1; Cottier, n. 17 above, at 239 n. 73. Germany chose to amend its constitutional prohibition on the extradition of nationals, although it is not certain that the relevant provision necessarily encompassed surrender to the ICC: Jarasch and Kress, n. 17 above, at 99–104.

[24] Such objections are contemplated for 'other forms of cooperation' under Art. 93, but are not mentioned in relation to arrest and surrender. Art. 72 ('National security') does apply to the entire Statute, but its procedures for consultation and maximizing cooperation would ensure that non-surrender could not be justified, as an accused has the right to silence (Art. 67(1)(g)) and testimony before the ICC or in respect of its proceedings is in any event subject to limitations, set out in Art. 72, aimed at protecting national security information (Art. 99(5)).

[25] Art. 98(1) (pp. 141–6 above); Art. 98(2) also limits the obligation to surrender by acknowledging the potentially overriding obligations contained *inter alia* in Status of Forces Agreements (Chapter VII, n. 66 below).

[26] Under Art. 93(1)(c), a request for the 'questioning of any person being investigated or prosecuted' entails an obligation to inform the person before questioning of their rights under Art. 55(2), including the right to be informed that there are grounds to believe he or she has committed a crime within the jurisdiction of the Court, the right to silence (without silence being a consideration in the determination of guilt or innocence), the right to legal assistance (without cost, where necessary), and the right to counsel, including the right to have counsel present during questioning. This obligation applies whether the questioning is to be done by ICC or by national officials.

[27] See the cooperation provisions in Canada's ICC legislation, ss. 56–69, New Zealand's legislation, ss. 24–31, 81–123, and the UK Act, ss. 27–41: Chapter V, n. 26 above.

Two other forms of cooperation are provided for outside of Part 9. These will entail changes to national law but do not bear directly on investigation and prosecution. First, Article 70 lists six offences against the administration of justice (giving false testimony, bribery, intimidation, etc.). The Statute calls upon States Parties to penalize such offences when committed on its territory or by one of its nationals and at the request of the Court to submit a case to their authorities for prosecution (Article 70(4)(b)).[28] Secondly, the Statute provides (in Part 10, Articles 103–11) arrangements relating to the execution by national authorities of ICC sentences. Only Article 109 affects all States, requiring them to enforce fines and forfeiture orders relating to 'proceeds, property and assets derived directly or indirectly' from the crime for which sentence was passed (Article 77(2)(b)); this will be essential to the Court's ability to compensate victims.[29] The other articles (especially 103–6 and 110) relate to sentences of imprisonment, and affect only States Parties that indicate to the Court their willingness to accept sentenced persons. Such States are obliged to meet basic international treaty standards relating to the treatment of prisoners, to cooperate with the Court in the supervision of the sentence, and to respect the sentence handed down by the Court, leaving review or reduction of it to the Court alone.[30]

It should be apparent from this discussion that the Rome Statute provides a sufficient framework of obligations, of considerable detail, but that both the goodwill and adequate legislative framework of States will be necessary to realize the ICC's potential.[31] Notwithstanding their obligations under the Statute, States will retain the decisive decision-making power at critical phases,[32] making the political context and the ultimate availability of enforcement essential. Should the measures available to the Assembly of States Parties prove inadequate (as often they must), the support of the Security Council will become determinative.

---

[28] Kenneth Harris, 'Comment on Art. 70', in Triffterer (1999), n. 16 above, at 923 (pointing out that it is the host State, the Netherlands, which may have most opportunity to prosecute offences committed on its territory). See Canada's ICC legislation, ss. 16–26; New Zealand's legislation, ss. 14–23, and the UK Act, ss. 54, 61: Chapter V, n. 26 above.

[29] See Canada's ICC legislation, ss. 27–32, 57–8; New Zealand's legislation, ss. 111–12, 126–35, and the UK Act, ss. 37–8: Chapter V, n. 26 above.

[30] See Canada's ICC legislation, ss. 34–41; New Zealand's legislation, ss. 139–56, and the UK Act, ss. 42–8: Chapter V, n. 26 above.

[31] In the view of Antonio Cassese, 'The Statute of the International Criminal Court: Some preliminary reflections' (1999) 10 E.J.I.L. 144, at 170, 'the framers of the Rome Statute were not sufficiently bold to jettison the sovereignty-oriented approach to state cooperation with the Court and opt for a "supra-national" approach. Instead of granting the Court greater authority over states, the draughtsmen have left too many loopholes permitting states to delay or even thwart the Court's proceedings.'

[32] For example, the provisions for cooperation in investigations provided by the Canadian and New Zealand legislation, as well as by the UK Act, Chapter V, n. 26 above, retain the element of ministerial discretion found in ordinary inter-State mutual assistance/extradition context, notwithstanding the obligatory nature of cooperation under the Rome Statute.

4. THE SECURITY COUNCIL

The Security Council will play a number of important functions with respect to the ICC, although the relationship between the Council and the Court, as set out in the Statute, reflects the wariness with which many viewed this relationship during the negotiations at Rome. The power of the Council acting under Chapter VII to refer situations to the Court (Article 13(b)) is treated above (at pp. 78–9), as is the Council's ability (under Article 16) to request a deferral of Court proceedings when a matter falls within the Council's Chapter VII mandate (pp. 81–2 above; see also p. 180). The still unresolved question concerning the significance of a Council determination that an act of aggression has taken place to the Court's eventual exercise of jurisdiction over that crime is touched on elsewhere.[33] A fourth function, relating to enforcement, is relevant here.

The Statute, in Article 87(5) and (7), limits the Court's referral to the Security Council of non-cooperation findings to situations 'where the Security Council referred the matter to the Court'. Of course, it is possible for the Court to exercise its jurisdiction pursuant to a State referral or a *proprio motu* action of the Prosecutor in a situation in which the Council is engaged under its Chapter VII mandate (provided only that the Council has not requested the deferral of ICC proceedings under Article 16). In such a situation, the words of the Statute imply that findings of non-cooperation would be referred only to the Assembly of States Parties, and not to the Council, because the latter did not 'refer the matter'. It nonetheless seems probable that the Court will be able to call upon the Council for its support more broadly, as Article 87(6) allows the Court to 'ask any intergovernmental organization to provide . . . forms of cooperation and assistance which may be agreed upon with such an organization and which are in accordance with its competence or mandate', and the Relationship Agreement between the ICC and the UN will include a broad commitment to cooperate on the part of the UN.[34] For its part, the Council has shown itself capable at least in limited circumstances of linking matters that 'shock the conscience of humanity' to its Chapter VII mandate.[35] This is fortunate, as the overriding nature of

---

[33] See Chapter II, nn. 83–5 and related text above.

[34] *Draft Relationship Agreement between the Court and the United Nations*, U.N. Doc. PCNICC/2001/1/Add.1 (8 January 2002), Art. 17 ('Cooperation between the Security Council of the United Nations and the Court'), para. 3 of this article links Security Council cooperation to Art. 87(5) and (7).

[35] See Chapter V, n. 8 above. Here one must be cautious. While it may be true that 'the conduct of a Government towards its own citizens which grossly and persistently violates firmly established international law' gives rise to Chapter VII authority owing to 'the historically demonstrable connection between the proscribed behaviour and a propensity to war' (Thomas M. Franck, *Fairness in the International Legal and Institutional System* (The Hague: Academy for International Law, 1993), at 204), not all violations even of international criminal law can be

Chapter VII powers and obligations will make it highly desirable for the Court's to call upon the Council for assistance, particularly where UN-mandated personnel are in a position to gather evidence, protect victims and witnesses, or arrest suspects.

While the potential for Security Council support for the ICC may thus exist, the likelihood of significant support for the Court in reality should not be exaggerated. The way in which the political calculations of permanent members of the Council have led to uneven support towards the ICTY has been reviewed above (pp. 151–5). There is no immediate reason to believe that the same calculations will not lead to similar results for the ICC. More fundamentally, there is a question whether the Council will ever avail itself of its power to refer cases or its related enforcement role, given the power and potential willingness of the United States to block these (Chapter IX). Thus, notwithstanding some changes in Security Council activities in the wake of the Cold War (pp. 185–92 below), its role as a bulwark of the international rule of law—understood as regular and impartial enforcement with respect to the 'core crimes'—cannot really be affirmed, with the result that even the equivocal support of Security Council forces may not be available to the ICC.[36]

5. CONCLUSIONS

Because decision-making on whether and how to enforce the non-cooperation decisions of the Court are left to the Assembly of States Parties and (where appropriate) to the Security Council, a range of extra-legal diplomatic, strategic, economic, and political considerations will inevitably come to bear as States factor their national interest into the enforcement equation.[37] The first conclusion to be drawn from this is that the ICC will be

expected to do so in practice. Even where their scale or intensity leads to action, Security Council initiatives will take into account a broad matrix of factors influencing peace in the circumstances, and placing a firm priority on rigorously pursuing prosecutions will not necessarily survive such calculus. A distinction between a normative peace interest (through accountability) and the actual establishment of peace is thus seen in the practice of the Council, and could be expected to survive even a major 'fairness' reform of the Council (which does not, in any event, appear likely at present). See Part III, nn. 3–6 and related text below.

[36] Franck (1993), n. 35 above, at 204.

[37] Bass (2000), n. 6 above, at 28, applies 5 theses in explaining the sufficiency of political will in past efforts at accountability for international crimes. These are that (1) 'it is only liberal states, with legalistic beliefs, that support *bona fide* war crimes tribunals'; (2) 'even liberal states tend not to push for a war crimes tribunal if so doing would put their own soldiers at risk'; (3) '[e]ven liberal states are more likely to be outraged by war crimes against their own citizens than war crimes against foreigners'; (4) 'even liberal states are most likely to support a war crimes tribunal if public opinion is outraged by the war crimes in question'; and (5) 'nonstate pressure groups can be effective in pushing for a tribunal, by shaming liberal states into action and providing expertise'. One might add to these higher-level 'national interest' factors such as the economic, strategic, and other political calculations that inform State decision-making.

most effective where the State on the territory or by the national of which the crime was (allegedly) committed is itself willing to enforce the requests of the Court. Such States are likely to be most willing where prior regimes, 'rogue' or disfavoured elements of the government, scapegoats, or non-State actors are under investigation. In other words, where it is in the State's interest, cooperation will occur; absent this, the pressure of other States will be decisive.

A second conclusion is that such pressure is unlikely to be forthcoming with the regularity sought by the rule of law. International pressure will undoubtedly be brought to bear and influence cooperation, and the ICC can be expected to help build a 'culture of accountability' that will help to increase and regularize such pressure. Nonetheless, the truly refractory State will not cooperate. Many cases will require the mobilization of coercive power, not infrequently in the context of maintaining or restoring international peace and security. International action against disruptions of peace and security will, as in the Former Yugoslavia, be a precondition for effective international criminal proceedings. In many instances, the ICC is unlikely to be effective (and *a fortiori* unlikely to deter) where such mobilization is absent or insufficient.

One might therefore conclude, thirdly, that while other, limited avenues of enforcement may be available, the Security Council as the *de facto* executive authority of the international system is the source from which regular enforcement would be most likely to emanate where there is determined non-cooperation. An important corollary of this is that some regularity in the management of international peace and security (and in the use of force required therefor) will ultimately be needed to underpin the rule of law in international criminal law.

If it is true that '. . . the effectiveness of both the judicial arm and the investigation arm of an international criminal tribunal depends heavily on state cooperation and is ultimately impeded by lack of state cooperation under the guise of state sovereignty',[38] the Rome Statute does not fundamentally change this state of affairs. The ICC will undoubtedly contribute to the *formal* rule of law in international criminal law (through its definitions of crimes, general principles, and so forth); that it will also contribute to the minimal level of consistent enforcement also called for by the rule of law cannot be assumed from the Statute itself. Rather, the promotion of regular and effective compliance will depend on the concerted political will of the members of the Assembly of States Parties and of the Security Council. Such a concerted will—'a culture of legality'—cannot arise from the formal qualities of the Statute alone, but depends on a number of factors lying outside the Statute and in some instances outside international law itself (see pp. 185–92 below).

---

[38] Cassese (1998), n. 3 above, at 12.

IX

Cornerstone or Stumbling Block? The United States and the ICC

1. INTRODUCTION

From the moment the final traits of the Rome Statute became apparent, the United States has sought accommodation of what it has called 'fundamental concerns'[1] with the text. In essence, and through various guises, the U.S. Administration has identified the need for an exemption for U.S. nationals from the already curtailed jurisdiction of the final compromise language (see pp. 80–2 above). During its term in office, the Clinton administration actively put forward proposals in the post-Rome negotiating process, without acknowledging that such an exemption would require an amendment to the Statute (in accordance with the stringent procedures set out in Articles 121–122),[2] while the Bush administration, reiterating the concerns, distanced itself from PrepCom negotiations almost entirely, and turned instead to the U.N. Security Council and to bilateral negotiations, where its influence was at a maximum.[3]

The stance of the United States has also been intensely frustrating for its negotiating partners in the Preparatory Commission. Charged by the General Assembly with seeking ways to 'enhance the effectiveness and acceptance of the Court',[4] while negotiating within the framework of the agreement adopted at Rome, national delegates have walked a tightrope between seeking to keep the U.S. engaged and respecting the integrity of the Rome Statute. Real incentives exist to engage U.S. support. These are both financial, as the burden on other developed countries would be substantially reduced with

---

[1] David J. Scheffer, 'The United States and the International Criminal Court' (1999) 93 A.J.I.L. 12, at 21; idem, 'Staying the Course with the International Criminal Court' (2001) 35 Cornell Int'l L.J. 47.

[2] See n. 32 below.

[3] Pam Spees, 'The Rome Statute of the International Criminal Court', in Nicole Deller, Arjun Makhijani, and John Burroughs, eds., *Rule of Power or Rule of Law? An assessment of U.S. policies and actions regarding security-related treaties* (Institute for Energy and Environment Research/Lawyers Committee on Nuclear Policy, 2002); John Washburn, 'The International Criminal Court Arrives—The U.S. Position: Status and prospects' (2002) 25 Fordham Int'l L.J. 873.

[4] The language is from the General Assembly resolutions convening the Preparatory Commission, and was included with the intention of keeping the U.S. engaged in the ICC process by providing the PrepCom with a mandate not provided for in the Final Act of the Rome Conference: See Resolutions 53/105, para. 4, 54/105, para. 3, 55/155, para. 4, Chapter IV, n. 22 above; Final Act, see Chapter II, n. 62 above.

U.S. support,[5] and political, as the regime of international justice would undoubtedly be stronger with the support of the sole global hegemon behind it. Nonetheless, the U.S. has rejected arguments that its reasons for supporting the Court outweigh its reasons for opposing it. Delegates have good reason to doubt[6] that any accommodation of the United States is possible on reasonable terms.

2. U.S. NEGOTIATING AIMS AND 'FLAWS' IN THE ROME STATUTE

When it refers to 'flaws' in the Rome Statute,[7] the U.S. refers primarily to the ICC's ability to exercise jurisdiction over the nationals of non-States Parties to the Statute without the consent of those States.[8] For the U.S. government, this raises fears of U.S. personnel[9] being investigated *inter alia* for war crimes by an international tribunal. That the Court would be able to do so only when the national of the non-party is suspected on reasonable grounds of committing genocide, crimes against humanity, or war crimes on the territory of a State Party (Articles 15, 53, and 58), and where the State of nationality (among others) is found unwilling or unable to proceed genuinely against the individual (Articles 17, 18, and 19), has not been considered sufficiently reassuring. For the States now moving towards ratification that supported this arrangement at Rome, the jurisdictional scheme is simply a delegation to the ICC of the territorial and national jurisdiction that States undoubtedly enjoy under international law: the ICC will do nothing more than what these States have the right to do, and only when they are unwilling or unable to do it.[10] The U.S. argues that the possible investigation and prosecution of its nationals without its consent is tantamount to the imposition of treaty obligations on a third State—something expressly disallowed by the Vienna Convention on the Law of Treaties.[11] For ICC supporters, to allow the State of national-

---

[5] Assuming a hypothetical budget of U.S.$ 100m and applying the U.N. scale of assessment, the discussion paper of the Project on International Courts and Tribunals indicates that 'the United States would take on 27.19 per cent of the Court's budget ($27,194,012.97), while Japanese and EU contributions would decrease to 22.37 and 39.41 per cent respectively' [compared to 30.73 and 54.14 per cent respectively without the U.S.; or 78.17 per cent for the E.U. alone if neither the U.S. nor Japan were parties].

[6] See below, at pp. 181–2.

[7] Scheffer (1999), n. 1 above, at 17.

[8] See pp. 80–1 above.

[9] Including high-ranking officials.

[10] Philippe Kirsch, 'The Rome Conference on the International Criminal Court: A comment' (November–December 1998) *Am. Soc. Int'l L. Newsletter* 1; see also Gerhardt Hafner, Kristen Boon, Anna Rübesame, and Jonathan Huston, 'A Response to the American View as Presented by Ruth Wedgwood' (1999) 10 E.J.I.L. 108 at 117.

[11] Scheffer (1999), n. 1 above, at 18. Gerhard Hafner draws the distinction between imposing criminal responsibility on the nationals of third States and imposing obligations on those States:

ity of the accused to decide whether its nationals would be prosecuted would be a retreat from the Nuremberg principle that an individual cannot find immunity behind the veil of the State.[12]

The United States' legal argument is widely thought to be weak, but arises from deeper concerns emanating in different forms from the U.S. Congress and the Executive. Objections from the conservative wing of the Congress typically express themselves in 'sovereignty'-based arguments about the exposure of U.S. military personnel to potentially anti-American, politically motivated judges and prosecutors, and about the lack of due process protections equivalent to those provided by the United States' Constitution.[13] These concerns are relatively widespread among conservative commentators,[14] but are not well supported among even sympathetic U.S. academics, who typically recognize that the Rome Statute offers significant safeguards (many based on U.S. proposals) and that constitutional concerns are misplaced.[15]

see Hafner *et al.* (1999), n. 10 above, at 117–18. The most detailed explication, broadly sympathetic to the U.S., of the legal argument is Madeline Morris, 'High Crimes and the International Criminal Court' 64 L. & Contemp. Probs at 13; see also Ruth Wedgwood, 'The International Criminal Court: An American view' (1999) 10 E.J.I.L. 93. For a short critique of the legality argument, see Diane F. Orentlicher, 'Politics by Other Means: The law of the International Criminal Court', (1999) 32 Cornell Int'l L.J. 489. The Bush administration has repeatedly relied on this argument of alleged illegality. In the words of Under Secretary of State Marc Grossman: 'The Court, as constituted today, claims the authority to detain and try American citizens, even though our democratically-elected representatives have not agreed to be bound by the treaty. While sovereign nations have the authority to try non-citizens who have committed crimes against their citizens or in their territory, the United States has never recognized the right of an international organization to do so absent consent or a UN Security Council mandate'—Under Secretary of State for Political Affairs Marc Grossman, *American Foreign Policy and the International Criminal Court*, Remarks to the Center for Strategic and International Studies (6 May 2002), available online at http://www.state.gov/p/9949.htm (last visited 21 July 2002). The United States has failed to provide reasoned support for this position, which is not considered credible among non-American lawyers.

[12] Orentlicher, n. 11 above, at 493–5.

[13] See 'Address by Senator Jesse Helms, Chairman, U.S. Senate Committee on Foreign Relations, before the United Nations Security Council, January 20, 2000' (available from Senator Helms' website: http://www.senate.gov/~helms/ (site last visited on 21 July 2002)).

[14] John Bolton, 'Reject and Oppose the International Criminal Court' in Alton Frye, ed., *Toward an International Criminal Court? Three options presented as presidential speeches* (New York: Council on Foreign Relations, 1999); Helle Bering, 'International Criminal Circus; Political correctness runs amok again' *Washington Times* (5 April 2000) A19; Jonathan Tepperman, 'Contempt of Court: How Jesse Helms and the State Department are helping future Melosovics escape justice' *Washington Monthly* (November 2000) 25.

[15] Ruth Wedgwood, a leading academic sympathizer with U.S. government concerns, starts from the position that the applicable standards are those pertaining to military courts martial and to cases of extradition to foreign States—where constitutional protections are weakest— rather than civilian trials for acts within the United States. On this basis, her analysis finds few grounds for constitutional objection: Ruth Wedgwood, 'The Constitution and the ICC' in Sarah B. Sewall and Carl Kaysen, eds., *The United States and the International Criminal Court: National security and international law* (Lanham, MA: Rowman and Littlefield, 2000) 119. See also 'Statement of Monroe Leigh on behalf of the American Bar Association, submitted to the Committee on International Relations, U.S. House of Representatives, regarding H.R. 4654, *American Servicemembers' Protection Act*' (25 July 2000) (on file).

Even given the Bush administration's political alignment with the Congressional right, Executive concerns tend to emanate primarily from the Department of Defense. Leading military and State Department decision-makers are concerned that the U.S. ability to project force abroad will be constrained by possible ICC investigation into the actions of U.S. personnel on the territory either of a party to the Statute or of a State consenting *ad hoc* to the Court's jurisdiction. The United States government, in the context of an overall aim of entrenching post-Cold War U.S. pre-eminence in international affairs, is seeking to prevent the emergence of a possible curb on the latitude available to the U.S. military in acting as an arm of U.S. foreign policy. That such latitude might encompass actions in at least the gray zone of legality could only exacerbate this concern.[16]

Before and during the Rome Conference, the United States aimed to shape a Court that it would be able to control, above all where proceedings against its nationals were concerned.[17] This aim was expressed through proposals that would require Security Council approval of proceedings related to a situation being dealt with by the Council under Chapter VII of the Charter (thus requiring the affirmative votes of its permanent members, including the United States), and that would require the State of nationality of the accused to recognize the Court's jurisdiction (through ratification or consent *ad hoc* under Article 12(3)) before the Court could act.

The U.S. was not successful in achieving its aim at Rome, and consequently voted against the adoption of the Statute. Rather than the Security Council having power to decide the Chapter VII situations against which the Court

[16] See, for example, Jules Lobel and Michael Ratner, 'Bypassing the Security Council: Ambiguous authorizations to use force, cease-fires and the Iraqi inspection regime' (1999) 93 A.J.I.L. 124; Bruno Simma, 'NATO, the UN and the Use of Force: Legal aspects' (1999) 10 E.J.I.L. 1. The connection between the ICC and use of force in the so-called 'war on terrorism' has been expressly made by U.S. Secretary of Defense Donald Rumsfeld: 'There is the risk that the ICC could attempt to assert jurisdiction over U.S. servicemembers, as well as civilians, involved in counter-terrorist and other military operations—something we cannot allow'— *Secretary Rumsfeld Statement on the ICC Treaty*, United States Department of Defense News Release No. 233-02 (6 May 2002), available online at http://www.defenselink.mil/news/May2002/b05062002_bt233-02.html (last visited 21 July 2002). The place of the ICC in the geopolitical framework of U.S. interests at the end of the twentieth century has, to the knowledge of this author, not been adequately explored to date. But see 'A World Court for Criminals' *Economist* (9 October 1999) 19 (that U.S. opposition to the Court is contrary to its larger interest in world order) and Wedgwood, n. 4 above (taking a sympathetic view of U.S. concerns), and in particular Sarah B. Sewall, Carl Kaysen, and Michael P. Scharf, 'The United States and the International Criminal Court: An overview' in Sewall and Kaysen (2000), n. 15 above, 1. For more general views finding an overriding U.S. interest in multilateralism see 'America's world' *Economist* (23 October 1999) 15 and Sherle R. Schwenninger, 'World Order Lost: American foreign policy in the post-Cold War world' (Summer 1999) World Policy J. 42. 'Multilateralist' discourse has, of course, waned, even as concerns about international checks on U.S. military action have grown, in the wake of the attacks on the United States of 11 September 2001.

[17] For the U.S. role at the Rome Conference, see Scheffer (1999) and (2002), both at n. 1 above, and Lawrence Weschler, 'Exceptional Cases in Rome: The United States and the struggle for an ICC', in Sewall and Kaysen (2000), n. 15 above, 85.

will proceed, the ICC has *carte blanche* to act within such situations (subject to the limits of the Statute) unless the Security Council makes the affirmative decision under Article 16 to request a one-year, renewable deferral (in which decision all permanent members must concur) (see pp. 81–2 above and p. 180 below). Under Article 12, the acceptance of the territorial State is enough to allow the ICC to exercise jurisdiction, even if without the approval of the State of nationality of an accused (see p. 81 above). Nonetheless, the text adopted on 18 July 1998 contained numerous provisions reflecting U.S. concerns and leaving only the narrowest window of vulnerability. Important provisions in this regard include the facts that, first, the discretion of the Prosecutor to initiate investigations *proprio motu* is controlled by a panel of judges in the Pre-Trial Chamber (Article 15). Secondly, even once an investigation begins, the complementarity provisions would allow the U.S., even as a non-party, to stop ICC proceedings at the earliest stage simply by asserting that it was investigating the matter itself.[18] Initial study indicates that the U.S., which probably has the most sophisticated military justice system in the world, is well prepared (at least in principle) to fulfil the role envisioned by the scheme of complementarity, provided the will were present.[19] Thirdly, the Rome Statute includes a provision in Article 98(2) that in effect allows the U.S. to enter into agreements (Status of Forces Agreements or other instruments) that would block surrender of its nationals to the ICC.[20] Nonetheless, the fact remains that the independent judges of the ICC will make the key decision as to whether a State was willing and able to proceed genuinely, and the officials of the ICC would be chosen by governments other than the U.S. As a result, and largely because of the vehemence of Defence Department and Congressional criticisms, the narrowness of its exposure has done little to assuage the U.S. administration.

---

[18] Arts. 18–20 (see pp. 87–93 above). Art. 18, which stems from a U.S. proposal, requires the Prosecutor to give notice to *all* States as soon as he or she decides that there is a reasonable basis for opening an investigation. The Prosecutor then has to defer the investigation if one of those States gives notice that it is investigating the matter itself, unless the Prosecutor gets the approval of the Pre-Trial Chamber to proceed (presumably, because the State is found unwilling or unable to proceed genuinely). These provisions put the Prosecutor under a burden to prove 'unwillingness' or 'inability' at a very early stage, before an investigation has even begun, making deferral to national authorities likely in all but the most egregious cases. If the accused is in the hands of the State of nationality at the time of deferral, and that State (e.g. the United States) is a non-party and not obliged to cooperate with the Court, it may be all but impossible to proceed subsequently.

[19] A judge of the U.S. Court of Military Appeals concludes that '[a]ny conduct by a service-member that would be subject to trial by the ICC as a war crime probably could also be made subject to trial by a general court-martial. . . .' but that '[a]s a matter of caution, some additions to the Uniform Code [of Military Justice] and to the Manual for Courts-Martial might be desirable in order to make even firmer the conclusion that, as to American servicemembers, the jurisdiction of courts-martial would be coextensive with that of the ICC': Robinson O. Everett, 'American Servicemembers and the ICC' in Sewall and Kaysen (2000), n. 15 above, 137 at 146.

[20] See Ch. VII, n. 65 below. See also discussion at pp. 148–9 above and pp. 179–81 below.

The aim of post-Rome Clinton administration efforts was to undertake an approach of 'constructive engagement' with the PrepCom in order to seek to raise the comfort level of ICC skeptics within the United States government, in particular by limiting the Court's effective powers with respect to non-State Parties. In its extreme form, this exercise sought a 'fix' in the form of a 'magic bullet' proposal that would resolve concerns through a *de facto* or *de lege* amendment to the Rome Statute. At the same time, there appears to have been debate within the relevant agencies of government as to what would constitute adequate 'protection' with respect to which concerns. Intimately tied to this debate was the question of the legal form such a 'fix' should take. If '100 per cent protection' were to be the watchword, then a protocol or an amendment to the Statute would have been necessary, with all the political hurdles this would present. If 'full protection' were to entail something less than this, then a binding understanding (of the PrepCom or of the eventual Assembly of States Parties) or an addition to the Rules of Procedure and Evidence or the Relationship Agreement between the ICC and the United Nations might have sufficed. Under the Bush administration, such efforts to obtain a 'fix' have been abandoned, and replaced by a stance of active hostility that has resulted in some gains in the U.S. quest for abstention from ICC jurisdiction.

Without exploring in detail the policies and institutional interests behind U.S. efforts, the following pages examine first the search, under the Clinton administration, for an accommodation of U.S. concerns in the context of the PrepCom, and secondly the blunter approach of the Bush administration, which has abandoned the ICC process as such. In the light of this, the conclusion argues that, while early reconciliation with the ICC might best serve long-term U.S. interests from one perspective, it is likely that an uneasy relationship between the two will persist for some time to come.

3. THE CLINTON ADMINISTRATION'S SEARCH FOR A NEGOTIATED 'FIX'

(a) The negotiating environment

Any Clinton administration proposal or proposals to reduce ICC jurisdiction over U.S. nationals would, if proposed to the PrepCom, have had to receive support from a controlling number of States engaged in the process. The U.S. would have to create a common understanding of the problem as well as sympathy towards its position from at least key leaders among the States involved. Such an effort would necessarily have been constrained by the international situation and by positions taken by those countries that would have to agree to any accommodation.

At the time of deposit of the Rome Statute's sixtieth instrument of ratification (p. 76 above), States Parties included permanent Security Council members France and the United Kingdom (with Russia a signatory), as well as the entire EU and all NATO members (except Turkey, and with Greece having signed but not yet ratified). Adherence to the Statute by these States created the political support and financial viability for the Court that other States needed as a precondition for own support. Partly as a result, many sub-Saharan African and Central and Eastern European States have accelerated their processes of ratification.[21] Despite slower progress in Asia and the Middle East, the first Assembly of States Parties, in September 2002, included representatives from all regions of the globe, in addition to the above-mentioned NATO and Security Council members.

From the point of view of the Clinton administration's efforts, the momentum towards the establishment of the ICC had the effect of reducing the inclination of signatory and ratifying States to modify arrangements under the Statute. The Like Minded Group of countries supporting the early establishment of an effective ICC publicly affirmed its support for the integrity of the Rome Statute in European, United Nations and other fora.[22] These countries could not be seen to retreat from this position without considerable loss of face. Supportive States, including those that regularly contribute troops to peace-keeping operations, decided and declared publicly that the package set out in the Statute provides adequate safeguards to meet their concerns.[23]

Moreover, leading countries of the Like-Minded Group were among the majority at the Diplomatic Conference that supported what amounted to universal jurisdiction for the Court,[24] that decisively rejected the suggestion that the exercise of jurisdiction should be based on consent of the State of nationality alone,[25] and that, without U.S. urging, might well have created an independent Prosecutor without the constraints now seen, particularly in

---

[21] The most current source of information on the state of signature and ratification is the web-site of the non-governmental Coalition for an International Criminal Court: www.iccnow.org. (site last visited on 21 July 2002). Of course, not all signatory States can be expected to ratify in the near term.

[22] The Like Minded group consists of over 60 States, and includes preservation of the integrity of the Rome Statute among its guiding principles: Chapter IV, n. 14 and related text above.

[23] Robin Cook, the UK Foreign Secretary, stated with reference to the U.S. concerns that '[w]e in Britain would not be exposing our servicemen to vexatious prosecution. We have signed up to the ICC because we are confident there is no risk of that': 'Cook Rallies to Genocide Court' *Guardian* (26 August 2000) 13.

[24] 'Proposal of the Republic of Korea', U.N. Doc. A/Conf.183/C.1/L.6 (1998), proposed that the Court be able to exercise its jurisdiction if any of 4 States was party to the Statute (or consented *ad hoc*): the territorial State, the State of nationality of the victim or of the accused, and the State with custody of the accused. According to NGO reports, this proposal was supported by 79% of States during the penultimate week and by 89% of States during the final week of the Diplomatic Conference: 'The Numbers: NGO Coalition Special Report on Country Positions' (10 July 1998) *Rome Treaty Conference Monitor* 1; 'NGO Coalition Special Report on Country Positions on L.59: The Virtual Vote' (15 July 1998) *Rome Treaty Conference Monitor* 1.

[25] 'Proposal of the United States of America', U.N. Doc. A/Conf.183/C.1/L.70 (15 July 1998).

Articles 15 and 18. These States have remained mindful that the jurisdictional arrangement is a compromise very much narrower than that favoured by the large majority at Rome, and is indeed one adopted primarily to placate the United States. The result is something of a stalemate on the ICC that promises to endure for some time after entry into force.

The Clinton administration was further hampered in its efforts to negotiate a 'fix' by the lack of any sufficient bargaining chip to offer its counterparts. Constructive U.S. engagement in the PrepCom sessions resulted in provisions of the Rules of Procedure and Evidence and the Elements of Crime that address various 'second-tier' U.S. concerns.[26] But because the PrepCom Rules and Elements were draft instruments which could conceivably be changed before adoption by the first Assembly of States Parties, and because its fundamental issue remained unresolved, the Clinton administration had an incentive to stay involved.[27] U.S. engagement made both withdrawal from the PrepCom and concerted opposition to the ICC, the main negative incentives available seem implausible.

As for positive incentives, the Clinton administration felt itself unable to offer a clear promise of signature in advance and chose to sign the Statute only at the last minute before the deadline passed on 31 December 2000.[28]

[26] For example, the U.S. had concerns about the potential abuse of Art 12(3), which allows non-party States to consent *ad hoc* to the Court's jurisdiction 'with respect to the crime in question'. The U.S. was concerned that the use of the word 'crime' rather than the word 'situation' could allow States maliciously to pick individual defendants for prosecution by the ICC (e.g. enemy nationals in their custody): Ruth Wedgwood, 'The United States and the International Criminal Court: Achieving a wider consensus through the "Ithaca package"' (1999) 32 Cornell Int'l L.J. 535, at 541. This concern was addressed in the negotiation of the draft Rules of Procedure and Evidence, Chapter IV, n. 16 above, which provide in Rule 44(2) that: 'When a State lodges, or declares to the Registrar its intent to lodge, a declaration with the Registrar pursuant to article 12, paragraph 3 . . . the Registrar shall inform the State concerned that the declaration under article 12, paragraph 3, has as a consequence the acceptance of jurisdiction with respect to the crimes referred to in article 5 of relevance to the situation and the provisions of Part 9, and any rules thereunder concerning States Parties, shall apply'. The words 'of relevance to the situation' indicate that both sides to a conflict and some adequate temporal and geographical scope is encompassed by *ad hoc* consent to the Court's jurisidiction.

[27] Resolution F of the Final Act of the Rome Conference, Chapter II, n. 62 above, declares in para. 5 that '[t]he Commission shall prepare proposals for . . . the draft texts of the Rules of Procedure and Evidence, Elements of Crimes, and other instruments. The PrepCom will remain in existence until the conclusion of the first session of the Assembly of States Parties: ibid., para. 8. While all States invited to participate in the Rome Conference (including all Member States of the UN) are entitled to participate in the PrepCom (ibid., para. 2), only States that have signed either the Final Act of the Rome Conference or the Rome Statute itself will be entitled to sit as observers in the Assembly of States Parties (Art. 112(1)), which will adopt the drafts prepared by the PrepCom (Art. 112(2)(a)).

[28] For example, U.S. statements on the ICC before the Sixth Committee of the General Assembly in 1999 and 2000 referred only to how the U.S. could 'embrace' or be a 'good neighbour' to the Court if its demands were met: (on file). In accordance with Art. 125(1), the Rome Statute closed for signature on 31 December 2000. The signature of the United States on 31 December 2000 was completely unexpected: see 'U.S. Signs Treaty for World Court to Try Atrocities' *New York Times* (1 January 2001) A1.

Much less was it able to offer eventual ratification, with its Senate Foreign Relations Committee chaired by a vehement opponent of the Court (Senator Jesse Helms of North Carolina) and, perhaps more importantly, while it was seeking concessions whose effect would be to exempt it *as a non-party* from the Court's jurisdiction over its nationals, giving it an incentive to remain indefinitely outside the regime. Moreover, the U.S. could not credibly offer the only 'carrot' remaining to it. Support for the Court[29]—while undoubtedly attractive to other States if offered concretely—is necessarily contingent on the changeable politics of the Executive and Congress, and cannot be guaranteed in advance.

In addition to isolation in its concerns and uncertainty in its bargaining power, the U.S. had to contend with a restrictive time frame. The Clinton administration's search for accommodation was conditioned by key dates. To the extent that a 'fix' involved the Rules of Procedure and Evidence, the deadline of 30 June 2000 for completion of draft Rules was a constraint.[30] Later PrepCom sessions were constrained by the pending entry into force of the Statute, with resulting limited time for drafting remaining instruments.[31] Without an express promise of signature in advance, the Clinton administration had little with which to win others to its cause before its mandate expired following the December 2000 PrepCom session.

Ultimately, the Clinton administration's search for a negotiated 'fix' was unsuccessful for a mix of formal and substantive reasons. Formally, the degree of available insulation from ICC jurisdiction would be highest with an amendment or a protocol to the Statute, which would have the effect of altering the institutional 'constitution' of the Court.[32] The argument challenging the legality of the Statute could have been intended in part to prepare the ground for such a remedy. The degree of sustained political support that would have been needed for this and the political cost for the Like Minded countries of entering into any apparent retreat from their position of support for the integrity of the Statute led the U.S. to abandon this option in favour of 'softer' ones (in particular, Rules of Procedure and Evidence and the

---

[29] Whether political, financial, or diplomatic.

[30] Resolution F of the Final Act, Chapter II, n. 62 above, para. 6, called on the PrepCom to adopt the draft Rules of Procedure and Evidence and Elements of Crime by 30 June 2000.

[31] Following adoption of the drafts of the Rules of Procedure and Evidence and Elements of Crime on 30 June 2000, Chapter IV, n. 26 above, the PrepCom turned its attention to the remaining instruments called for under Resolution F, para. 5, of the Final Act, Chapter II, n. 62 above. It subsequently formed working groups for, drafted and adopted the Financial Regulations and Rules, the Agreement on the Privileges and Immunities of the Court, the Relationship Agreement between the ICC and the UN, the Rules of Procedure of the Assembly of States Parties, principles for the Headquarters Agreement between the ICC and the Netherlands, a first-year budget of the Court, and more.

[32] Substantive amendments require the affirmative vote of two-thirds of the Assembly of States Parties, followed by ratification by seven-eighths of them, creating a very high threshold for changing the Statute (Art. 121(5)). A protocol to the Statute would presumably require signature and ratification by all States Parties.

Relationship Agreement between the ICC and the UN). Substantively, the resistance of Like Minded governments to arguments of U.S. exceptionalism obliged the United States, under Clinton, to frame its proposals in general terms; at the same time, no principled general accommodation could be found that would meet U.S. needs without opening a loophole through which myriad injustices would flow.

During the Clinton administration's campaign of 'constructive engagement' in the PrepCom negotiations (from 1998 to the end of 2000) four major attempts directed at U.S. concerns surfaced. None was successful, owing largely to a combination of political resistance, lack of incentive, and clear inconsistency with the Rome Statute.

(b) Broadening deference to States through the Rules of Procedure and Evidence

At the PrepCom session held in December 1999 the United States introduced a proposal for the Rules of Procedure and Evidence that would have in part addressed its concerns.[33] The proposal dealt with Articles 17, 18(1), (2), and (3), and 19(10). In its key provision, the U.S. suggested adding three broad factors to be taken into account in determining admissibility under Article 17. These include the independence of the country's justice system, the past practice of that system, and whether the State in question has communicated to the Court that the acts in question were performed in the course of official duties.[34] These proposed factors did not sit easily with the factors under Article 17 (see pp. 88–93 above), for example by adding promises of future investigation to the present or past proceedings contemplated by the Statute. Most importantly, the principle of complementarity applies to *specific proceedings* (Articles 17(2) and 20(3)) where the U.S. proposal would have required the ICC to judge the general independence and effectiveness of national justice systems: a controversial role and a time-consuming task for the ICC. For this and other reasons, the proposal met with significant resis-

---

[33] Proposal of the United States of America, U.N. Doc. PCNICC/1999/WGRPE/DP.45 (2 December 1999).

[34] Rule for article 17(1)(a)

In determining, under article 17(1)(a) or (b) or (c), whether a case is inadmissible, the Court shall take into account, *inter alia*, the following:

- The independence of the State's applicable justice system, including its court martial system;
- Whether in the past the State has genuinely investigated or prosecuted similar conduct, whether official or non-official, by its military personnel or citizens; and
- Whether the State has communicated in writing to the Office of the Prosecutor that the person concerned was acting in the course of his or her official duties authorized by such State with respect to the matter under investigation and that the State shall immediately investigate pursuant to its processes, or has investigated or shall continue to investigate, fully such person's actions and, if warranted, shall prosecute expeditiously such person for any crime within the jurisdiction of the Court.'

tance from other States, with the result that only a harmless residual rule was adopted in the final draft package of the Rules.[35]

(c) An exemption from surrender for 'official acts'

With the failure of its December 1999 effort, which amounted only to an indirect attempt to reduce the Court's jurisdiction over its nationals by broadening the 'complementarity' criteria, the U.S. presented a more direct proposal. The informal proposal circulated by the United States delegation at the March 2000 PrepCom is a good illustration of problems that arose with attempts to find accommodation for its concerns. The proposal had two parts, formal and substantive. The substance of the proposal was intended to be included in the Relationship Agreement between the UN and the ICC, which began negotiation at the November–December 2000 session of the PrepCom. Formally, and to give the substantive provision in the Relationship Agreement a point of entry into the Statute, the U.S. sought a rule of procedure to make clear that the Relationship Agreement would be considered an 'international agreement' for the purposes of Article 98(2), which exempts States from their obligation to surrender an individual to the ICC in case of conflicting obligations, and which was intended to make allowance for Status of Forces Agreements or SOFAs.[36] By ensuring that the Relationship Agreement was encompassed by Article 98(2), the U.S. planned to insert a provision in that Agreement that would block surrender of its nationals to the ICC. It proposed that where the national of a non-party is involved, and the State of nationality acknowledges that the individual was acting under its 'overall direction', the Court would not proceed with a request for surrender unless either the State of nationality consents, or the Security Council passes a resolution against the directing State under Chapter VII of the Charter, authorizing the continuation of proceedings. While the proposal would only stop the Court at the stage of surrender, thus allowing investigations to proceed up to that stage, the three key features of this proposal gave rise to familiar difficulties.

First, the ability of a State of nationality of the accused to acknowledge its overall direction over the individual is the 'official acts' exception that was

[35] Rule 51 of the Draft Rules of Procedure, Chapter IV, n. 26 above, reads:

Information provided under article 17

In considering the matters referred to in article 17, paragraph 2, and in the context of the circumstances of the case, the Court may consider, *inter alia*, information that the State referred to in article 17, paragraph 1, may choose to bring to the attention of the Court showing that its courts meet internationally recognized norms and standards for the independent and impartial prosecution of similar conduct, or that the State has confirmed in writing to the Prosecutor that the case is being investigated or prosecuted.

[36] See n. 20 above. The first (informal) formulation of the proposed rule to this paragraph reads as follows: 'The Court shall proceed with a request for surrender or an acceptance of a person into the custody of the Court only in a manner consistent with its obligations under the relevant international agreement' (on file).

proposed by the U.S. and subsequently rejected at Rome.[37] The requirement that a non-party State acknowledge that an individual was engaged in official acts would ostensibly limit the exception to situations in which a State was willing so to acknowledge. However, the proposal: would have allowed States to block ICC jurisdiction over their nationals (and for the most serious crimes conceivable), would have done so when those crimes were allegedly committed on the territory of a State Party to the Statute (which would normally itself be able to exercise jurisdiction), would not have required the State of nationality to investigate or prosecute itself, and would have provided no effective control to ensure that the acknowledgement was made in good faith. For many of those who rejected this concept at Rome, it would be a clear retreat from the Nuremberg principles to allow the State of a person accused of genocide, crimes against humanity, or war crimes to block proceedings in this way. The second feature of the proposal, State of nationality consent, raised the same objection and was similarly rejected at Rome.[38]

The third key feature, that of Security Council approval, revisited the position advanced by the U.S. through the early stages of the Rome Conference.[39] Whatever the weight of arguments about the priority owing to the Security Council in its actions to maintain or restore international peace and security under Chapter VII of the Charter, the granting of control over Court proceedings to the Security Council was strongly resisted throughout negotiations. Such control would have allowed inequitable immunity of the nationals of permanent members of the Council (as well as the nationals of their proxy and client States) and was thus criticized for institutionalizing inequality before the law. This critique was inflamed by the North–South issues heaped on the argument by members of the Non Aligned Movement and others. Given that the issue of Security Council control was debated and settled at Rome, bestowing upon the Council a right to delay Court proceedings by Chapter VII resolution (Article 16) (pp. 81–2 above), U.S. ability to win support to revisit this issue was utterly inadequate.

Despite these shortcomings, the adoption of a Rule of Procedure seen by the U.S. as laying the foundation for further negotiations towards an exemption in the Relationship Agreement kept the underlying strategy, if not the exact terms, of this proposal alive.[40]

[37] 'Proposal of the United States of America', U.N. Doc. A/Conf.183/C.1/L.90 (16 July 1998).

[38] Proposal L.70, n. 25 above.

[39] The analogy is not exact, since the March 2000 proposal would only require Security Council approval once the Court was to seek surrender of the accused, rather than prevent proceedings from the start. The proposal is also narrower than the previous position, in that it would require a Security Council resolution taking measures *against the State of nationality* as a precondition to the surrender of nationals of that State to the Court. Proceedings could continue as prescribed by the Statute with respect to nationals of e.g. the State on the territory of which the crime was alleged.

[40] Rule 195, Chapter IV, n. 26 above, states: 'The Court may not proceed with a request for the surrender of a person without the consent of sending State if, under article 98, paragraph 2,

(d) A seven-year opt-out from ICC jurisdiction over war crimes

With the approach of the November-December 2000 PrepCom session and concerns about an intensive U.S. campaign to win the second part of its 'March proposal' in the Relationship Agreement between the UN and the ICC, an alternative proposal was briefly discussed. This would have allowed signatories that had not yet ratified to file a declaration resulting in a seven-year exemption from ICC jurisdiction over war crimes.[41] This would have extended Article 124 of the Statute, which allows States Parties the same prerogative.[42] A justification put forward for the proposal was based on Article 36 of the Vienna Convention of the Law of Treaties, which allows States Parties to extend the benefit of a treaty to non-States Parties in certain circumstances.[43] Whether this foundation was solid or not, the proposal never emerged formally, as it would have required the U.S. to commit itself to signing the treaty before the deadline for signature on 31 December 2000. Although the U.S. did subsequently sign,[44] it was not prepared, in early December, to offer to do so in exchange for a time-limited and subject matter-limited protection entailed by this option.[45]

---

such a request would be inconsistent with obligations under an international agreement pursuant to which the consent of a sending State is required prior to the surrender of a person of that State to the Court'. Delegates at the June PrepCom were careful to insert language in the final report of the session indicating that adoption of Rule 9.19 did not entail any concession of substance ('It was generally understood that Rule 9.19 should not be interpreted as requiring or in any way calling for the negotiation of provisions in any particular international agreement by the Court or by any other international organization or State'): *Proceedings of the Preparatory Commission at its Fifth Session (12–30 June 2000)*, U.N. Doc. PCNICC/2000/L.3/Rev.1 (6 July 2000), at 3.

[41] See Diane Orentlicher, 'International Criminal Tribunals: An institution the United States can support', paper presented at *America's national interests in multilateral engagement: A bipartisan dialogue* (Harvard University, John F. Kennedy School of Government, 14–15 May 2000) (on file).

[42] 'Notwithstanding article 12, paragraphs 1 and 2, a State, on becoming a party to this Statute, may declare that, for a period of seven years after the entry into force of this Statute for the State concerned, it does not accept the jurisdiction of the Court with respect to the category of crimes referred to in article 8 when a crime is alleged to have been committed by its nationals or on its territory. A declaration under this article may be withdrawn at any time. The provisions of this article shall be reviewed at the Review Conference convened in accordance with article 123, paragraph 1.'

[43] Vienna Convention on the Law of Treaties, (1969) 1155 U.N.T.S. 331, Art. 36(1): 'A right arises for a third state from a provision of a treaty if the parties to the treaty intend the provision to accord that right either to the third state, or to a group of states to which it belongs, or to all states, and the third state assents thereto. Its assent shall be presumed so long as the contrary is not indicated, unless the treaty otherwise provides.'

[44] 'U.S. Signs Treaty', n. 29 above.

[45] 'TPI: Les Etats-Unis Refusent la Proposition Suisse' *Le Temps* (Switzerland) (11 December 2000).

(e) A broader deference to 'responsible nations'

By the beginning of the November–December 2000 PrepCom, the United States had received sufficiently strong signals criticizing its March proposal that it did not pursue its original plans.[46] It recognized that an attempt to win acceptance of its proposal, or any near variant of it, would be unsuccessful. Consequently, it presented at the last available moment a two-part proposal that was appended to the proceedings of the session without any discussion. As a result of their lack of examination in the Working Group, no support for the proposal could be claimed outside the U.S., although at the same time it was not rejected. The apparent tactic was to keep a door open for a return to the proposal in future, while avoiding any outright rejection that would force the U.S. to acknowledge that its efforts could not lead to success. If head of delegation Ambassador David Scheffer intended to present President Clinton with an argument for signature, this strategy was probably the only one available. While U.S. signature would have been most likely following a concession to its proclaimed needs, it is clear that signature would be politically improbable following a clear rejection of their key proposal. This situation left the U.S. only with an ambiguous middle ground open to it, in which future options would not be prejudiced, if not assured, and signature could in principle be given without closing the door to any future administration's quest for exemption.

The proposal aims to gain 'responsible nations'—States that contribute to measures to enforce international peace and security—some special consideration from the ICC. It seeks to achieve this in two parts, one procedural and the other substantive. The procedural mechanism is to *require* what the Statute merely *permits*, by indicating in the Relationship Agreement that the Court shall exercise its discretion under Article 19(1) to determine admissibility,[47] and that it shall do so prior to seeking the surrender of a suspect,

---

[46] These criticisms included a joint EU statement delivered privately at the end of May 1999, stating that the proposal in its current form was 'unacceptable': (on file). In addition to the comment of UK Foreign Secretary Cook, n. 23 above, Canadian Foreign Minister Lloyd Axworthy stated bluntly that '. . . there has to be flexibility on the U.S. side. They have to adjust their sights now too and recognize that they are not going to get an exemption from this court. That's pretty clear. They've been told that': 'U.S. Resists War-Crimes Court as Canada Conforms', *New York Times* (22 July 2000), and a number of countries made clear their feelings when the ICC was discussed at the Sixth Committee in October 2000: France on behalf of the European Union ('The European Union Reiterates its Commitment to the Integrity of the Statute . . .', Statement of France on behalf of the European Union, 18 October 2000), and South Africa ('. . . we will not support any attempts that will seek to limit the jurisdictional scope of the International Criminal Court as contained in the Rome Statute', Statement in the Sixth Committee by the Representative of South Africa, 18 October 2000) (on file).

[47] ART. 19(1) reads: 'The Court shall satisfy itself that it has jurisdiction in any case brought before it. The Court may, on its own motion, determine the admissibility of a case in accordance with article 17.'

where that individual has acted outside his or her State of nationality.[48] In itself, this would afford the U.S. no comfort, as the Court would merely apply the criteria of 'unwillingness' and 'inability' set down in Article 17, and these criteria do not assure the U.S. of the deference it requires.[49] Thus the U.S. put forward the second, substantive part of the proposal, which indicates a broadening of the factors considered by the Court in determining admissibility to take account of the State's role in contributing to international peace and security.[50] While the exact terms of the substantive part of the proposal were left for possible future negotiations (which the Bush administration chose not to take up), the intent of the Clinton administration's proposal was to have the Court, before requesting surrender of a U.S. national, take into account the special responsibilities that the U.S. claims to have in relation to the international use of force.

The proposal itself appeared to carry little weight with delegates, and for several reasons. First, to make mandatory the discretionary power of the Court to determine admissibility under Article 19(1), even if under limited circumstances, appeared to be a matter more appropriate for amendment to the Statute than for inclusion in the Relationship Agreement. Secondly, the limited circumstances to which this provision would have applied (i.e. where a suspect acts outside his or her State of nationality), and the rationale offered (that it would 'encourage contributions by States to promote international peace and security') were not seen to justify the measure by Like Minded States. Countries that support the Court include major troop contributors like Australia, Canada, France, and the United Kingdom, and these have never expressed concerns about the operation of the Court interfering with the peace-keeping functions of their armed services. Moreover, the broad right of States to intervene before the Court and seek admissibility determinations is such that admissibility will ordinarily be settled before a surrender

---

[48] *Discussion paper proposed by the Coordinator*, U.N. Doc. PCNICC/2000/WGICC-UN/RT.1 (7 December 2000), Annex, 'Additional article':

In order to encourage contributions by States to promote international peace and security, and unless there has been a referral to the Court pursuant to Article 13(b) of the Statute, the United Nations and the Court agree that the Court shall determine on its own motion pursuant to Article 19(1) the admissibility of a case in accordance with Article 17 when there is a request for the surrender of a suspect who is charged in such case with a crime that occurred outside the territory of the suspect's State of nationality.

[49] One might argue that a mandatory pre-surrender determination of admissibility would provide clarity to States engaged in the international use of force. Such an argument neglects the fact that States will already be invited to seek deferral of ICC proceedings under Art. 18 (n. 18 above) and that proceedings related to Art. 18 will often involve or give rise to admissibility proceedings at the very outset of an investigation, which would ordinarily precede identification of an individual suspect and preparation of surrender request.

[50] 'Proposal submitted by the United States of America', U.N. Doc. PCNICC/2000/DP.1 (7 December 2000): 'The United States of America proposes for the consideration of the Preparatory Commission the development of factors for the Court that may be relevant for the investigation, prosecution and surrender of suspects, including the context within which an alleged crime has occurred and a State's contribution to international peace and security'.

request is prepared, making the provision unnecessary.[51] Finally, inviting the PrepCom to negotiate terms on which the Court would or would not defer to States' efforts regarding international peace and security would prove too contentious for timely resolution and threatened to draw the Court into an inherently politicized area of decision-making.

In addition to these difficulties, the U.S. administration had little to offer its negotiating partners in exchange for the concession they were asked to make. While it unexpectedly signed the Statute on 31 December 2000, no realistic prospect of ratification then appeared, with continuing deep hostility towards the ICC in the U.S. Congress; moreover, any promise of *ad hoc* support for the Court would have been premature before the ICC itself was in operation, and could not have bound a subsequent Administration. Conversely, a threat of sustained opposition to ratification was unlikely to prevent or seriously retard entry into force, given current momentum. This lack of bargaining power made the viability of the proposals all the more suspect.

4. THE U.S. UNDER THE BUSH ADMINISTRATION

That the final proposal of the Clinton administration was unlikely to be successful mattered less than the fact that the United States left the PrepCom process at the end 2000 with the groundwork in place for the incoming Bush administration to take up the policy of 'constructive engagement', had it so chosen. That the Bush administration chose instead to abandon the process, and that other governments have become comfortable going forward with entry into force and the process of establishing the institution even without the United States, have made any return to efforts for a negotiated 'fix' highly unlikely.

The initial stance of the Bush administration, over the early course of 2001, was one of withdrawal from the ICC-related PrepCom process and of slow stocktaking, as the administration worked to develop a policy distinct from its predecessor. The attacks directed against the United States on 11 September 2001 and the ensuring retaliation against Afghanistan suspended this process into the early months of 2002. As it became clearer, however, that the deposit of the sixtieth instrument of ratification and the entry into force of the Statute were a pending reality, increased statements of concern about the ICC began to issue from Washington. It soon became apparent that the Bush administration was planning to denounce the signature that the Clinton administration had given the Rome Statute on 31 December 2000.[52]

---

[51] See n. 49 above.

[52] James Bone and Richard Beeston, 'U.S. Rejects World Court for Fear of Partisan Lawsuits' *Times* (London) (30 March 2002); Elizabeth A. Neuffer, 'U.S. to Back Out of World Court Plan—Envoy: Bush team may "unsign" treaty' *Boston Globe* (29 March 2002).

The trigger for the U.S. 'unsigning' of the Statute was the simultaneous deposit of ten instruments of ratification at a special ceremony held at the United Nations on 11 April 2002.[53] This event—bringing the number of ratifications beyond the sixty needed—ensured that the Statute would enter into force on 1 July 2002. In response, on 6 May 2002 the U.S. delivered a letter to United Nations Secretary General Kofi Annan declaring that the United States 'does not intend to become a party to the treaty' and that consequently 'the United States has no legal obligations arising from its signature on 30 December 2000'.[54] Secretary of Defense Donald Rumsfeld asserted that the action 'effectively reverses the previous U.S. Government decision to become a signatory',[55] reflecting the unprecedented—and therefore controversial—U.S. reliance on Article 18 of the Vienna Convention on the Law of Treaties for authority to undo the obligation, incurred on signature, to respect the object and purpose of a treaty.[56] On the same day U.S. Under-Secretary of State Marc Grossman detailed a series of U.S. policy commitments related to international justice that attempted to frame the 'unsigning' as part of what purported to be an ongoing U.S. commitment to accountability for international crimes.[57]

Foreshadowing actions to follow, the U.S. in its policy statement declared that it would '[w]ork together with countries to avoid any disruptions caused by the Treaty, particularly those complications in U.S. military cooperation with friends and allies that are parties to the treaty'. A similar reference to possible agreements that would address U.S. concerns about the Court was made at the same time in a State Department *démarche* instructing U.S. embassies around the world to convey the policy position to their accrediting governments. This proved to be the opening salvo in a U.S. campaign to secure agreements to bar the surrender of U.S. nationals to the ICC under Article 98(2) of the Statute.[58]

---

[53] See Ch. IV, n. 30 above.

[54] Under Secretary of State for Arms Control and International Security, John R. Bolton, *International Criminal Court: Letter to UN Secretary General Kofi Annan* (6 May 2002), available online at http://www.state.gov/r/pa/prs/ps/2002/9968.htm (last visited 21 July 2002).

[55] *Secretary Rumsfeld Statement on the ICC Treaty*, n. 16 above.

[56] 'A State is obliged to refrain from acts which would defeat the object and purpose of a treaty when . . . (a) it has signed the treaty or has exchanged instruments constituting the treaty subject to ratification, acceptance or approval, until it shall have made its intention clear not to become a party to the treaty . . .' *Vienna Convention on the Law of Treaties*, (1969) 1155 U.N.T.S. 331, Art. 18. The European Union noted 'that this unilateral action may have undesirable consequences on multilateral treaty-making and generally on the rule of law in international relations': *Declaration by the EU on the position of the US towards the International Criminal Court* (13 May 2002), available on-line at http://www.ue2002.es/principal.asp?idioma-ingles (last visited 21 July 2002).

[57] *American Foreign Policy and the International Criminal Court*, n. 11 above. After rehearsing familiar criticisms of the 'unchecked' 'flawed' ICC, the statement promotes national accountability processes as a more appropriate alternative to the ICC. That such processes frequently fail, and that the ICC aims primarily to promote such processes, is not acknowledged.

[58] See Ch. VII, n. 65 above.

Such agreements were not, however, the United States' first choice as a vehicle for securing immunity from the ICC. While recognized by the Statute, and potentially enduring, they are limited to ICC requests directed to the countries that enter into them. Moreover, they do not ensure that the ICC will not commence an investigation or issue an indictment against a U.S. national, only that the Court will not insist on the individual's handover where an Article 98(2) agreement is in place; in Defense Department minds, this conjures the fear of international war crimes investigations directed against the actions of U.S. civilian and military officials. These shortcomings led the U.S. to put its initial energy after the May 6 policy announcement into a more ambitious strategy involving the Security Council.

After a false start with a Security Council resolution renewing the UN mission in East Timor,[59] the U.S. pushed for language in a resolution renewing the mandate of the UN mission in Bosnia-Herzegovina that would bar ICC action with respect to peacekeeping forces engaged there. The United States announced that it would veto the resolution unless its demand for an exemption from ICC jurisdiction were met. It subsequently did so. After two tense weeks and numerous government statements objecting to the U.S. initiative, a compromise resolution was agreed upon.[60]

Resolution 1244 of 12 July 2002 cites Article 16 of the Rome Statute (see pp. 81–2 above) and requests the ICC to refrain from commencing or proceeding with an investigation or prosecution of any case involving current or former officials or personnel from a contributing State that is not party to the Rome Statute, for a period of one year from 1 July 2002; it also expresses the intention of the Council to renew the resolution 'for as long as may be necessary'. However, the resolution did not give the United States the perpetual, self-renewing resolution for which it hoped, and rallying the necessary votes for a renewal is always uncertain. Because the resolution turns Article 16 to a use for which it was never intended, and because it can be read as implying that ICC investigations threaten international peace and security (when one of the Court's stated purposes, on the contrary, is to reinforce peace) it can only be deeply troubling for Rome Statute supporters. At the same time, the resolution offers the United States only a temporary and unstable form of exemption that can do little to satisfy the Defense and State Departments.

These limits to the 'cover' provided by resolution 1244 led the Bush administration to engage in an intensive effort to secure 'Article 98 agreements' with as many nations as possible. This proved easy with a non-State Party and

---

[59] 'U.S. Fails in U.N. to Exempt Peacekeepers From New Court' *New York Times* (18 May 2002).

[60] S.C. Res. 1422 (12 July 2002). See Judy Dempsey, 'Little Applause on Criminal Court Deal' *Financial Times* (15 July 2002); 'Europeans Give UN Court Deal Lukewarm Reception' *New York Times* (13 July 2002).

close U.S. ally like Israel, but has been more difficult with other countries. Romania agreed to such a text, under U.S. pressure related to its effort to join NATO, but subsequently appeared ambivalent about the decision when the EU expressed its disapproval. As efforts continued with countries from around the world, the prospects for the U.S. in this effort were less than clear, notwithstanding the threat to withhold U.S. military aid, as allowed by the American Servicemembers Protection Act, signed by President Bush on 2 August 2002.[61]

The aggressiveness of the Bush administration in seeking to shape the ICC in conformity with U.S. foreign policy interests does not mean that eventual U.S. cooperation with the ICC cannot be anticipated. Such cooperation can only realistically be expected, however, where contrary U.S. interests are not engaged, and where the ICC 'threat' to U.S. military action has been neutralized. Ratification of the Rome Statute by the United States, with the acceptance that this would entail of ICC oversight of military and civilian judicial processes, must be seen as a very dim prospect indeed.

5. THE ARGUMENT FOR U.S. SUPPORT

With the abandonment of the search for a full 'fix' for the United States on one hand, and its consistent rejection on the other—on the grounds that it would amount to a re-opening of the Statute or a reversal of the 'Nuremberg precedent'—the U.S. will, if it is ever to reconcile itself to the existence of the ICC, have to content itself with the fruits of its 'constructive engagement' strategy, which has resulted in a mosaic of provisions in the Statute, Rules, Elements of Crimes, and other PrepCom texts. These should leave the U.S. with a considerable degree of reassurance, even if exposure to the Court's jurisdiction (at least in principle, and narrowly) remains.

Such exposure to ICC jurisdiction is not incompatible with U.S. support for the Court, any more than it is for French, UK, or Senegalese support. The institutional interest of the Defense Department in preserving its latitude as U.S. foreign policy's enforcer of last resort in the post-Cold War environment makes its opposition to the ICC rational, from a certain 'realist' point of view. This is ultimately only one of several U.S. interests, however. If one accepts that the ICC is going to come into existence—as now one must—and in a

---

[61] Ian Traynor, 'East Europeans Torn on the Rack by International Court Row' *The Guardian* (17 August 2002). The American Servicemembers Protection Act bars U.S. cooperation with the ICC, and requires the cut-off of U.S. military assistance to countries that ratify the Rome Statute, unless the President waives this requirement 'in the national interest'. NATO members and major U.S. allies such as Israel are exempted from this restriction: American Servicemembers Protection Act of 2002, P.L. 107–206, signed into law on 2 August 2002.

form that leaves a degree of U.S. exposure to its jurisdiction, U.S. opposition to the Court becomes questionable. Such a stance would be difficult to maintain and could be argued to entail significant disadvantages for the U.S. by preventing participation in the Assembly of States Parties, even as an observer (to engage in oversight of the Court, influence the negotiation of a definition of the crime of aggression, and participate in the appointment of judges and other senior officials). Full U.S. opposition would, moreover, feed the claim that the U.S. was opposed to 'the rule of law' or to accountability for the worst violations of human rights.

The most compelling reason for rejecting an 'all or nothing' approach to the ICC is the likelihood of an eventual warming of U.S. relations with the ICC. For some State Department planners, eventual U.S. support, or at least, eventual U.S. ability to avail itself of the Court, must have a certain appeal. When the next Kosovo, East Timor, Rwanda, or Sierra Leone erupts on the international stage, the U.S. are unlikely to refuse to support accountability merely because the ICC is the only viable means of attaining it. Future *ad hoc* tribunals, already considered unlikely, will be even less likely with permanent Security Council members France and the United Kingdom as Parties to the Rome Statute, which offers a structure for accepting Security Council referrals without the cost of establishing new tribunals. Even were the U.S. to resist the temptation to acquiesce in a Security Council referral, and instead rely on its veto, *proprio motu* actions by the Prosecutor and State referrals might still arise. Where the crime was egregious and the public clamour for justice significant, it would surely be politically attractive for the U.S. to provide diplomatic or other support, rather than leave its allies to take credit for promoting accountability.

Other States involved in the process recognize the substantial reasons for eventual U.S. support for the Court. This does not mean that *bona fide* efforts will not be made to increase the 'comfort level' of the U.S. (particularly while supportive American voices remain in the minority); it is only that States see little reason to weaken a Court that the U.S. is unlikely to oppose and has a number of good reasons to support. The Bush administration's distance from the process only defers the question for another day.

6. CONCLUSION

While the long-term interest of the U.S. might dictate a stable order of law and good relations with its allies, it is unlikely that such appeals will move policy-makers for the foreseeable future. The result is a range of options from opposition, to simple neglect, to eventual *ad hoc* cooperation with the Court. It seems clear that ICC supporters have come to the conclusion that the the institution will be viable without the support of the global hegemon, and that, while U.S. engagement would be an asset, no reasonable price for winning its support has yet been put forward. The judgement to date has been that, while the ICC might be weaker without the United States' involvement, it enjoys sufficient support not to fall victim to the same fate as the League of Nations, and that the legitimacy the ICC gains through maintaining the integrity of the Statute compensates for the loss of U.S. backing. Whether the ICC will have the balance of legitimacy, durability, and effectiveness needed over the long term, and where the point lies at which the United States or the Like Minded group would put aside their efforts to win or to resist exemption respectively, remains to be seen.

At present the U.S. is bound up in more than a debate about the jurisdiction of the Court. It is caught up in a series of processes that will ultimately shape the U.S. role in the geopolitical environment of the twenty-first century. The respective values of multilateralism and unilateralism, of 'isolationism' and the support for an infrastructure of global governance, of 'soft power' and the role of the military, are all under debate, with a significant push from the U.S. response to the events of 11 September 2001. The U.S. stance towards the ICC is caught up in these debates, but this issue alone seems unlikely to be settled until the turbulence of early twenty-first century international relations and of the United States' role therein abates.

Part III

Conclusion: Systemic Change and International Justice

It becomes apparent from the studies in Part II above that the role of States in making key decisions affecting the credibility of international criminal law remains a central fact of the emerging system of international justice, and that this fact sits uneasily with any assertion that the international rule of law is gaining strength. The needs of justice will have to compete with other priorities in the decision-making of States. This is particularly visible in the area of cooperation and enforcement (Chapter VIII), although the tension between different functional regimes is also seen clearly in the area of immunities (Chapter VII). To a large extent, the consistent enforcement of international criminal law will ultimately depend on coherence in the practice of States acting individually and collectively, notably through the ICC Assembly of States Parties and the UN Security Council. Yet irregularity in the practice of both the latter bodies can confidently be predicted, given the State-centric and interest-driven decision-making built into each, and also given the flexible framework of both the Rome Statute and the UN Charter.

If, to the extent of this State-centred flexibility, the regular enforcement of international criminal law is undermined, may it nonetheless be said that the system is moving or may move in a direction likely to support more regular enforcement in the long term? The answer to this question depends on one's view of the impact of three major themes in recent debates, namely the end of the Cold War, the decline of sovereignty, and globalization. A bold view of each of these closely inter-related themes could support belief in the imminent emergence of a robust international criminal justice system. Nevertheless, and without attempting the extensive and necessarily cross-disciplinary discussion that a proper assessment would require, a more nuanced approach appears to be justified.

The end of the Cold War brought with it a change in the way that issues were articulated, given priority, and responded to at the international level. It has led to some attenuation of the link between territorial integrity and international stability, and has supported an increased willingness to consider intervention and the altering of borders.[1] More to the point, the collapse of

---

[1] J. Samuel Barkin, 'The Evolution of the Constitution of Sovereignty and the Emergence of Human Rights Norms' (1998) 27 *Millennium* 229, esp. 243–6.

the system of superpower confrontation has allowed human rights to take a more prominent place in the discourse and the practice of States and international organizations. The result is a cementing of human rights among the factors contributing to the international legitimacy (and particularly the recognition) of States. As a result, the international community and individual States will find it easier to justify intervening in the affairs of governments that abuse human rights, especially where the abuses are egregious.[2] The course and pace of development in international law and the action of international institutions have clearly been altered by this geopolitical change. The increasing prominence, expansion, and refinement of international criminal law, and the project of establishing an ICC (itself seldom opposed *per se* during its development, however divergent visions of the Court were) were also facilitated by this change.

At the same time, the importance of the Cold War's end as a matter of *legal* change should not be exaggerated. The conditions inherent in the post-War order (dividing prohibitions and their enforcement, norms and behaviour, and ultimately law and politics) have not themselves ceased to exist since 1989. Decisions in interpreting or applying the law, as well as action authorized through the Security Council, the Assembly of States Parties, or NATO, unilaterally or otherwise, will continue to depend significantly on the auto-interpretation of self-interested States and on their calculus of national strategic, economic, and political costs and benefits, even if the costs and benefits have altered in significant respects with the end of the Cold War. In particular, the Security Council will continue to be influenced in its Chapter VII practice by the national interests of its permanent members, largely free of outside review and imminent reform.[3] While the decline of East–West confrontation may have lessened tensions, allowed norms to be elaborated, and created a greater potential for consensus in some areas, the translation of these effects into regular enforcement is not a necessary consequence of any post-1989 'new world order'.[4] A convergence of interests (particularly among

---

[2] Barkin (1998) at 246–9 (limiting 'human rights' to civil and political rights).

[3] This is not to say that Security Council decision-making is completely anarchic. The permanent members cannot simply push their initiatives through. Even once united themselves they must secure the affirmative votes of 4 of the remaining members to make a majority. These members are drawn in accordance with a fixed quota from the different geographic regions, and come to the Council with their own national aims. The decisions of the Security Council must be perceived to be *bona fide*, *intra vires*, and legitimate to attract compliance: see Thomas M. Franck *Fairness in the International Legal and Institutional System* (The Hague: Academy for International Law, 1993), at 190–2. At the same time, the 'dominant role of the permanent five, the secrecy of the Council's procedures, the lack of a clearly delimited competence and the absence of what might be called a legal culture within the Council' must continue to raise doubts: Martti Koskenniemi, 'The Police in the Temple: Order, justice and the UN—A dialectical view' (1995) 6 E.J.I.L. 325, at 327; see also Barkin (1998), n. 1 above, at 250–1.

[4] Franck (1993), n. 3 above, at 189–221, initiates an examination of Security Council action to early 1993 by asking: 'Does the practice of the Security Council permit the conclusion that it has exercised its exceptional enforcement powers legitimately and fairly? Does it, for example, treat

the P5) sufficient to support the claim that a secure and regular practice with respect to collective security is emerging, would appear to be a remote prospect.[5] The enforcement of international law, like collective security, has been elusive for reasons other than East-West polarity alone.[6]

The same can be said of the 'decline of sovereignty' and globalization. The term 'globalization' may be 'the cliché of our times',[7] but the notion does provide a heading for much-needed analysis of the transformations that advances in communications, transportation, and other technologies are visiting upon the political and social realms. While globalization does have a certain power in framing analysis of undoubtedly real transformations in a number of areas (notably economic trade and production), the 'distinctive attributes of contemporary globalization . . . by no means simply prefigure the demise of the nation-state or even the erosion of state power'.[8] On the contrary, 'processes of globalization are closely associated with, although by no means the sole cause of, a transformation or reconstitution of the powers of the modern nation-state . . .', at least in developed States.[9] The better view is that the foreseeable future does not hold the realistic prospect of a significant replacement or realignment of the institution of sovereignty, at least in any

like cases alike?' The mention of 'like cases' highlights the congruity between Franck's treatment of 'legitimacy' and the notion of the rule of law (see n. 16 below). Franck detects the emergence of a principled approach to the use of Chapter VII in the Council's treatment of 'Governments demonstrably in gross violation of fundamental norms of international law' and 'especially egregious civil wars' (ibid., at 196), but his study is methodologically flawed in that he only examines cases where Chapter VII was invoked and/or a 'threat to the peace, breach of the peace, or act of aggression' specifically found. He does not consider those cases in which the Council failed to act, either because of the veto of a permanent member or because the issue was never taken up or did not proceed as far as a vote. His examination is therefore incapable of reliably answering the question that it poses.

[5] Moreover, even were it not, some would argue that the Security Council is structurally suited, at best, only to maintain a minimal and minimally fair degree of order, and not to pursue justice in a wider sense: Koskenniemi (1995), n. 3 above.

[6] Higgens makes the important points that '[a] . . . consequence [of the failure of the UN to put in place the collective security apparatus foreseen in the Charter] was that the United Nations decided that the absence of agreements under Article 43 [for standing military contribution arrangements] made impossible an obligatory call upon members to participate in military enforcement', and that the end of the Cold War has not made effective Art. 43 agreements more likely: see Rosalyn Higgens, 'Peace and Security: Achievements and failures' (1995) 6 E.J.I.L. 445, at 447, 451. Higgens goes on to remark, ibid., at 456, that '[b]y failing to go back to these possibilities at the end of the Cold War the Security Council has deliberately ensured that it will not have an effective enforcement capability, in which military action could be rapidly ordered, and perceived as being on behalf of, and participated in by, the UN membership as a whole'. Instead, 'enforcement will only take place when there is a perceived national interest in doing so on the part of the major military powers': ibid., at 459. See also Christoph Schreuer, 'The Waning of the Sovereign State: Towards a new paradigm for international law?' (1993) 4 E.J.I.L. 447, at 467.

[7] David Held *et al.*, *Global Transformations: Politics, economics and culture* (Cambridge: Polity, 1999), at 1; Held *et al.*, wisely point out, ibid., at 436, that 'no single coherent theory of globalization exists'.

[8] Ibid., at 436.

[9] Ibid.

sense relevant to the establishment of the preconditions for regular, impartial enforcement of international criminal law.[10] Bearing in mind the distinction between sovereignty and autonomy (pp. 58–62 above), it is much easier to assert a reduction in the latter than it is a decline in the former. A decline of sovereignty, in the sense of a loss of exclusive authority within State jurisdiction, would imply a corresponding increase in authority at some other level of the system. Of course, no cosmopolitan or supra-State institutional order can be said to be emergent at present,[11] even if international obligations increasingly condition sovereignty.[12]

The end of the Cold War and the process of globalization may not themselves establish on a *formal* level the preconditions necessary for the regular enforcement of international criminal law. Nonetheless, the effect of global communications on the growth of international civil society (particularly the media and human rights NGOs) and on an intensified interdependency between States has (noticeably since the Cold War's end) created a new 'legitimation environment' in which States are under increased pressure to justify their decisions and account for their conduct towards their own citizens.[13] If deep changes to the international system are not presently foreseeable, the question then arises whether these changes in the decision-making environment of States may, given the norms that have been elaborated and the systems that are being put in place, significantly heighten support for enforcement by increasing the pressure on decision-makers.[14] In other words, can the

[10] This assertion would, of course, have to be backed up with empirical research before it could be offered other than conditionally. As Thomson remarks, 'an assessment of the current and future prospects of sovereignty depends upon a theoretically coherent conception of sovereignty which is both consistent with history and amenable to empirical analysis': Janice E. Thomson, 'State Sovereignty in International Relations: Bridging the gap between theory and empirical research' (1995) 39 Int'l Studies Q. 213, at 213.

[11] Thomson (1995), n. 10 above, at 214 ('a shift from sovereignty to some other form of global political organization would entail one or more of the following: the loss of state's exclusive authority to recognize sovereignty; transfer of meta-political authority to nonstate actors or institutions; end of the state's monopoly on legitimate coercion; and deterritorialization of states' authority claims'), and 229 (expressing serious doubt that any such changes are endangering sovereignty); also Schreuer (1993), n. 6 above, at 448 ('International law has increased in volume, but has mostly remained a law that is applicable between States. Sovereignty . . . has been harnessed to some extent, but its core has remained intact'). See also Hedley Bull, *The Anarchical Society: A study of order in world politics* (London: Macmillan, 1977), at 248–56.

[12] Barkin (1998), n. 1 above, at 249, explicitly relates this to the ICC:

. . . the reappearance of war crimes tribunals in the 1990s . . . and the absence of any widespread contestation over the idea of an International Criminal Court . . . does not suggest a diminution of sovereignty any more than did the creation of the International Court of Justice earlier this century; both institutions are founded on, rather than being contestations of, the idea that the sovereign state is at the core of international politics . . . . states remain fully sovereign, but that full sovereignty is itself dependent on legitimate constitutionality.

[13] 'Reflexivity' in Giddens' discourse: Anthony Giddens, *The Consequences of Modernity* (Stanford, CA: Stanford U.P., 1990), at 36–45.

[14] Without drawing the connection to globalization and the increasing role of civil society, Schreuer (1993), n. 6 above, at 453, foresees the development of such a system:

. . . there is mounting evidence that the process of redistributing authoritative functions will continue and that the vertical element in a preponderantly horizontal order will continue to grow. The sovereign State is still the

current international system be said to be developing towards a 'culture of accountability' in a strong sense? Such a culture would be one of voluntary compliance or of voluntary cooperation on enforcement to at least the minimum level necessary to have the 'rule' or governance of law at all, and appears to be an indispensable precondition to the rule of law in the existing international system. While the extent to which the relevant pressure will lead to regular, impartial enforcement of international criminal law remains to be seen, and no attempt can be made to answer the question here, a few relevant remarks may be ventured.

First, the concepts of rule of law, accountability, and legality can be expected to form an increasingly entrenched part of international discourse as a standard of legitimacy, largely as a result of the impact of the ICC on national and international law, practice, and discourse. The strengths of the Rome Statute (its allocation to the Court of the competence to interpret the Statute and to decide whether reasonable grounds exist to believe that a crime has been committed in a given situation, whether a State is willing to proceed genuinely, and whether a State is cooperating adequately), the wide support for the Rome Statute, and the related amendments of national law (at pp. 92–3 and 155–9 above) ensure the basis of accountability discourse as a theme of national and international life. This is likely to have positive effects. The degree to which States feel compelled to adjust their law and practice, however, will depend ultimately on the number of States ratifying the Statute, the rigour with which the Court interprets and applies it, and the action of the Assembly of States Parties in response to any non-cooperation. The effect of the ICC, as magnified by the media and NGOs, is likely to have clear effects of increasing the prominence of rule of law discourse while remaining ultimately dependent on a convergence of interests and action on the part of States.

Secondly, a robust 'culture of accountability' would, however, ultimately necessitate a convergence of interests sufficient to lead to a sustained endorsement by at least a critical mass of States concerning the use of international coercive power, and ultimately the system for managing international peace and security and the use of force, with greater regularity than it has been used to present. From this it follows that the rule of law in international criminal law could emerge only as part of a more consistent treatment of peace and security matters by the international community. This means that the ultimate (not necessarily near-term) support of the United States, and with it that of the Security Council, is probably an essential condition of the ICC's

chief pillar of our international system, and there is no evidence that it is crumbling or is in danger of collapse. Rather, the static weight it has carried is gradually being shifted to other, for the time being, still lesser pillars. This process is gradual and irregular. It will proceed more rapidly in some regions than in others and it is likely to assume a variety of forms. The picture emerging from all this is still somewhat diffuse, but it is distinct enough to warrant a re-examination of a number of assumptions about international law to which we have become accustomed.'

ultimate success as a core and not a peripheral part of the system for regulating international life. Events will have to prove whether the influence of domestic and international pressures will be enough to persuade the P5 to deploy the system's action accordingly. Yet from this perspective, and despite improvements following the end of the Cold War, the deep entrenchment of a culture of accountability, with its implicit convergence of international values and interests, must at present appear a remote possibility.[15]

Thirdly, it should be noted that, in the pursuit of international as of national justice, legitimacy and the rule of law are not identical or interchangeable.[16] The rule of law promises clarity, order, and predictability, and by holding out a means of promoting fairness or justice, helps legitimate the State (at the domestic level). Yet fairness and governance, and not just the rule of law, similarly contribute to legitimacy.[17] Perceptions of legitimacy,

[15] In the early post-Cold War years, Thomas Franck wrote, in Franck (1993), n. 3 above, at 221: 'As the United Nations system increasingly comes to operate as it was intended, the rule of law imposed on the political process by the Charter will assume increasing importance'. This shows some of the euphoria characteristic of its time. It is has been apparent for some time that it is at best unproven that the UN system will in future 'operate as it was intended', at least so far as the role of the Security Council and the collective security function of the Organization is concerned: see Higgens (1995), n. 6 above, at 456 ('[f]or all the rhetoric at the end of the Gulf War that the UN would now be able to act as it was meant to under the Charter, and enforce the peace, it is clearly not so'). At the same time, Franck's assertion that 'the rule of law imposed on the political process by the Charter will assume increasing importance' is less implausible. The end of the Cold War has taken the force out of arguments formerly used for bypassing the system, and expectations of accountability have commensurately risen, raising the pressure on the Security Council to take action effectively and on a consistent basis. The issue of accountability, anchored in the activity of the ICC, will undoubtedly be one factor influencing pressures directed at the Council. Such developments are informal rather than legal or structural, however: see n. 6 above.

[16] David Beetham, *The Legitimation of Power* (London: Macmillan, 1991), at 68–9 ('. . . appeal to the law can never provide more than a primary, and therefore provisional, ground for legitimacy. . . . rules cannot justify themselves simply by being rules, but require justification by reference to considerations which lie beyond them'); also Dencho Georgiev, 'Politics or Rule of Law: Deconstruction and legitimacy in international law' (1993) 4 E.J.I.L. 1, at 12–13. Thomas Franck, in his extensive considerations of legitimacy and fairness in international legal studies, does not treat the concept of the rule of law: *The Power of Legitimacy Among Nations* (New York: Oxford U.P. 1990), and (1993), n. 3 above. His four-pronged concept of legitimacy largely overlaps with it, however, as 'determinacy' (specificity of norms), 'coherence' (treating like cases alike and making decisions not capriciously but on the basis of generally recognized principles of differentiation), and 'adherence' (the 'vertical nexus between a single primary rule of obligation . . . and a pyramid of secondary rules about how the community makes, interprets and applies such rules') all overlap with accepted conceptions of the rule of law (Chapter III, n. 4 above); only 'symbolic validation' (symbols, pedigrees, and rituals forming part of 'the anthropology of law') is outside its ambit: Franck (1993), n. 3 above, at 48–61. See Franck (1990), above in this n., at 49–194, for a full discussion. Rather than follow Franck by in effect restricting legitimacy to formal criteria largely congruent with the rule of law, a broader approach to explaining compliance is adopted in the text above.

[17] Franck considers fairness and legitimacy to be distinct: Franck (1993), n. 3 above, at 43. Others treat determinacy, non-retroactivity, and other principles normally clustered under the rule of law as 'fairness principles': Andrew Ashworth, *Principles of Criminal Law* (Oxford: Clarendon, 1991), at 59ff. Distinct or not, the relevant point here is that both fairness and the rule of law contribute to the legitimacy of laws and a legal system. Governance as a factor in

and with them compliance, are also affected by the use or threat of coercion and the individual interests of legal subjects.[18] It follows that a formalistic approach to the rule of law (or 'legitimacy', in Franck's formulation) is incapable of explaining compliance in an adequate way, as it fails to take into account the full range of contributing factors.

Fourthly, it follows that a full understanding of the preconditions for legitimacy and compliance would involve a wide-ranging and necessarily interdisciplinary inquiry. Future work aimed at devising viable approaches to the enormous array of problems facing the field of international justice, as it moves into its 'practical' phase, should therefore pursue questions concerning compliance from the perspective of 'real world' pressures on the making, interpretation, and application of international law. Such work would ideally profit from an increasingly systematic interaction between international law and related disciplines such as political science, international relations, history, and institutional sociology. Legitimacy in international law may primarily be the intersubjective understanding of States, but its legitimacy also depends on the perceptions of all those who contribute to the process of opinion- and will-formation on the part of States. Moreover, the decision-making procedures of differently situated countries are permeable to different degrees and in different ways, varying in their level of susceptibility to media, NGO, economic, political, and strategic pressures, and effective work on deepening the entrenchment of international justice in the international system would have to take this into account.[19] Furthermore, future work must begin from the premise that our understanding of the interrelationship of peace and justice is at a relatively early stage. While prosecution rose in the last decade of the twentieth century to find its place in the 'tool kit' of those engaged in maintaining or restoring peace, its utility, cost-effectiveness, and contextual limits are not well understood or widely agreed upon. It is

---

legitimation refers to the fact that not all rules whereby positions of power are filled are of equal legitimacy. The extent to which laws and the legal system are perceived as legitimate by those to whom the law is addressed will be affected by the practices and institutional arrangements pertaining to how laws are proposed, debated, passed, and applied, as well as to how disputes about them are adjudicated or otherwise resolved: both Beetham, n. 16 above, and Jürgen Habermas, 'On the Idea of the Rule of Law' (Kenneth Baynes, trans.), in Sterling M. McMurrin, ed., *The Tanner Lectures on Human Values* (vol. VIII) (Cambridge, Mass. Cambridge U.P., 1988) focusing on national legal process, have insisted upon the importance of democratic participation in law-making.

[18] Beetham (1991), n. 16 above, at 27.

[19] Thus, any account of State behaviour and decision-making in this area would have to consider internal as well as external pressures in a manner similar to that increasingly pursued by political scientists like Fred Halliday, *Rethinking International Relations* (London: Macmillan, 1994) and Thomson (1995), n. 10 above; '. . . factors internal to States will play an increasingly important role in determining international society's "shared conceptual universe" and, therefore, how States and other actors at the international level behave': Michael Byers, *Custom, Power and the Power of Rules: International relations and customary international law* (Cambridge: Cambridge U.P., 1999), at 220.

probable that less should be made of the divide assumed in the accountability literature between international 'law' and 'politics'; it is also likely that international peace and security, and the value of flexibility needed to address them, have not been given due priority.[20] In any event, much more work, and of greater scope, remains to be done if international justice is to attain firm roots and achieve its potential in the present world order. The early jurisprudence of the ICC will provide one opportunity to begin proposing approaches to the outstanding problems.

Far from attempting to break ground in the broader framework of studies just outlined, the present work has merely aimed to show a few of the key difficulties facing international criminal law, a field that has grown enormously in recent years. The legal field of international criminal law is part of the broader, emerging field of international justice which, as in the other quintessentially contemporary fields of trade and the environment, encompasses not just legal but institutional, social, and political dimensions that bear critically on the manner in which and the extent to which international law can become entrenched in the 'real world' of State practice. The key difficulties treated in this work were selected for their ability to illustrate the main points at which sovereignty, or the State-centred character of the international system, stands between doctrines of international criminal law and their (reasonably) regular enforcement. In a very real sense, the idenification of the problems undertaken by this work merely opens the door to the next, more challenging phase, in which consensus on the legal solutions and political commitment to the regime of international justice will have to be secured in practice.

---

[20] The search for a pure international rule of law might, from this perspective, be viewed in part as 'yet another reformulation of the liberal impulse to escape politics', in which case it and the international redistribution of power it would require (but seldom admits) would have to be recognized as part of an ultimately political project: Martti Koskenniemi, 'The Politics of International Law' (1990) 1 E.J.I.L. 4, at 6, 31.

Sources

A. INTERNATIONAL INSTRUMENTS, INCLUDING RESOLUTIONS AND DECLARATIONS OF INTER-GOVERNMENTAL ORGANIZATIONS[1]

African Charter on Human and Peoples' Rights, 27 June 1981, O.A.U. Doc. CAB/LEG/67/3 Rev.5, 21 I.L.M. 59.

Agreement between the Parties to the North Atlantic Treaty Regarding the Status of their Forces (19 June 1951), (1953) Canada T.S. No. 13.

Agreement between the United Nations and the Government of Sierra Leone on the establishment of a Special Court for Sierra Leone, 16 January 2002 (available on-line at 'http://www.sierra-leone.org/specialcourtstatute.html').

Agreement for the Prosecution and Punishment of Major War Criminals of the European Axis, 8 August 1945, 82 U.N.T.S. 279.

Allied Control Council Law No. 10, Punishment of persons guilty of war crimes, crimes against peace and against humanity, 20 December 1945, 3 *Official Gazette of the Control Council for Germany* (31 January 1946) *reprinted in* Bassiouni (1992) 590.

American Convention on Human Rights, 22 November 1969, O.A.S.T.S. 36, O.A.S. Off. Rec. OEA/Ser.L/V/II.23, doc.21, rev.6, (1970) 9 I.L.M. 673.

Charter of the International Military Tribunal for the Far East, 19 January 1946, T.I.A.S. 1589, established by the *Proclamation by the Supreme Commander for the Allied Powers*, Tokyo (19 January 1946), *reprinted in* Bassiouni (1992) 604, 606.

Charter of the United Nations, 26 June 1945, 1 U.N.T.S. xvi.

Convention Against Torture and Other Cruel, Inhuman or Degrading Treatment or Punishment, 10 December 1984, 1465 U.N.T.S. 85, 23 I.L.M. 1027.

Convention for the suppression of unlawful acts against the safety of civil aviation, 23 September 1971, 974 U.N.T.S. 177.

Convention for the Suppression of Unlawful Seizure of Aircraft, 16 December 1970, 860 U.N.T.S. 105.

Convention on Prohibitions and Restrictions on the Use of Certain Conventional Weapons Which May Be Deemed to Be Excessively Injurious or to Have Indiscriminate Effects, 10 October 1980, 1342 U.N.T.S. 137, 19 I.L.M. 1523.

Convention on Special Missions, 8 December 1969, 1400 U.N.T.S. 231, 9 I.L.M. 127.

Convention on the non-applicability of statutory limitations to war crimes and crimes against humanity, 26 November 1968, 754 U.N.T.S. 73, (1969) 8 I.L.M. 68.

Convention on the Prevention and Punishment of the Crime of Genocide, (9 December 1948), 78 U.N.T.S. 277.

Convention on the Law of the Sea, 10 December 1982, 516 U.N.T.S. 205.

Convention Respecting the Laws and Customs of War on Land, 18 October 1907, 1 Bevans 631.

Convention with Respect to the Laws and Customs of War on Land, 29 July 1899, 1 Bevans 247.

---

[1] Not all cited resolutions of the Security Council and the General Assembly are listed.

European Convention for the Protection of Human Rights and Fundamental Freedoms, 4 November 1950, 213 U.N.T.S. 221, E.T.S. 5.

European Convention on the Suppression of Terrorism, 27 January 1977, 1137 U.N.T.S. 93, 90 E.T.S. 3.

Final Act of the United Nations Diplomatic Conference of Plenipotentiaries on the Establishment of an International Criminal Court, 17 July 1998, U.N. Doc. A/Conf.183/10.

Geneva Convention for the Amelioration of the Condition of the Wounded and Sick in Armed Forces in the Field, 12 August 1949, 75 U.N.T.S. 31.

Geneva Convention for the Amelioration of the Condition of the Wounded, Sick and Shipwrecked Members of the Armed Forces at Sea, 12 August 1949, 75 U.N.T.S. 85.

Geneva Convention Relative to the Treatment of Prisoners of War, 12 August 1949, 75 U.N.T.S. 135.

Geneva Convention Relative to the Protection of Civilian Persons in Time of War, 12 August 1949, 75 U.N.T.S. 287.

Inter-American Convention to Prevent and Punish Torture, 9 December 1985, P.A.U.S.T. 67, 25 I.L.M. 519.

International Convention Against the Taking of Hostages, 17 December 1979, Annex to G.A. Res. 34/146, U.N. Doc. A/34/46, G.A.O.R., 34th Sess., Supp. No. 46 at 245, (1979) 18 I.L.M. 1456.

International convention for the suppression of the financing of terrorism, adopted by G.A. Res. 54/109 (9 December 1999).

International convention for the suppression of terrorist bombings, adopted by G.A. Res. 52/164 (15 December 1997).

International Convention on the Suppression and Punishment of the Crime of Apartheid, 30 November 1973, 1015 U.N.T.S. 243.

International Covenant of Civil and Political Rights, 16 December 1966, 999 U.N.T.S. 171.

Principles of international cooperation in the detection, arrest, extradition and punishment of persons guilty of war crimes and crimes against humanity, G.A. Res. 3074 (XXVIII) (3 December 1973).

Protocol Additional to the Geneva Conventions of 12 August 1949, and Relating to the Protection of Victims of International Armed Conflicts, 8 June 1977, 1125 U.N.T.S. 3.

Protocol Additional to the Geneva Conventions of 12 August 1949, and Relating to the Protection of Victims of Non-International Armed Conflicts, 12 December 1977, 1125 U.N.T.S. 609.

Regulation No. 2000/15 on the establishment of panels with exclusive jurisdiction over serious criminal offences, U.N. Doc. UNTAET/REG/2000/15 (6 June 2000).

Regulation No. 2000/16 on the organization of the Public Prosecution Service in East Timor, U.N. Doc. UNTAET/REG/2000/16 (6 June 2000).

Rome Statute of the International Criminal Court, 17 July 1998, U.N. Doc. A/Conf.183/9, as corrected by the procés-verbaux of 10 November 1998 and 12 July 1999.

Rules of Procedure and Evidence (ICTY Doc. No. IT/32/Rev.18) (14 July 2000).

Statute of the International Criminal Tribunal for the Prosecution of Persons Responsible for Genocide and Other Serious Violations of International Humanitarian Law Committed in the Territory of Rwanda and Rwandan Citizens Responsible for

Genocide and Other Such Violations Committed in the Territory of Neighbouring States, between 1 January 1994 and 31 December 1994, 8 November 1994, U.N. Doc. S/Res/955 (1994), Annex.

Statute of the International Tribunal for the Prosecution of Persons Responsible for Serious Violations of International Humanitarian Law Committed in the Territory of the Former Yugoslavia since 1991, 25 May 1993, U.N. Doc. S/Res/827 (1993), Annex.

Universal Declaration of Human Rights, G.A. Res. 217A (III) (10 December 1948), U.N. Doc. A/810.

Vienna Convention on Diplomatic Relations (18 April 1961), 500 U.N.T.S. 95.

Vienna Convention on the Law of Treaties, (1969) 1155 U.N.T.S. 331.

Vienna Declaration and Programme of Action, U.N. Doc. A/Conf.157/23 (12 July 1993).

B. NATIONAL LAWS AND LEGISLATIVE BILLS

Canada, *Crimes Against Humanity and War Crimes Act*, Statutes of Canada 2000, c.24; *Criminal Code*, R.S. 1985, c.C–46.

Cambodia, *Law on the establishment of extraordinary chambers in the courts of Cambodia for the prosecution of crimes committed during the period of Democratic Campuchea* (available online at 'http://go.to/CambodiaToday').

Belgium, *Loi relative à la répression des violations graves de droit international humanitaire* (10 February 1999), (23 March 1999) *Moniteur belge*, s. 7.

Finland, *Act on the implementation of the provisions of a legislative nature of the Rome Statute of the International Criminal Court and on the application of the Statute*, No. 1284/2000 (28 December 2000), available on-line at 'http://www.legal.coe.int/criminal/icc/Default.asp?fd=docs&fn=Docs.htm'.

France, *Loi constitutionelle nr. 99–568 du 8 juillet 1999*, (9 juillet 1999) *Journal Officiel de la République française* (lois et décrets), p. 10175.

New Zealand, *International Crimes and International Criminal Court Act 2000*, 1 October 2000.

Norway, *Act No. 65 of 15 June 2001 relating to the implementation of the Statute of the International Criminal Court of 17 July 1998 (the Rome Statute) in Norwegian law*, available on-line at 'http://www.legal.coe.int/criminal/icc/Default.asp?fd=docs&fn=Docs.htm'.

——*General Civil Penal Code*, Pt. 1, ch. 1, s.12(4).

Sweden, *Penal Code*, ch. 2, s. 3(7).

South Africa, *International Criminal Court Bill*, 2001 Bill No. 42, online at http://www.parliament.gov.za/bills/2001/b42–01.pdf.

United Kingdom, *International Criminal Court Act 2001*, Royal Assent 11 May 2001.

United States, *Destruction of Aircraft or Aircraft Facilities*, 18 U.S.C. §32; *Torture*, 18 U.S.C. §2340; *Genocide*, 18 U.S.C.A. §1091; *War Crimes*, 18 U.S.C.A. §2441.

C. DECISIONS OF NATIONAL AND
INTERNATIONAL COURTS AND TRIBUNALS

Application of the Convention on the prevention and punishment of the crime of genocide (Bosnia and Herzegovina v. *Yugoslavia (Serbia and Montenegro)), Further Requests for the Indication of Provisional Measures, Order of 13 September 1993,* (1993) I.C.J. Rep. 325.

Arrest Warrant of 11 April 2000 (Democratic Republic of the Congo v. *Belgium), Judgment,* 14 February 2002.

Attorney-General of the Government of Israel v. *Adolph Eichmann,* (12 Dec. 1961) 36 I.L.R. 18 (Isr. Dist. Ct.—Jerusalem), *aff'd* (27 May 1962) 36 I.L.R. 277 (Isr. Sup. Ct.).

Barayagwiza v. *Prosecutor, Decision (Prosecutor's Request for Review or Reconsideration)* (ICTR Case No. 97–19-AR72) (31 March 2000) (Appeals Chamber).

The Barcelona Traction, Light and Power Company, Limited (Belgium v. *Spain) (Second phase), Judgment (5 February 1970),* (1970) I.C.J. Rep. 4.

Demjanjuk v. *Petrovsky,* 776 F.2d 571, 582 (6th Cir. 1985), *cert. denied,* 475 U.S. 1016 (1986).

Hugo Leonardo et al., Rep. No. 29/92, Cases no. 10.029 *et al.,* (1992–1993) Ann. Rep. Inter-Am. Comm'n H.R. 154, O.A.S. Doc. No. OEA/Ser.L/V/II.83, doc. 14, corr.1 (12 March 1993).

In re List (Hostage Case), (1946–1949) 11 Trials of War Criminals 757 (U.S. Mil. Trib.—Nuremberg, 1948).

Ministère Public et François Diouf contre Hissene Habré, (Arrêt no. 135 du 04–07–2000) (Cour d'Appel de Dakar, Senegal).

Prosecutor v. *Barayagwiza, Decision on Review and/or Reconsideration* (ICTR Case No. 97–19-AR72) (14 September 2000) (Appeals Chamber).

Prosecutor v. *Furundzija, Judgment* (ICTY Case No. IT–95–17/1) (10 December 1998).

Prosecutor v. *Jean Kambanda, Judgment and Sentence* (ICTR Case No. 97–23-S) (4 September 1998).

Prosecutor v. *Milosevic et al., Indictment* (ICTY Case No. IT–99–37) (24 May 1999).

Prosecutor v. *Dusko Tadic a.k.a. 'Dule', Decision on the Defence Motion for Interlocutory Appeal on Jurisdiction* (ICTY Case No. IT–94-I) (2 October 1995) (Appeals Chamber).

Prosecutor v. *Tihomir Blaskic, Judgement on the Request of the Republic of Croatia for Review of the Decision of Trial Chamber II of 18 July 1997* (ICTY Case No. IT–95–14) (29 October 1997) (Appeals Chamber).

R. v. *Bow Street Metropolitan Stipendiary Magistrate and others,* ex parte *Pinochet Ugarte,* [1998] 4 All E.R. 897, [1998] 3 W.L.R. 1456 (H.L.).

R. v. *Bow Street Metropolitan Stipendiary Magistrate and others,* ex parte *Pinochet Ugarte (Amnesty International and others intervening)* (No. 2), [1999] 1 All E.R. 577, [1999] 2 W.L.R. 272 (H.L.).

R. v. *Bow Street Metropolitan Stipendiary Magistrate and others,* ex parte *Pinochet Ugarte (Amnesty International and others intervening)* (No. 3), [1999] 2 All E.R. 97 (H.L.).

The Steamship Lotus (France v. *Turkey),* (1927) P.C.I.J. Ser. A, No. 10.

Tachiona et al. v. *Mugabe et al.*, Decision and Order, 31 October 2001 (00 Civ. 6666 [VM], unreported) (U.S. Dist. Ct., S.D.N.Y.).

Traité portant statut de la Cour pénale internationale (22 January 1999), Decision 98-408 DC (Conseil Constitutionnel, France).

United States diplomatic and consular staff in Tehran (United States of America v. *Iran), Judgment of 24 May 1980*, (1980) I.C.J. Reports 3.

United States v. *Calley*, (1973) 46 C.M.R. 1131, *aff'd* (1973) 22 U.S.C.M.A. 534, 48 C.M.R.

Valasquez Rodriguez Case, Judgment, 29 July 1988 (1988) Ann. Rep. Inter-Am. Courtt H.R., Appendix VI, at 35, OAS Doc. No. OAS/Ser.L/V/III.19, doc. 13 (31 August 1988).

D. BOOKS, JOURNAL ARTICLES, NON-GOVERNMENTAL REPORTS

Georges Abi-Saab, 'The Uses of Article 19' (1999) 10 E.J.I.L. 339.

Paul Ames, 'Rwandan nuns, man lose appeals' (9 January 2002) Associated Press.

Amnesty International, *Universal Jurisdiction: The duty of states to enact and implement legislation* (AI Index No. IOR 53/002/2001) (London: AI, 2001).

——*Establishing a just, fair and effective international criminal court* (AI Index No. IOR 40/05/94) (London: AI, 1994).

——*Fair trials manual* (AI Index POL 30/02/98) (AI: London, 1998).

——*The International Criminal Court: Fundamental principles concerning the elements of genocide* (AI Index: IOR 40/01/99) (London: AI, 1999).

——*The International Criminal Court: Making the right choices, Part III* (AI Index IOR 40/013/97) (London: AI, 1997).

——*International criminal tribunals: Handbook for government cooperation* (AI Index: IOR 40/07/96) (London: AI, 1996).

Andrew Ashworth, *Principles of criminal law* (Oxford: Clarendon, 1991).

Kelly Dawn Askin, *War crimes against women: Prosecution in international war crimes tribunals* (The Hague: Kluwer, 1997).

J. Craig Barker, *The Abuse of diplomatic privileges and immunities: A Necessary evil?* (Aldershot: Dartmouth, 1996).

——'The Future of former Head of State immunity after *Ex parte Pinochet*' (1999) 48 I.C.L.Q. 937.

J. Samuel Barkin, 'The Evolution of the constitution of sovereignty and the emergence of human rights norms' (1998) 27 Millennium 229.

Gary Jonathan Bass, *Stay the hand of vengeance: The Politics of war crimes tribunals* (Princeton: Princeton U.P., 2000).

Peter Evans Bass, 'Ex-Head of State immunity: A Proposed statutory tool of foreign policy' (1987) 97 Yale L.J. 299.

M.C. Bassiouni, *Crimes against humanity under international law* (Dordrecht: Martinus Nijhoff, 1992).

——*Crimes against humanity in international criminal law*, 2d ed. (The Hague: Kluwer, 1999) ['Bassiouni (1999a)'].

——*International criminal law: A Draft international criminal code* (Alphen aan den Rijn, The Netherlands: Sijthoff & Noordhoff, 1980).

M.C. Bassiouni, *International criminal law conventions and their penal provisions* (Irvington-on-Hudson, NY: Transnational, 1997).

——ed., *The International Criminal Court: Observations and issues before the 1997–98 Preparatory Committee; and administrative and financial implications* (1997) 13 Nouvelles Études Pénales.

——ed., *International criminal law* (3 vols.) (Dobbs Ferry, NY: Transnational, 1986).

——ed., *International Criminal Law*, 2d ed., (3 vols.) (Ardsley, NY: Transnational, 1999) ['Bassiouni (1999b)'].

——ed., *The Statute of the International Criminal Court: A Documentary History* (Ardsley, NY: Transnational, 1998).

——& Peter Manikas, *The Law of the International Criminal Tribunal for the Former Yugoslavia* (Irvington-On-Hudson, NY: Transnational, 1996).

——& Madeline H. Morris, eds., *Accountability for international crimes and serious violations of fundamental human rights* (1996) 59 L. & Contemp. Probs.

——& Ekkehart Müller-Rappard, eds., *European inter-State cooperation in criminal matters: The Council of Europe's legal instruments* (Dordrecht: Martinus Nijhoff, 1993).

——& Edward M. Wise, *Aut dedere aut judicare: The Duty to extradite or prosecute in international law* (Dordrecht: Martinus Nijhoff, 1995).

David Beetham, *The Legitimation of power* (London: MacMillan, 1991).

Rudolf Bernhardt, ed., *Encyclopedia of Public International Law*, 2d ed. (Amsterdam: Elsevier, 1997).

R. Bhattacharyya, 'Establishing a Rule-of-Law International Criminal Justice System' (1996) 31 Texas Int'l L.J. 57.

Derek William Bowett, 'Crimes of state and the 1996 Report of the International Law Commission on State Responsibility' (1998) 9 E.J.I.L. 163.

A.C. Brackman, *The Other Nuremberg: The Untold story of the Tokyo war crimes trials* (London: Collins, 1989).

Jürgen Bröhmer, *State immunity and the violation of human rights* (The Hague: Martinus Nijhoff, 1997).

Bruce Broomhall, Claus Kress & Flavia Lattanzi, eds., *Constitutional issues, cooperation and enforcement*, Vol. 2 of *The ICC and Domestic Legal Orders* (Nomos, forthcoming 2003).

Ian Brownlie, *International law and the use of force by States* (Oxford: Clarendon, 1963).

——*Principles of public international law*, 5th ed. (Oxford: Clarendon, 1998) ['Brownlie (1998a)'].

——*The Rule of law in international affairs: International law at the fiftieth anniversary of the United Nations* (The Hague: Martinus Nijhoff, 1998).

——*System of the law of nations: State responsibility, Part I* (Oxford: Clarendon, 1983).

——ed., *Basic documents in international law* (4th ed.) (Oxford: Clarendon, 1995).

Thomas Buergenthal, 'The United Nations Truth Commission for El Salvador' (1994) 27 Vanderbilt J. Transnat'l L. 497.

Hedley Bull, *The Anarchical society: A Study of order in world politics* (London: Macmillan, 1977).

Michael Byers, *Custom, power and the power of rules: International relations and customary international law* (Cambridge: Cambridge U.P., 1999).

Thomas Carothers, 'The Rule of law revival' (1998) 77 Foreign Affairs 95.

Antonio Cassese, *International law in a divided world* (Oxford: Clarendon, 1986).

—— 'On the current trends towards criminal prosecution and punishment of breaches of international humanitarian law' (1998) 9 E.J.I.L. 2.

—— 'The Statute of the International Criminal Court: Some preliminary reflections' (1999) 10 E.J.I.L. 144.

—— *Violence and law in the modern age* (Princeton, NJ: Princeton U.P., 1988).

A. Chayes & A.H. Chayes, *The New sovereignty: Compliance with international regulatory agreements* (Cambridge, MA: Harvard U.P., 1995).

Roger S. Clark, 'Countering transnational and international crime: Defining the agenda', in Peter J. Cullen & William C. Gilmore, eds., *Crime sans frontiers: International and European legal approaches* (Hume Papers on Public Policy, Vol. 6, Nos. 1 & 2) (Edinburgh: Edinburgh University Press, 1998) 20.

—— 'The Development of international criminal law', paper presented at the conference 'Just Peace? Peace making and peace building in the new millennium', Massey University, Auckland, New Zealand, 24–28 April 2000 (unpublished).

—— 'The Proposed International Criminal Court: Its establishment and its relationship with the United Nations' (1997) 8 Crim. L. Forum 1.

William M. Cohen, 'Principles for establishment of a rule of law criminal justice system' (1993) 23 Georgia J. Int'l & Comp. L. 269.

Peter J. Cullen & William C. Gilmore, eds., *Crime sans frontiers: International and European legal approaches* (Hume Papers on Public Policy, Vol. 6, Nos. 1 & 2) (Edinburgh: Edinburgh University Press, 1998).

Eileen Denza, *Diplomatic law: A Commentary on the Vienna Convention on Diplomatic Relations*, 2d ed. (Oxford: Clarendon, 1998).

—— '*Ex parte Pinochet*: Lacuna or leap?' (1999) 48 I.C.L.Q. 949.

Yoram Dinstein, *War, aggression and self-defence* (Cambridge: Grotius, 1988).

—— & M. Tabory, ed., *War crimes in international law* (The Hague: Martinus Nijhoff, 1996).

Nicholas R. Doman, 'Aftermath of Nuremberg: The Trial of Klaus Barbie' (1989) 60 Colo. L. Rev. 449.

Ronald Dworkin, *Law's empire* (Cambridge, MA: Belknap, 1986).

—— ed., *The Philosophy of law* (Oxford: Oxford U.P., 1977).

Bardo Fassbender, 'The United Nations Charter as a constitution of the international community' (1998) 36 Columbia J. Transnat'l L. 529.

John Finnis, *Natural law and natural rights* (Oxford: Clarendon, 1980).

M.R. Fowler & J.M. Bunck, *Law, power and the sovereign State: The Evolution and the application of the concept of sovereignty* (University Park, PA: Pennsylvania State University Press, 1995).

Hazel Fox, 'The Pinochet Case No.3' (1999) 48 I.C.L.Q. 687.

Thomas M. Franck, *Fairness in the international legal and institutional system* (General Course on Public International Law) (Offprint from *Recueil des cours*, Vol. 240 [1993-III]) (The Hague: Academy for International Law, 1993).

—— *The Power of legitimacy among nations* (New York: Oxford U.P., 1990).

Alton Frye, ed., *Toward an International Criminal Court? Three options presented as presidential speeches* (New York: Council on Foreign Relations, 1999).

Lon L. Fuller, *The Morality of Law* (New Haven: Yale University Press, 1964).

——'Positivism and fidelity to law: A Reply to Professor Hart' (1958) 71 Harvard L. Rev. 630.

Giorgio Gaja, 'Should all references to international crimes disappear from the ILC Draft Articles on State Responsibility?' (1999) 10 E.J.I.L. 365.

Robert P. George, ed., *Natural law theory: Contemporary essays* (Oxford: Clarendon, 1992).

Dencho Georgiev, 'Politics or rule of law: Deconstruction and legitimacy in international law' (1993) 4 E.J.I.L. 1.

H.H. Gerth & C. Wright Mills, eds., *From Max Weber: Essays in sociology* (New York: Oxford U.P., 1946).

Anthony Giddens, *The Consequences of modernity* (Stanford, CA: Stanford U.P., 1990).

——*The Nation-State and violence (A Contemporary critique of historical materialism,* Vol. II) (Berkeley: U. of California P., 1987).

George Ginsburgs & V.N. Kudriavtsev, eds., *The Nuremberg trial and international law* (Dordrecht: Martinus Nijhoff, 1990).

Silvia A. Fernández de Gurmendi, 'The Working Group on Aggression at the Preparatory Commission for the International Criminal Court' (2002) 25 Fordham Int'l L.J. 589.

Jürgen Habermas (William Rehg, trans.), *Between facts and norms: Contributions to a discourse theory of law and democracy* (Cambridge, MA: MIT, 1998).

——(Kenneth Baynes, trans.), *Law and morality*, in Sterling M. McMurrin, ed., *The Tanner Lectures on Human Values* (Vol. VIII) (Cambridge, MA: Cambridge U.P., 1988) 217.

Gerhardt Hafner, Kristen Boon, Anna Rübesame & Jonathan Huston, 'A Response to the American view as presented by Ruth Wedgwood' (1999) 10 E.J.I.L. 108.

Fred Halliday, *Rethinking international relations* (London: Macmillan, 1994).

H.L.A. Hart, *The Concept of law*, 2d ed. (Oxford: Clarendon, 1994).

F.A. Hayek, *The Constitution of liberty* (London: Routledge & Kegan Paul, 1960).

——*The Road to serfdom* (London: Routledge & Kegan Paul, 1944).

Herman A.M. von Hebel, Johan G. Lammers, & Julien Schukking, eds., *Reflections on the International Criminal Court: Essays in honour of Adriaan Bos* (The Hague: T.M.C. Asser Press, 1999).

David Held, David Goldblatt, Anthony McGrew & Jonathan Perraton, *Global transformations: Politics, economics and culture* (Cambridge: Polity, 1999).

Jesse Helms, 'Address by Senator Jesse Helms, Chairman, U.S. Senate Committee on Foreign Relations, before the United Nations Security Council, January 20, 2000' (available from Senator Helms' website: http://www.senate.gov/~helms/).

Louis Henkin & John L. Hargrove, eds., *Human rights: An Agenda for the next century* (Washington, DC: Am. Soc. Int'l L., 1994).

Rosalyn Higgins, 'Peace and security: Achievements and failures' (1995) 6 E.J.I.L. 445.

Peter W. Hogg, *Constitutional law of Canada*, 3d ed. (Scarborough, Ont.: Carswell, 1992).

John Hopkins, 'Case and comment: Former head of foreign state—extradition—immunity' (1999) Camb. L.J. 461.

Interights, 'Responding to September 11: The Framework of international law' (October 2001), on-line at 'http://www.interights.org/about/Sept%2011%20Parts%20I-IV.htm#PART%20IV'.

International Commission of Jurists, *The Rule of law in a free society: A Report of the International Congress of Jurists, New Delhi, India, January 5–10, 1959* (Geneva: I.C.J., 1959).

International Council on Human Rights Policy, *Thinking ahead on universal jurisdiction: Report of a meeting hosted by the International Council on Human Rights Policy, 6–8 May 1999* (1999).

International Law Association, Committee on International Human Rights Law and Practice, *The Exercise of universal jurisdiction in respect of gross human rights offences: Final report* (London: Report of the Sixty-Ninth International Law Association Conference, 2000).

Robert H. Jackson, Quasi-States: Sovereignty, international relations and the Third World (Cambridge: Cambridge U.P., 1988).

John Calvin Jeffries, 'Legality, vagueness and the construction of penal statutes' (1985) 71 Virg. L. Rev. 189.

Sir Robert Jennings & Sir Arthur Watts, eds., *Oppenheim's international law,* 9th ed. (London: Longman, 1996).

Christopher C. Joyner, ed., *Reining in impunity for international crimes and serious violations of fundamental human rights: Proceedings of the Siracusa Conference, 17–21 September 1998* (1998) 14 Nouvelles Études Pénales.

N. Jørgensen, *The Responsibility of States for international crimes* (Oxford: Oxford U.P., 2000).

Benedict Kingsbury, 'The Concept of compliance as a function of competing conceptions of international law' (1998) 19 Michigan J. of Int'l L. 345.

Philippe Kirsch, 'The Rome Conference on the International Criminal Court: A Comment' (November–December 1998) *Am. Soc. Int'l L. Newsletter* 1.

——& John T. Holmes, 'The Rome Conference on an International Criminal Court: The Negotiating Process' (1999) 93 A.J.I.L. 2.

Martti Koskenniemi, 'The Police in the temple: Order, justice and the UN—A dialectical view' (1995) 6 E.J.I.L. 325.

——'The Politics of international law' (1990) 1 E.J.I.L. 4.

Claus Kress & Flavia Lattanzi, eds., *The Rome Statute and domestic legal orders: General aspects and constitutional issues,* vol. 1 (Baden-Baden: Nomos, 2000).

Neil J. Kritz, ed., *Transitional justice: How emerging democracies reckon with former regimes* (Washington, DC: U.S. Institute of Peace, 1995).

Anne Marie Latcham, 'Duty to punish: International law and the human rights policy of Argentina' (1989) 7 Boston U. Int'l L.J. 355.

Flavia Lattanzi & William A. Schabas, eds., *Essays on the Rome Statute of the International Criminal Court* (Vol. 1) (Ripa Fagnano Alto: Il Sirente, 1999).

Roy S. Lee, ed., *The International Criminal Court: Issues, negotiations, results* (The Hague: Kluwer, 1999).

Monroe Leigh, 'Statement of Monroe Leigh on behalf of the American Bar Association, submitted to the Committee on International Relations, U.S. House of

Representatives, regarding H.R. 4654, *American Servicemembers' Protection Act'* (25 July 2000) (on file).

Jennifer J. Llewellyn & Robert Howse, 'Institutions for restorative justice: The South African Truth and Reconciliation Commission' (1999) 49 U. Toronto L.J. 355.

Jules Lobel & Michael Ratner, 'Bypassing the Security Council: Ambiguous authorizations to use force, cease-fires and the Iraqi inspection regime' (1999) 93 A.J.I.L. 124

T.L.H. McCormack & G.J. Simpson, eds., *The Law of war crimes: National and international approaches* (The Hague: Kluwer, 1997).

Michael B. McDonough, 'Privileged Outlaws: Diplomats, crime and immunity' (1997) 20 Suffolk Transnat'l L. Rev. 475.

Peter Malanczuk, *Akehurst's modern introduction to international law*, 7th ed. (London: Routledge, 1997).

Jerrold L. Mallory, 'Resolving the confusion over head of state immunity: The Defined right of kings' (1986) 86 Columbia L. Rev. 169.

Juan E. Méndez, 'Accountability for past abuses' (1997) 19 H.R. Quarterly 255.

—— *Truth and partial justice in Argentina* (New York: America's Watch, 1987).

Theodor Meron, 'Is international law moving towards criminalization?' (1998) 9 E.J.I.L. 18 ['1998a'].

—— *War crimes law comes of age: Essays* (Oxford: Clarendon, 1998) ['1998b'].

Kurt Mills, *Human rights in the emerging global order: A New sovereignty?* (London: Macmillan, 1998).

R.H. Minear, *Victors' justice: The Tokyo war crimes trial* (Princeton, NJ: Princeton U.P., 1971).

Madeline Morris, ed., *The United States and the International Criminal Court* (2001) 64 Law & Contemporary Problems.

Virginia Morris & Michael P. Scharf, *The International Criminal Tribunal for Rwanda* (2 vols.) (Irvington-on-Hudson, NY: Transnational, 1998).

Rein Müllerson, *Ordering anarchy: International law and international society* (The Hague: Martinus Nijhoff, 2000).

Aryeh Neier, *War crimes: Brutality, genocide, terror, and the struggle for justice* (New York: Random House, 1998).

P.M. North & J.J. Fawcett, *Cheshire and North's Private International Law*, 12th ed. (London: Butterworths, 1992).

J. Oraá, *Human Rights in States of Emergency in International Law* (Oxford Monographs in International Law) (Oxford: Clarendon,1992).

D. Orentlicher, 'International criminal tribunals: An Institution the United States can support', paper presented at *America's national interests in multilateral engagement: A Bipartisan dialogue* (Harvard University, John F. Kennedy School of Government, 14–15 May 2000) (on file).

—— 'Politics by other means: The Law of the International Criminal Court', (1999) 32 Cornell Int'l L.J. 489.

—— 'Settling accounts: The Duty to prosecute human rights violations of a prior regime' (1991) 100 Yale L.J. 2537.

Alain Pellet, 'Can a State commit a crime? Definitely, yes!' (1999) 10 E.J.I.L. 425.

Michael Plachta, '(Non-)extradition of nationals: A Never-ending story?' (1999) 13 Emory International Law Review 77.

Kenneth C. Randall, 'Universal jurisdiction under international law' (1988) 66 Tex. L. Rev. 785.

John Rawls, *A Theory of justice* (Oxford: Oxford U.P., 1972).

Rosemary Rayfuse, 'The Draft Code of Crimes against the Peace and Security of Mankind: Eating Disorders at the International Law Commission' (1997) 8 Crim. L. Forum 43.

Joseph Raz, 'The Politics of the rule of law' (1990) 3 Ratio Juris 331.

——'The Rule of law and its virtue' (1977) 93 L.Q.R. 195.

The Redress Trust, *Universal jurisdiction in Europe: Criminal prosecutions in Europe since 1990 for war crimes, crimes against humanity, torture and genocide* (London: The Redress Trust, 1999).

Restatement (third) of the foreign relations law of the United States (1986).

Darryl Robinson, 'Defining 'crimes against humanity' at the Rome Conference' (1999) 93 A.J.I.L. 43.

Naomi Roht-Arriaza, ed., *Impunity and human rights in international law and practice* (New York: Oxford University Press, 1995).

Cesare Romano, Thordis Ingadottir, *The Financing of the International Criminal Court: A Discussion paper* (New York: Project on International Courts and Tribunals, New York University, 2000).

James N. Rosenau, *Turbulence in international politics: A Theory of change and continuity* (Princeton: Princeton U.P., 1990).

Robert Rosenstock, 'An International criminal responsibility of States?' in *International law on the eve of the twenty-first century: Views from the International Law Commission* (New York: United Nations, 1997).

Alfred P. Rubin, *The Law of Piracy*, 2d ed. (Irvington-on-Hudson, NY: Transnational, 1997).

Yves Sandoz, *et al.*, eds., *Commentary on the Additional Protocols of 8 June 1977 to the Geneva Conventions of 12 August 1949* (Geneva: I.C.R.C./Martinus Nijhoff, 1987).

William A. Schabas, *Genocide in international law: The Crime of crimes* (Cambridge: Cambridge U.P., 2000).

Michael P. Scharf, 'The Amnesty exception to the jurisdiction of the International Criminal Court' (1999) 32 Cornell Int'l L. J.

——'The ICC's jurisdiction over the nationals of non-party States: A Critique of the U.S. position' (2000) 63 L. & Contemp. Probs.

David J. Scheffer, 'Staying the Course with the International Criminal Court' (2001) 35 Cornell Int'l L.J. 47.

——'The United States and the International Criminal Court' (1999) 93 A.J.I.L. 12.

Peter A. Schey, Dinah L. Shelton, & Naomi Roht-Arriaza, 'Addressing human rights abuses: Truth commissions and the value of amnesty' (1997) 19 Whittier L. Rev. 325.

Christoph Schreuer, 'The Waning of the sovereign State: Towards a new paradigm for international law?' (1993) 4 E.J.I.L. 447.

G. Schwarzenberger, 'The Problem of an international criminal law' (1950) 3 Current Leg. Probs. 262.

Sarah B. Sewall & Carl Kaysen, eds., *The United States and the International Criminal Court: National security and international law* (Lanham, MA: Rowman and Littlefield, 2000).

William Shawcross, *Deliver us from evil: Peacekeepers, warlords and a world of endless conflict* (New York: Simon & Schuster, 2000).

I.A. Shearer, *Extradition in international law* (Manchester: Manchester U.P., 1971).

Bruno Simma, ed., *The Charter of the United Nations: A Commentary* (Oxford: Oxford U.P., 1995).

——'NATO, the UN and the use of force: Legal aspects' (1999) 10 E.J.I.L. 1.

Pam Spees, 'The Rome Statute of the International Criminal Court', in Nicole Deller, Arjun Makhijani, and John Burroughs, eds., *Rule of power or rule of law? An Assessment of U.S. policies and actions regarding security-related treaties* (Institute for Energy and Environment Research/Lawyers Committee on Nuclear Policy, 2002).

W.J. Stankiewitz, ed., *In defense of sovereignty* (New York: Oxford U.P., 1969).

Lyal S. Sunga, *Individual responsibility in international law for serious violations of human rights* (Dordrecht: Martinus Nijhoff, 1992).

Telford Taylor, *The Anatomy of the Nuremberg trials* (New York: Alfred A. Knopf, 1992).

Janice E. Thomson, 'State sovereignty in international relations: Bridging the gap between theory and empirical research' (1995) 39 Int'l Studies Q. 213.

C. Tomuschat, 'International crimes by States: An Endangered species?', in K. Wellens (ed.), *International law: Theory and practice: Essays in honour of Eric Suy* (The Hague, Nijhoff, 1998).

Otto Triffterer, 'Efforts to recognize and codify international crimes (General Report, Part I)', in *International crimes and domestic criminal law* (1989) 60 Revue Internationale de Droit Penal 29.

——ed., *The Rome Statute of the International Criminal Court: Observers' notes, article by article* (Baden-Baden: Nomos, 1999).

E.C.S. Wade & A.W. Bradley, *Constitutional and administrative law*, 11th ed. (London: Longman, 1993).

Colin Warbrick, 'The United Nations system: A Place for criminal courts?' (1995) 5 Transnat'l L. & Contemp. Probs. 237.

John Washburn, 'The International Criminal Court arrives—the U.S. position: Status and prospects' (2002) 25 Fordham Int'l L.J. 873.

Sir Arthur Watts, 'The Legal position in international law of Heads of States, heads of governments and foreign ministers' (1994) III *Recueil des Cours* 9.

Ruth Wedgwood, 'Courting disaster: The US takes a stand', (March 2000) *Foreign Service J.* 34.

——'The International Criminal Court: An American view' (1999) 10 E.J.I.L. 93.

——'International criminal law and Augusto Pinochet' (2000) 40 Virg. J. Int'l L. 829.

——'The United States and the International Criminal Court: Achieving a wider consensus through the 'Ithaca package'' (1999) 32 Cornell Int'l L.J. 535.

Joseph H.H. Weiler, Antonio Cassese & Marina Spinedi, eds., *International crimes of State: A Critical analysis of the ILC's Draft Article 19 on State Responsibility* (New York: Walter de Gruyter, 1989).

Ernest J. Weinrib, 'Legal formalism: On the immanent rationality of law' (1989) 97 Yale L.J. 949.

M. Weller, 'The Reality of the emerging universal constitutional order: Putting the pieces together' (1997) Cambridge Rev. Int'l Studies.

Leila Sadat Wexler, 'The Interpretation of the Nuremberg principles by the French Court of Cassation: From Touvier to Barbie and back again' (1994) 32 Colum. J. Transnat'l L. 289.

——'Reflections on the trial of Vichy collaborator Paul Touvier for crimes against humanity in France' (1995) 20 J.L. & Soc. Inq. 191.

James F. Willis, *Prologue to Nuremberg: The Politics and diplomacy of punishing war criminals of the First World War* (Westport, CN: Greenwood, 1982).

Salvatore Zappalà, 'Do Heads of State in office enjoy immunity from jurisdiction for international crimes? The Ghaddafi case before the French Cour de Cassation' (2001) 12 E.J.I.L. 595.

E. REPORTS OF GOVERNMENTS AND INTER-GOVERNMENTAL ORGANIZATIONS, DRAFT INSTRUMENTS, PROPOSALS, ETC.

Bureau Proposal, U.N. Doc. A/Conf.183/C.1/L.59 (10 July 1998).

Chairman's suggestions for articles 21, 26 and 28, U.N. Doc. A/Conf. 183/C.1/WG.GP/ L.1 (15 June 1998).

Decisions taken by the Preparatory Committee at its session held from 11 to 21 February 1997, U.N. Doc. A/AC.249/1997/L.5 (1997).

Discussion Paper, U.N. Doc. A/Conf.183/C.1/L.53 (6 July 1998).

Discussion paper proposed by the Coordinator, U.N. Doc. PCNICC/1999/WGCA/ RT.1 (9 December 1999).

Discussion paper proposed by the Coordinator, U.N. Doc. PCNICC/2000/WGICC-UN/RT.1 (7 December 2000).

Draft Relationship Agreement between the Court and the United Nations: Discussion paper proposed by the Coordinator, U.N. Doc. PCNICC/L.4/Rev.1/Add.1 (14 December 2000).

Draft report of the Drafting Committee to the Committee of the Whole, U.N. Doc. A/Conf.183/C.1/L.65/Rev.1 (14 July 1998).

Draft Statute for the International Criminal Court, U.N. Doc. A/Conf.183/C.1/L.76/ Add.3 (16 July 1998).

Fifth annual report of the International Criminal Tribunal for the Prosecution of Persons Responsible for Genocide and Other Serious Violations of International Humanitarian Law Committed in the Territory of Rwanda and Rwandan Citizens Responsible for Genocide and Other Such Violations Committed in the Territory of Neighbouring States between 1 January and 31 December 1994, for the period 1 July 1999 to 30 June 2000, U.N. Doc. A/55/435 (2 October 2000).

Finalized Draft Rules of Procedure and Evidence, U.N. Doc. PCNICC/2000/1/Add.1 (2 November 2000).

Finalized Draft Text of the Elements of Crimes, U.N. Doc. PCNICC/2000/INF/3/ Add.2 (6 July 2000).

First report on the Draft Code of Offences Against the Peace and Security of Mankind, U.N. Doc. A/CN.4/364 (29 April 1983).

General Comment No.20(44) (Article 7), U.N. Doc. CCPR/C/21/Rev.1/Add.3 (7 April 1992).

Historical review of developments relating to aggression, U.N. Doc. PCNICC/2002/ WGCA/L.1 (24 January 2002); addendum to same, U.N. Doc. PCNICC/2002/ WGCA/L.1/Add.1 (18 January 2002).

Letter from President McDonald to the President of the Security Council concerning outstanding issues of State non-compliance (2 November 1999) (ICTY Press Rel. JL/P.I.S./444-E).

Model Agreement Between the United Nations and the Member States Contributing Personnel and Equipment to United Nations Peace-Keeping Operations, U.N. Doc. A/46/185 (23 May 1991).

Model Status-of-Forces Agreement for Peace-Keeping Operations, U.N. Doc. A/45/594 (9 October 1990).

Model Treaty on Mutual Assistance in Criminal Matters, 14 December 1990, Annex to G.A. Res. 45/117, U.N. Doc. A/45/49, G.A.O.R., 45th Sess., Supp. No. 49A, at 215.

Office of the Special Coordinator in the Occupied Territories, *Rule of law development in the West Bank and Gaza Strip: A Development assistance survey* (Rimal, Gaza: UNESCO, 1997).

Proceedings of the Preparatory Commission at its Fifth Session (12–30 June 2000), U.N. Doc. PCNICC/2000/L.3/Rev.1 (6 July 2000).

Proposal submitted by Algeria, India, Sri Lanka and Turkey, U.N. Doc. A/CONF.183/C.1/L.27 (29 June 1998).

Proposal submitted by Barbados, Dominica, India, Jamaica, Sri Lanka, Trinidad and Tobago and Turkey, U.N. Doc. A/CONF.183/C.1/L.71 (14 July 1998).

Proposal of Germany, U.N. Doc. A/AC.249/1998/DP.2 (1998).

Proposal submitted by Germany, U.N. Doc. PCNICC/2000/WGCA/DP.4 (13 November 2000).

Proposal submitted by India, Sri Lanka and Turkey, U.N. Doc. A/CONF.183/C.1/ L.27/Rev. 1 (6 July 1998).

Proposal of the Republic of Korea, U.N. Doc. A/Conf.183/C.1/L.6 (18 June 1998).

Proposal of the United States of America, U.N. Doc. A/Conf.183/C.1/L.70 (15 July 1998).

Proposal of the United States of America, U.N. Doc. A/Conf.183/C.1/L.90 (16 July 1998).

Proposal of the United States of America, U.N. Doc. PCNICC/1999/WGRPE/DP.45 (2 December 1999).

Proposal submitted by the United States of America, U.N. Doc. PCNICC/2000/DP.1 (7 December 2000).

Reference document on the crime of aggression, prepared by the Secretariat, U.N. Doc. PCNICC/2000/WGCA/INF/1 (27 June 2000).

Report of the Ad Hoc Committee on the Establishment of an International Criminal Court, U.N. Doc. A/50/22, G.A.O.R., 50th Sess., Supp. No. 22 (1995).

Report of the Committee Against Torture, U.N. Doc. A/45/44, G.A.O.R., 45th Sess., Supp. No.44 (1990).

Report of the International Law Commission covering its second session, U.N. Doc. A/1316, 5 G.A.O.R. Supp. No.12 (1950).

Report of the International Law Commission covering the work of its sixth session, 3 June—28 July 1954, U.N. Doc. A/2693, G.A.O.R., 9th Sess., Supp. No. 9 (1954).

Report of the International Law Commission on the work of its twenty-eighth session, 3 May–23 July 1976, U.N. Doc. A/31/10, G.A.O.R., 31st Sess., Supp. No. 10 (1976).

Report of the International Law Commission on the work of its forty-fifth session, U.N. Doc. A/48/10, G.A.O.R., 48th Sess., Supp. No. 10 (1993).

Report of the International Law Commission on its Forty-sixth Session, U.N. Doc. A/49/10, G.A.O.R., 49th Sess., Supp. No. 10 (1994).

Report of the International Law Commission on the work of its forty-eighth session, 6 May–26 July 1996, U.N. Doc. A/51/10, G.A.O.R. 51st Sess., Supp. No. 10 (1996).

Report of the International Law Commission on the work of its fiftieth session, 20 April–12 June 1998, 27 July–14 August 1998, U.N. Doc. A/53/10, G.A.O.R., 53d Sess., Supp. No. 10 (1998).

Report of the International Law Commission on the work of its fifty-third session, 23 April–1 June, 2 July–10 August 2001, U.N. Doc. A/56/10, G.A.O.R., 56th Sess., Supp. No. 10 (2001).

Report of the International Tribunal for the Prosecution of Persons Responsible for Serious Violations of International Humanitarian Law Committed in the Territory of the Former Yugoslavia since 1991, U.N. Doc. A/54/187 (25 August 1999).

Report of the Inter-Sessional Meeting from 19 to 30 January 1998 in Zutphen, the Netherlands, U.N. Doc. A/AC.249/1998/L.13 (1998).

Report of the Preparatory Committee on the Establishment of an International Criminal Court, U.N. Doc. A/51/22, G.A.O.R., 51st Sess., Supp. No. 22, (1996) (2 Vols.).

Report of the Preparatory Committee on the Establishment of an International Criminal Court, U.N. Doc. A/Conf.183/2/Add.1 (1998).

Report of the Secretary-General on measures to eliminate international terrorism, U.N. Doc. A/56/160 (3 July 2001).

Report of the Secretary-General on the establishment of a Special Court for Sierra Leone, U.N. Doc. S/2000/915 (4 October 2000).

Report of the Secretary-General on the United Nations Transitional Administration in East Timor (for the period 27 July 2000 to 16 January 2001), U.N. Doc. S/2001/42 (16 January 2001).

Report of the Secretary-General on the United Nations Transitional Administration in East Timor (for the period 16 October 2001 to 18 January 2002), U.N. Doc. S/2002/80 (17 January 2002).

Report of the Secretary-General pursuant to paragraph 2 of Security Council Resolution 808 (1993), U.N. Doc. S/25704.

Report of the Working Group on General Principles of Criminal Law, U.N. Doc. A/Conf.183/C.1/WGGP/L.4 (18 June 1998).

Report of the Working Group on Measures to Eliminate International Terrorism, U.N. Doc. A/C.6/56/L.9 (29 October 2001), paras. 11–14 and Annex 1.

Terrorism and human rights: Progress report prepared by Ms Kalliopi K. Koufa, Special Rapporteur, U.N. Doc. E/CN.4/Sub.2/2001/31 (27 June 2001), paras. 24–81.

Trial of the Major War Criminals before the International Military Tribunal, Nuremberg, 14 November 1945—1 October 1946 (Nuremberg: I.M.T., 1947).

Truth and Reconciliation Commission of South Africa Report (5 Vols.) (London: MacMillan, 1998).

United Nations Commission on the Truth for El Salvador, *From madness to hope: The 12-year war in El Salvador*, U.N. Doc. S/25500 (1993).

F. PRESS RELEASES, ARTICLES, ETC.

'An African Pinochet' *New York Times* (11 February 2000) A30.

'America's world' *The Economist* (23 October 1999) 15.

'Annan: Cambodia must change its position if it wants U.N. to help set up a tribunal' Associated Press (14 March 2002).

'A World court for criminals' *The Economist* (9 October 1999) 19.

Helle Bering, 'International criminal circus; political correctness runs amok again' *The Washington Times* (5 April 2000) A19.

James Bone & Richard Beeston, 'US rejects world court for fear of partisan lawsuits' *The Times* (London) (30 March 2002).

David Bosco, 'Dictators in the dock' *American Prospect* (14 August 2000) 26.

'Cook rallies to genocide court' *The Guardian* (26 August 2000) 13.

Barbara Crosette, 'War crimes tribunal becomes reality, without U.S. role' *New York Times* (12 April 2002).

Keith Harper, 'Violence threatens booming world sea trade' *The Guardian* (18 September 1999).

International Maritime Organization, 'IMO acts to combat piracy' (Press Release, February 1998).

Michael Kinsley, 'Defining terrorism: It's essential. It's also impossible' *Washington Post* (5 October 2001) p. A37.

Elizabeth A. Neuffer, 'US to Back Out of World Court Plan—Envoy: Bush team may 'unsign' treaty' (29 March 2002).

'NGO Coalition Special Report on Country Positions on L.59: The Virtual Vote' *Rome Treaty Conference Monitor* (15 July 1998) 1.

Katie Nguyen 'Belgian Court Sets May 15 for Sharon Hearing' (6 March 2002) Reuters.

'The Numbers: NGO Coalition Special Report on Country Positions' *Rome Treaty Conference Monitor* (10 July 1998) 1.

Andrew Osborn & Suzanne Goldenberg, 'Massacre survivors seek trial of Sharon in Belgium' (19 June 2001) *The Guardian*.

'The Politics of justice at the International Criminal Tribunal for Rwanda' *Internews* (29 February 2000).

'Rwanda normalizes relations with UN Tribunal' *Internews* (10 February 2000).

Sherle R. Schwenninger, 'World order lost: American foreign policy in the post-Cold War world' (Summer 1999) World Policy J. 42.

Marlise Simons, 'Mother Superior guilty in Rwandan killings' (9 June 2001) *New York Times* A4.

Jonathan Tepperman, 'Contempt of court: How Jesse Helms and the State Department are helping future Milosovics escape justice' *Washington Monthly* (November 2000) 25.

'TPI: Les Etats-Unis refusent la proposition suisse' *Le Temps* (Switzerland) (11 December 2000).

United Nations, 'Press Briefing by the Under-Secretary-General for Legal Affairs and United Nations Counsel' (13 July 2000).

——'Ratification ceremony at UN paves way for International Criminal Court', UN Press Release (11 April 2002).

——'Secretary General says establishment of International Criminal Court is major step in march towards universal human rights, rule of law', U.N. Press Release L/2890 (20 July 1998).

——'United Nations and Government of Sierra Leone sign agreement establishing Special Court', UNAMSIL Press Release (16 January 2002) (available online at 'http://www.un.org/Depts/dpko/unamsil/DB/160102a.htm').

'U.S. Frees Accused Torturer' *Washington Post* (11 March 2000) A1.

'U.S. resists war-crimes court as Canada conforms' *New York Times* (22 July 2000).

'U.S. Signs Treaty for World Court to Try Atrocities' *The New York Times* (1 January 2001) A1.

'United States Department of Defense News' Release No. 233–02, 'Secretary Rumsfeld Statement on the ICC Treaty' (6 May 2002), available on line at http://www. defenselink.mil/news/May2002/605062002_bt233-02.html

Index

Lightning Source UK Ltd.
Milton Keynes UK
04 April 2011

170373UK00002B/28/P

9 780199 274246